MYTHS, DREAMS AND MYSTERIES

MYTHS, DREAMS AND MYSTERIES

*The Encounter
between Contemporary Faiths
and Archaic Realities*

MIRCEA ELIADE

Translated by
PHILIP MAIRET

HARPER TORCHBOOKS
Harper & Row, Publishers
New York and Evanston

R. N. Rior

Mythology,
dreams,
mysteries -- religious

THE LIBRARY OF RELIGION AND CULTURE
General Editor: Benjamin Nelson

MYTHS, DREAMS AND MYSTERIES

This book was originally published by Gallimard, Paris, under
the title *Mythes, Rêves et Mystères*. The English translation
was first published by Harvill Press, London, and Harper &
Row, Publishers, New York, in 1960.

First HARPER TORCHBOOK edition published 1967 by Harper &
Row, Publishers, Incorporated, New York, N.Y. 10016

Library of Congress Catalog Card Number: 60–15616.

CONTENTS

Contents

Foreword
to the English Translation

RE-READING the following pages after an interval of three years, I decided that it would be useful to introduce them by an additional preface. The one to the French edition gives too little prominence to the links between the major themes of the book. In writing it I limited myself to discussion of the differences of structure between myths and dreams, and then to comparison of the respective points of view of the historian of religions and of the depth-psychologist. These are indeed highly important questions, and, since they are more or less directly involved in almost every chapter, it was advisable that an attempt to systematise them should be made at the beginning of the book. But on the other hand, the preface to the French edition might give rise to a misunderstanding: it might be thought that the confrontation between the two worlds, of myths and of dreams, was the principal object of our research, whereas it constitutes only one aspect of this. The central theme of the present work is, in fact, the meeting and confrontation of the two types of mentality which might be called, for simplicity's sake, the traditional and the modern; the first being characteristic of man in archaic and Oriental societies, the second of man in modern societies of the Western type.

As we know, the meeting and confrontation of these two types of civilisation count among the most significant events of the last quarter of a century. This confrontation is developing on two distinct planes and as a consequence of different sets of circumstances. On the one hand, the "exotic" and "primitive" peoples have now come within the orbit of history, so that

Western man is obliged to enquire into their systems of values, if he is to be able to establish and maintain communication with them. On the other hand, a whole series of changes has taken place in the cultural outlook of Europeans, changes which preceded the non-European peoples' entry into history, but which have, in a sense, paved the way for that event, or have at least prepared Western people to face and understand it. Indeed, the rise of the sciences of comparative religion, of ethnology and Orientalism, as well as the development of depth-psychology and the systematic study of symbolism, have considerably helped the West to enter into the spiritual universe of "exotic" and "primitive" peoples. On several occasions I have emphasised the cultural importance of the recent entry of Asia into History, and of the appearance of States constituted by ethnic groups which, until about a dozen years ago, belonged to the "primitive world". For some time past, the West has been no longer the only "maker of History". Which means, among other things, that Western culture will be in danger of a decline into a sterilising provincialism if it despises or neglects the dialogue with the other cultures. Hermeneutics is Western man's response—the only intelligent response possible—to the solicitations of contemporary history, to the fact that the West is forced (one might almost say, condemned) to this encounter and confrontation with the cultural values of "the others".

Fortunately, as I have just said, certain great cultural movements of this century—the several revivals of religion, depth-psychology, the discoveries of surrealism and of the most advanced painting, the researches of ethnology, etc.—have prepared the ground and, on the whole, have made it easier for us to understand psychological attitudes which at first sight seem "inferior", "strange" or disconcerting. It is true that, most of the time, encounters and comparisons with non-Western cultures have not made all the "strangeness" of these cultures evident. But this is due to the fact that the encounters have been made through their more Westernised representatives, or in the mainly external spheres of economics or politics. We may say that the Western world has not yet, or not generally, met with authentic representatives of the "real" non-Western traditions. But this encounter is, in the end, inevitable. Even supposing that, one day soon, all the traditional societies now beginning to play an active part in history must end by becoming radically Westernised—in other words, assuming that the non-Western peoples are fated to lose their place in History except in so far as they become Westernised—even then the encounter and comparison with the authentic traditions of the non-Western world could not be avoided. We cannot tell what the cultural ambience of these exotic peoples will be like in the future, but only yesterday it was radically different from that of the West. And sooner or later, the knowledge of the history of those peoples, and therefore the understanding of their authentic cultural creations, are tasks we shall no longer be able to shirk. The true meeting and the real confrontation will come about in any case. One day the West will have to know and to understand the existential situations and the cultural universes of the non-Western peoples; moreover, the West will come to value them as integral with the history of the human spirit and will no longer regard them as immature episodes or as aberrations from an exemplary History of man—a History conceived, of course, only as that of Western man.

Furthermore, this confrontation with "the others" helps Western man better to understand himself. The effort expended in correctly understanding ways of thinking that are foreign to the Western rationalist tradition—an effort which is, primarily, that of deciphering the meanings of myths and symbols—is repaid by a considerable enrichment of consciousness. It is true that modern European culture has already several methods for the exploration of the world of symbols and myths. One has only to remember the patient researches and the working hypotheses elaborated by psychoanalysis. And, from a certain point of view, we may say that the first systematic analysis and exegesis of these "alien" worlds, of the unconscious from which the symbols and the myths arise, were effected by Freud.

But the work of the depth-psychologists, considerable though it is, does not exhaust the possibilities of our encounter with the "strangers". The psychologists have applied themselves to studying the structure of symbols and the dynamism of myths in order to grasp the dynamism of the unconscious. But the confrontation with the non-European cultures governed by symbols and nourished by myths, takes place upon another plane: it is no longer a question of "analysing" these cultures as one would analyse the dreams of an individual in order to "reduce" them to symptoms expressive of certain modifications in the depths of his psyche. Here it is a case of considering the non-European peoples' cultural creations in themselves; that is, as the expressions of a particular genius; and of striving to understand them with the same intellectual passion that we would apply to the understanding of Homeric man, or of the prophets of Israel, or of the mystical philosophy of Meister Eckhardt. In other words, we have to approach the symbols, myths and rites of the Oceanians or the Africans—as, fortunately, we are beginning to do—with the same respect and the same desire to learn that we have devoted to Western cultural creations, even when those rites and myths reveal "strange", terrible or aberrant aspects. But now, it is no longer for the psychologist to interpret these, by showing how such nocturnal aspects are inseparable from profound dramas enacted in the unconscious: this time, the symbols, myths and rituals have to be judged as cultural values—in the final analysis as the privileged expressions of the existential situations of peoples belonging to various types of society, and impelled by historical forces other than those which have shaped the history of the Western world.

This effort, rightly to understand peoples demonstrably "other" than we ourselves, who are the heirs of Greece and of Judæo-Christianity, has the effect, as I have said, of enriching the Western consciousness. Such encounters may even lead to a renewal of the problematics of philosophy, just as the discovery of exotic and primitive arts half a century ago opened up new perspectives to the European world of art. To me it seems, for instance, that a closer study of the nature and function of symbols might well stimulate Western philosophic thinking and widen its horizons. Since I am primarily a historian of religions, it is in the perspective of that discipline that I have presented, in this book, some of the results arrived at by hermeneutics. But this is not to say that the interpretation or the evaluation of symbols or myths is the prerogative of the historian of religions. After all, this is a matter of the enlargement of human knowledge which is in the interest of all the disciplines of the mind. It concerns, moreover, the eventual discovery of fresh sources of inspiration for philosophical meditation. We know that such sources of inspiration are unforeseeable. Who could have imagined, thirty years ago, that the pre-Socratics would ever be thought capable of regenerating philosophical investigation? Yet the latest researches of Heidegger are developing in that direction.

In any case, the reactions of Western philosophers confronted by archaic and Oriental ways of thought belong to the future, and we have no right to anticipate them. It is a significant fact, however, that recent exegesis has led historians of religions to give prominence to the audacious "primitive" and Oriental conceptions of the structure of human existence, of the fall into temporality and of the need to know "death" before gaining access to the world of the Spirit. These they recognise as fairly close approximations to ideas which are arising today at the very heart of Western philosophical problematics. And when one rediscovers, in the archaic and Oriental religious ideologies, conceptions comparable to those of Western "classical" philosophy, the comparison is no less significant, since these conceptions are not derived from the same presuppositions. For example, when Indian thought, and also certain "primitive" mythologies, proclaim that the decisive action which inaugurated the present condition of man took place in a non-temporal past, and therefore that *the essential precedes the actual condition of man* (*cf.* Chapter II below), it should be of the highest interest to a Western philosopher or theologian to learn in detail how they arrived at that conception, and for what reasons.

But above all, it is the ideas of death and resurrection that will interest the modern Western man. Not, indeed, in order to borrow them, but to meditate upon, and try to decipher them. These conceptions express human situations that the Western world has long since left behind and, as such, they are unusable by the modern man of the West. On the other hand, their inexhaustible content and the hermeneutic interpretation of it can greatly stimulate philosophic thinking. For example, we cannot minimise the fact that the archaic and Oriental cultures succeeded in conferring positive values on anxiety, death, self-abasement, and upon chaos (see especially the following Chapters VII, VIII and IX). In a period of crisis, such as we are now passing through, it is not only useful, but may be necessary to know how, and starting from what presuppositions, cultures as different as those of the primitives and of the Indians came to attach values to situations which, for the modern man, are only terrifying, absurd or demonic.

If the discovery of the unconscious has compelled Western man to confront his own individual, secret and larval "history", the encounter with non-Western cultures will oblige him to delve very profoundly into the history of the human spirit, and will perhaps persuade him to admit that history as an integral part of his own being. As the author of this book sees it, the history of religions is worthy to become, one day, our guide upon these far journeys, and to serve as interpreter in our encounters with the most "alien" among "the others".

October 1959
University of Chicago

Preface
to the original Edition

THE CHAPTERS of this book do not presume to constitute a systematic study of the relations between certain constituents of the religious universe—such as myths and mysteries—and the universe of dreams. That is a problem that may fascinate the psychologist, or even the philosopher, but one that is less essential for the historian of religions, and it is in this capacity that I prepared the studies now to be read. Not, indeed, that the historian of religions has nothing to learn from all the recent discoveries of depth-psychology. But neither is he obliged to forsake the perspective appropriate to his own task of understanding the different religious worlds revealed by his documents.

To do this would be to take on the psychologist's work, and it is safe to say that he would gain nothing by it. He has before now met with misfortune when, believing it might be of benefit to his own discipline, he has tackled its subject-matter as a sociologist or ethnologist, only to arrive at bad sociology or bad ethnology. Assuredly, all the disciplines of the mind and all the sciences of man are equally precious and their discoveries mutually so, but this solidarity does not mean confusion. What is important is to integrate the results of the diverse applications of the mind without confounding them. The surest method, in the history of religions as in all else, is still that of studying a phenomenon in its own frame of reference, with freedom afterwards to integrate the results of this procedure in a wider perspective.

There is hardly one of the writings here brought together that does not include some allusions to, and brief comparisons between, the activities of the unconscious and the characteristics of religion. But it is the fifth chapter, above all, which is meant to elucidate the relations between the dynamism of the unconscious—as it manifests itself in dreams and in the imagination—and the structures of the religious universe. Their mutual confrontation could have been undertaken in respect of every one of the themes discussed in this book. For there is no mythic motive or scenario of initiation which is not also presented, in one way or another, in dreams and in the working of the imagination. In the oneiric universe we find again and again the symbols, the images, the figures and the events of which the mythologies are constituted. Upon this discovery, due to the genius of Freud, all the depth-psychologies have been working for half a century. The great temptation, into which nearly all the psychologists have fallen, has been to try to derive the Figures and the Events of mythology from the contents and the dynamic of the Unconscious. From a certain point of view the psychologists are right; it is indeed possible to homologise the *function* of the Figures and the *results* of the Events upon the parallel planes of unconscious activity and of religion and mythology. But we ought not to confuse homologisation with reduction. It is when the psychologist "explains" a mythological Figure or Event by reducing it to a process of the unconscious, that the historian of religions—and perhaps not he alone—hesitates to follow him. At bottom, such explanation by reduction would be equivalent to explaining *Madame Bovary* as an adultery. But *Madame Bovary* has an unique existence in its own frame of reference, which is that of a literary creation, of a creation of the mind. That *Madame Bovary* could only have been written in Western bourgeois society of the nineteenth century, when adultery constituted a problem *sui generis*—that is quite another problem, belonging to the sociology of literature, but not to the æsthetics of the novel.

The myth defines itself by its own mode of being. It can only be grasped, as a myth, in so far as it *reveals* something as having been *fully manifested*, and this manifestation is at the same time *creative* and *exemplary*, since it is the foundation of a structure of reality as well as of a kind of human behaviour. A myth always narrates something as having *really happened*, as an event that took place, in the plain sense of the term—whether it deals with the creation of the World, or of the most insignificant animal or vegetable species, or of an institution. The very fact of *saying* what happened reveals *how* the thing in question was realised (and this *how* stands equally for *why*). For the act of coming to be is, at the same time, the emergence of a reality and the disclosure of its fundamental structures. When the cosmogonic myth tells us how the world was created, it is also revealing the emergence of that totality of the real which is the Cosmos, and its ontological laws: it shows in what sense the World *is*. Cosmogony is also ontophany, the plenary manifestation of Being. And since all myths participate in some sort in the cosmological type of myth—for every account of what came to pass in the holy era of the Beginning (*in illo tempore*) is but another variant of the archetypal history: how the world came to be—it follows that all mythology is ontophany. Myths reveal the structure of reality, and the multiple modalities of being in the world. That is why they are the exemplary models for human behaviour; they disclose the *true* stories, concern themselves with the *realities*. But ontophany always implies theophany or hierophany. It was the Gods or the semi-divine beings who created the world and instituted the innumerable modes of being in the world, from that which is uniquely human to the mode of being of the insect. In revealing the history of what came to pass *in illo tempore*, one is at the same time revealing an irruption of the sacred into the world. When a God or a civilising Hero ordained a mode of behaviour—for instance, a particular way of taking food—he not only assured the reality of that behaviour (for until then the practice in question was non-existent, was not in use and so was "unreal"), but by the very fact that this behaviour was his invention, it is also theophany, a divine creation. By feeding himself in the same manner as the God or civilising Hero, man repeats their gestures and, in some sort, participates in their presence.

The following pages deal sufficiently with the structure and function of myths for us to content ourselves here with a few general observations. What has just been said is enough to indicate the radical difference in ontological significance between myths and dreams. There is no myth which is not the unveiling of a "mystery", the revelation of a primordial event which inaugurated either a constituent structure of reality or a kind of human behaviour. Thence it follows that, because of its own mode of being, the myth cannot be particular, private or personal. It can establish itself as a myth only to the extent that it reveals the existence and the activity of super-human beings behaving in an *exemplary manner*; and this—at the level of primitive spirituality—is as much as to say, behaving in a *universal manner*, for a myth becomes a model for "the whole world" (which is how one thinks of the society one belongs to) and a model for "eternity" (because it came to pass *in illo tempore* and does not participate in the temporal). Lastly, there is also a special emphasis, which is important: the myth is assumed by man in as much as he is a whole being; it is not addressed to his intelligence or his imagination only. When no longer assumed to be a revelation of the "mysteries" the myth becomes "decadent", obscured; it turns into a tale or a legend.

No long analysis is needed to show that a dream cannot attain to any such ontological status. It is not lived by the *whole man* and therefore cannot succeed in transforming a particular situation into one that is exemplary and universally valid. Admittedly, a dream may be deciphered, interpreted, and may thereby transmit its message in a more explicit manner. But in itself, considered simply in its own universe, the dream lacks the constitutive dimensions of the myth—those of the exemplary and the universal. It is not assumed to be an unveiling of the nature of reality, nor is it the revelation of a type of behaviour which, being instituted by the Gods or civilising Heroes, imposes itself as exemplary.

Nevertheless, it has been possible to show a continuity between the oneiric and the mythological universes, just as there is a homology between mythological Figures and Events and the personages and happenings in dreams. It has also been shown that the categories of space and time become modified in dreams, in a way which to some degree resembles the abolition of Time and Space in myths. Moreover, it has been found that dreams and other processes in the unconscious may present, as it were, a "religious aura"; not only are their structures comparable to those of mythology, but the experience of living through certain contents of the unconscious is, as the depth-psychologists see it, homologous with the experience of the sacred. Some have concluded, perhaps rather prematurely, that the creations of the unconscious are the "raw material" of religion and of all that religion includes—symbols, myths, rituals, etc. But we have just shown, adducing *Madame Bovary* as an example, why the explanation of a reality by the "raw material" that it includes and presupposes need hardly detain us. The homology of the persons and the events of a myth with those of a dream does not imply any fundamental identity between them. One can never repeat this truism too often, for the temptation is always to explain the activities of the spirit by reducing them to some pre-spiritual "origin".

The "religious aura" surrounding certain contents of the unconscious does not surprise the historian of religions: he knows that religious experience engages the whole of a man, and therefore stirs the depths of his being. This is not to say that religion can be reduced to its irrational components, but simply that one recognises the religious experience for what it is—an experience of existence in its totality, which reveals to a man his own mode of being in the World. We are however in agreement in regarding the contents and structures of the unconscious as the results of immemorial experiences of critical situations. Every existential crisis brings once again into question both the reality of the world and the presence of man in the world. The crisis is, indeed, "religious" because, at the archaic levels of culture, "being" is fused together with the "holy". For all primitive mankind, it is religious experience which lays the foundation of the World. It is ritual orientation, with the structures of sacred space which it reveals, that transforms "Chaos" into the "Cosmos" and, therefore, renders human existence possible—prevents it, that is, from regression to the level of zoological existence. Every religion, even the most elementary, is an ontology: it reveals the *being* of the sacred things and the divine Figures, it shows forth *that which really is*, and in doing so establishes a World which is no longer evanescent and incomprehensible, as it is in nightmares, and as it again becomes whenever existence is in danger of foundering in the "Chaos" of total relativity, where no "Centre" emerges to ensure orientation.

In other words, in so far as the unconscious is the "precipitate" of innumerable limit-situations, it cannot *not* resemble a religious universe. For religion is the exemplary solution of every existential crisis. Religion "begins" when and where there is a total revelation of reality; a revelation which is at once that of the sacred—of that which supremely *is*, of what is neither illusory nor evanescent—and of man's relationship to the sacred, a relationship which is multiple, changing, sometimes ambivalent, but which always places man at the very heart of the real. This double relationship at the same time renders existence human, "open" to the values of the Spirit. On the one hand, the sacred is, supremely, the *other* than man—the transpersonal, the transcendent —and, on the other hand, the sacred is the exemplary in the sense that it establishes patterns to be followed: by being transcendent and exemplary it compels the religious man to come out of personal situations, to surpass the contingent and the particular and to comply with general values, with the universal.

It is in this sense that we must understand the "religious aura" around certain contents of the unconscious: the religious experience is at once a total crisis of existence and the exemplary solution of that crisis. The solution is exemplary because it unveils a World which is no longer private and opaque, but transpersonal, significant and sacred, being the work of the Gods. And it is by the exemplary character of the religious solution that one can best judge the distance that separates the universe of the unconscious from the universe of religion. The religious solution lays the foundation for an exemplary behaviour, and, in consequence, compels the man to reveal himself as both the real and the *universal*. It is only after this revelation has been assumed by man in his entire being that one can speak of religion. All religious structures and forms, rudimentary though they may be, participate in this ontological status. If, in a primitive society, some tree or other is regarded as the "Tree of the World", it follows that, thanks to the religious experience which originated that belief, it is possible for the members of this society to attain to a metaphysical understanding of the Universe; for the symbolism of the Tree of the World has revealed to them that a particular object may signify the whole of the cosmos; and thereby the individual experience is "awakened" and transmuted into spiritual action. Thanks to the religious symbolism of the Tree of the World, man succeeds in living the universal. But this must be a total experience: it is the religious vision of the world and the ideology derived from it which have enabled the man to bring his individual experience to fulfilment, to "open" it towards the universal.

Since we have chosen as an example the image of the Tree, let us see what is its function in the realm of the unconscious. We know that such images occur fairly frequently in dreams; this is one of the images recurrent in our deeper life, and its appearance indicates, it seems, that the drama which is being enacted in the unconscious—one that concerns the integrity of psycho-mental activity, and therefore of the person's whole existence—is on the way to finding a positive solution. That is to say, the meaning which is becoming decipherable at the level of oneiric or imaginative experience is integrating itself in the scale of values which, upon the plane of religious experience, is revealed by the symbolism of the Tree. Now, in mythologies and religions, the principal meanings of the Tree-symbolism—otherwise complex enough—are bound up with the ideas of periodic and unending renewal, of regeneration, of "the source of life and youth", of immortality and of absolute reality. Yet, so long as the image of the Tree is not revealing itself in its symbolic aspect—that is, not awakening the whole consciousness of the man and "opening" it to the universal—one cannot say that it has completely fulfilled its function. By emerging into his dreams, the image of the Tree has "saved" the man only in part from his individual predicament—has made him able, for example, to integrate a crisis in the depths and to recover his psychic balance, which was more or less seriously menaced. But, not having been accepted in its symbolic sense, the image of the Tree has not succeeded in revealing the universal, and therefore has not lifted the man up to the plane of the Spirit, as religion, however rudimentary, always does.

This may serve to indicate the perspective in which it is useful and fruitful to draw comparisons between the two universes of the historian of religions and of the depth-psychologist respectively. But there can be no question of confusing their frames of reference, nor their scales of value nor, above all, their methods.

June, 1956
Le Val d'Or

CONTEMPORARY
FAITHS

I

The Myths of the Modern World

WHAT EXACTLY is a myth? In the language current during the nineteenth century, a "myth" meant anything that was opposed to "reality": the creation of Adam, or the invisible man, no less than the history of the world as described by the Zulus, or the *Theogony* of Hesiod—these were all "myths". Like many another cliché of the Enlightenment and of Positivism, this, too, was of Christian origin and structure; for, according to primitive Christianity, everything which could not be justified by reference to one or the other of the two Testaments was untrue; it was a "fable". But the researches of the ethnologists have obliged us to go behind this semantic inheritance from the Christian polemics against the pagan world. We are at last beginning to know and understand the value of the myth, as it has been elaborated in "primitive" and archaic societies—that is, among those groups of mankind where the myth happens to be the very foundation of social life and culture. Now, one fact strikes us immediately: in such societies the myth is thought to express the *absolute truth*, because it narrates a *sacred history*; that is, a transhuman revelation which took place at the dawn of the Great Time, in the holy time of the beginnings (*in illo tempore*). Being *real* and *sacred*, the myth becomes exemplary, and consequently *repeatable*, for it serves as a model, and by the same token as a justification, for all human actions. In other words, a myth is a *true history* of what came to pass at the beginning of Time, and one which provides the pattern for human behaviour. In *imitating* the exemplary acts of a god or of a mythic hero, or simply by recounting their adventures, the man of an archaic society detaches himself from profane time and magically re-enters the Great Time, the sacred time.

23

Clearly, what we are dealing with here is a complete reversal of values; whilst current language confuses the myth with "fables", a man of the traditional societies sees it as the *only valid revelation of reality*. Little time was lost before conclusions were drawn from this discovery. Little by little, one ceased to insist upon the fact that the myth narrates impossibilities or improbabilities: one was content to say that it constituted a way of thinking different from ours, but that in any case we ought not to treat it *a priori* as an aberration. One went still further; one tried to integrate the myth into the general history of thought, by regarding it as the most important form of collective thinking. And, since "collective thinking" is never completely abolished in any society, whatever its degree of evolution, one did not fail to observe that the modern world still preserves some mythical behaviour: for example, the participation of an entire society in certain symbols has been interpreted as a survival of "collective thinking". It was not difficult to show that the function of a national flag, with all the affective experiences that go with it, was in no way different from the "participation" in any of the symbols of the archaic societies. This was as much as to say that, *upon the plane of social living*, there was no break in the continuity between the archaic world and the modern world. The one great difference was that of the presence, in the majority of the individuals who constitute modern societies, of a personal thinking that was absent, or almost so, among the members of traditional societies.

This is not the place to begin a discussion of the general considerations raised by this "collective thinking". Ours is a more modest problem: if the myth is not just an infantile or aberrant creation of "primitive" humanity, but is the expression of *a mode of being in the world*, what has become of myths in the modern world? Or, more precisely, what has taken the *essential* place occupied by the myth in traditional societies? For, if certain "participations" in myths and collective symbols still survive in the modern world, they are far from filling the central part played by the myth in traditional societies; in comparison with these, our modern world seems destitute of myths. It has even been held that the diseases and crises of modern societies are rightly attributable to the absence of a mythology appropriate to them. When Jung entitled one of his books *Modern Man in Search of a Soul*, he implied that the modern world—in crisis ever since its profound break with Christianity—is in quest of a new myth, which alone could enable it to draw upon fresh spiritual resources and renew its creative powers.[1]

It is true that, at least apparently, the modern world is not rich in myths. It was said, for instance, of the General Strike, that this was one of the rare myths created by the modern world. But that was a misunderstanding: it was supposed that an *idea*, accessible to a considerable number of individuals and therefore "popular", could become a *myth* for the simple reason that its realisation was projected into a more or less remote future. But that is not the way myths are "created". The general strike might be an instrument of political combat, but it has no mythical precedents, and that alone is enough to exclude it from mythical status.

Very different is the case of Marxian communism. Let us leave aside all question of the philosophic validity of Marxism and of its historic destiny, and consider only the mythological pattern of communism and the eschatological meaning of its popular success. For whatever we may think of the scientific claims of Marx, it is clear that the author of the *Communist Manifesto* takes up and carries on one of the great eschatological myths of the Middle Eastern and Mediterranean world, namely: the redemptive part to be played by the Just (the "elect", the "anointed", the "innocent". the "missioners", in our own days by the proletariat), whose sufferings are invoked to change the ontological status of the world. In fact, Marx's classless society,

[1]By the "modern world", we mean contemporary Western society; but also a certain state of mind which has been formed by successive deposits ever since the Renaissance and the Reformation. The active classes of the urban societies are in this sense " modern "—that is, the mass of mankind which has been more or less directly shaped by education and official culture. The rest of the population, especially in central and south-eastern Europe, still maintains its attachment to a traditional and half-Christian spiritual universe. The agricultural societies are, as a rule, passive towards History; most of the time they merely undergo it, and when directly involved in the great historical turmoils (for instance, the barbarian invasions of late antiquity), their reaction is that of passive resistance.

and the consequent disappearance of all historical tensions, find their most exact precedent in the myth of the Golden Age which, according to a number of traditions, lies at the beginning and the end of History. Marx has enriched this venerable myth with a truly messianic Judæo-Christian ideology; on the one hand, by the prophetic and soteriological function he ascribes to the proletariat; and, on the other, by the final struggle between Good and Evil, which may well be compared with the apocalyptic conflict between Christ and Antichrist, ending in the decisive victory of the former. It is indeed significant that Marx turns to his own account the Judæo-Christian eschatological hope of an *absolute goal of History*; in that he parts company from the other historical philosophers (Croce, for instance, and Ortega y Gasset), for whom the tensions of history are implicit in the human condition, and therefore can never be completely abolished.

In comparison with the grandeur and the vigorous optimism of the communist myth, the mythology propagated by the National Socialists seems peculiarly inept; and this not only because of the limitations of the racial myth (how could one imagine that the rest of Europe would voluntarily accept submission to a master-race?), but above all because of the fundamental pessimism of the Germanic mythology. In its effort to abolish Christian values and rediscover the spiritual sources of "the race"—that is, of Nordic paganism—Nazism was obliged to try to reanimate the Germanic mythology. But from the point of view of the depth-psychologists, such an effort was, in effect, an invitation to collective suicide; for the *eschaton* prophesied and expected by the ancient Germans was the *ragnarök*—that is, a catastrophic *end of the world*. This included a gigantic combat between the gods and the demons, ending in the death of all the gods and all the heroes and a final regression of the world into chaos. It is true that, after the *ragnarök*, the world was to be reborn, regenerated (for the ancient Germans, too, knew the doctrine of the cosmic cycles, the myth of recurrent creations and destructions of the world); nevertheless, to substitute Nordic mythology for Christianity was to replace an eschatology rich in promises and consolations (for to the Christian, the "end of the world" completes and at the same time regenerates History) by an *eschaton* that was frankly pessimistic. Translated into political terms, this substitution almost amounted to saying: Give up your old Judæo-Christian stories, and re-kindle, in the depths of your souls, the beliefs of your ancestors the Germans; then prepare yourselves for the last grand battle between our gods and the demonic forces: in that apocalyptic battle our gods and our heroes and we ourselves with them will all perish; that will be the *ragnarök*; but another world will be born later on. The wonder is, how such a pessimistic vision of the end of history could ever have fired the imagination of even a portion of the German people; and the fact that it did so has not yet ceased to raise problems for the psychologists.

2

Apart from these two political myths, modern societies do not seem to have entertained any others of comparable range. We are thinking of the myth as *a type of human behaviour* and, at the same time, as *an element of civilisation*—that is, of the myth as one finds it in traditional societies. For at the level of *individual experience* it has never completely disappeared: it makes itself felt in the dreams, the fantasies and the longings of the modern man; and an abundant psychological literature has now accustomed us to rediscoveries of both the big and the little mythologies in the unconscious and half-conscious activity of every individual. But what now interests us above all is to find out what it is, in the modern world, that fills the *central* position occupied by the myth in traditional societies. In other words, while recognising that the great mythical themes continue to repeat themselves in the obscure depths of the psyche, we still wonder whether the myth, as an exemplary pattern of human behaviour, may not also survive among our contemporaries in more or less degraded forms. It seems that a myth itself, as well as the symbols it brings into play, never quite disappears from the present world of the psyche; it only changes its aspect and disguises its operations. Would it not be instructive to prolong the enquiry and unmask the operations of myths upon the *social plane*?

Here is one example. It is clearly the case that certain festivals observed in the modern world, though apparently secular, still preserve a mythical structure and function: the rejoicings over the New Year, or the festivities following the birth of a child, or the building of a house, or even the removal into a new flat, show the obscurely-felt need for an *entirely new beginning*, of an *incipit vita nova*—that is, of a complete regeneration. Remote as these profane rejoicings may be from their mythic archetype—the periodic repetition of the creation[1]—it is none the less evident that modern man still feels the need for periodic re-enactments of such scenarios, however secularised they have become. There are no means of estimating how far modern man is still aware of any mythological implications of his festivities; what matters to us is that such celebrations still have a resonance, obscure but profound, throughout his being.

That is but one example; it may enlighten us, however, with regard to what appears to be a general situation: that certain mythical themes still survive in modern societies, but are not readily recognisable since they have undergone a long process of laicisation. This has long been known: indeed, modern societies might be simply defined as those which have pushed the secularisation of life and of the Cosmos far enough: the novelty of the modern world consists in its revaluation, at the secular level, of the ancient sacred values.[2] What we want to know, however, is whether anything else of the "mythical" survives in the modern world, besides what presents itself merely in the form of proce-

---

[1] *Cf.* my book *The Myth of the Eternal Return*, Trans. by W. R. Trask, London, 1955, pp. 83ff.

[2] This process is very well exemplified by the transformation of the values ascribed to Nature. We have not abolished the relationship of sympathy between man and Nature; nor was that possible. But this relationship has changed in value and in its orientation; for the magico-religious sympathy we have substituted emotion, either æsthetic or simply sentimental; sporting and hygienic appreciation, etc.; while contemplation of Nature has been ousted by observation, experiment and calculation. It could not be said of a physicist of the Renaissance, or of a naturalist of our own days, that he did not "love Nature"; but in this "love" one could no longer find anything of the spiritual attitude of the man in the archaic societies—such as that which is still maintained in European agricultural societies.

dures and values re-interpreted to fit the secular plane. If all the phenomena were of that description, we should have to agree that the modern world was radically opposed to all the historic forms that had preceded it. But the very presence of Christianity excludes such a hypothesis. Christianity admits none of the secularised views of the Cosmos or of life which are characteristic of all "modern" culture.

The question this raises is not a simple one; but since the Western world, or a great part of it, still claims to be Christian, it cannot be evaded. I shall not insist upon what are at present called the "mythical elements" in Christianity. Whatever may be said about these "mythical elements" it is a long time since they were Christianised, and, in any case, the importance of Christianity must be judged in another perspective. But, from time to time, voices are raised asserting that the modern world is no longer, or is not yet, Christian. For our present purpose we need not concern ourselves with those who put their hopes in *Entmythologisierung*, who believe it is necessary to "de-mythologise" Christianity to recover its essential truth. Some think just the opposite. Jung, for instance, believes that the crisis of the modern world is in great part due to the fact that the Christian symbols and "myths" are no longer lived by the whole human being; that they have been reduced to words and gestures deprived of life, fossilised, externalised and therefore no longer of any use for the deeper life of the psyche.

To us the question presents itself differently: to what extent is Christianity maintaining, in modern secularised and laicised society, a spiritual horizon comparable to that of archaic societies, where the myth predominates? Let us say at once that Christianity has nothing to fear from such a comparison: its specificity is assured, it is guaranteed by *faith* as the category *sui generis* of religious experience, and by its valorisation in *history*. With the exception of Judaism, no other pre-Christian religion has set a value on history as a direct and irreversible manifestation of God in the world, nor on faith—in the sense inaugurated by Abraham —as a unique means of salvation. Consequently the Christian polemic against the religious world of paganism is, historically speaking, obsolete: Christianity is no longer in danger of being confused with any other religion or gnosis whatsoever. This having been said, and in view of the discovery, which is quite recent, that the myth represents a certain mode of being in the world, it is no less true that Christianity, *by the very fact that it is a religion*, has had to preserve at least one mythic attitude— the attitude towards liturgical time; that is, the rejection of profane time and the periodical recovery of the Great Time, *illud tempus* of "the beginnings".

For the Christian, Jesus Christ is not a mythical personage: on the contrary, he is a historical personage; his greatness itself is founded upon that absolute historicity. For the Christ not only made himself man, "man in general", but accepted the historical condition of the people in whose midst he chose to be born; and he had recourse to no miracle to escape from that historicity— although he worked plenty of miracles in order to modify the "historical situations" of others—by curing the paralytic, raising Lazarus, etc. Nevertheless, the religious experience of the Christian is based upon an imitation of the Christ as *exemplary pattern*, upon the liturgical repetition of the life, death and resurrection of the Lord and upon the *contemporaneity* of the Christian with *illud tempus* which begins with the Nativity at Bethlehem and ends, provisionally, with the Ascension. Now, we know that the initiation of a transhuman model, the repetition of an exemplary scenario and the breakaway from profane time through a moment which opens out into the Great Time, are the essential marks of "mythical behaviour"—that is, the behaviour of the man of the archaic societies, who finds the very source of his existence in the myth. One is always *contemporary with a myth*, during the time when one repeats it or imitates the gestures of the mythic personages. Kierkegaard's requirement of the true Christian was that he should be a contemporary of the Christ. But even one who is not a "true Christian" in Kierkegaard's sense still is, and cannot *not* be, a contemporary of Christ; for the liturgical time in which the Christian *lives* during the divine service is no longer profane duration but is essentially sacred time, the time in which the Word is made flesh, the *illud tempus* of the Gospels. A Christian is not taking part in a commemoration of the Passion of Christ, as he might be joining in the annual celebration of the Fourth of July or the Eleventh of November, for example. He is not commemorating an event but re-actualising a mystery. For the Christian, Jesus dies and resurrects before him *hic et nunc*. Through the mystery of the Passion or of the Resurrection, the Christian dispels profane time and is integrated into time primordial and holy.

It is needless to insist upon the radical differences that divide Christianity from the archaic world: they are too obvious to give rise to misunderstandings. But there remains the identity of behaviour that we have just recalled. To the Christian, as to the man of the archaic societies, time is not homogeneous: it is subject to periodical ruptures which divide it into "secular duration" and a "sacred time", the latter being indefinitely reversible, in the sense that it repeats itself to infinity without ceasing to be the same time. It is said that Christianity, unlike the archaic religions, proclaims and awaits the end of Time; which is true of the "profane duration", of History, but not of the liturgical time inaugurated by the Incarnation. The Christological *illud tempus* will not be done away with at the end of History.

These few cursory observations have shown us in what sense Christianity is prolonging a "mythical" conduct of life into the modern world. If we take account of the true nature and function of the myth, Christianity does not appear to have surpassed the mode of being of archaic man; but then it could not. *Homo naturaliter Christianus*. It remains, however, to enquire what has taken the place of the myth among those of the moderns who have preserved nothing of Christianity but the dead letter.

3

It seems unlikely that any society could completely dispense with myths, for, of what is essential in mythical behaviour—the exemplary pattern, the repetition, the break with profane duration and integration into primordial time—the first two at least are consubstantial with every human condition. Thus, it is not so difficult to recognise, in all that modern people call instruction, education and didactic culture, the function that is fulfilled by the myth in archaic societies. This is so not only because myths represent both the sum of ancestral traditions and the norms it is important not to transgress, and because their transmission— generally secret, initiatory—is equivalent to the more or less official "education" of a modern society. The homology of the respective functions of the myth and of our public instruction is verified above all when we consider the origins of the exemplary models upheld by European education. In antiquity there was no hiatus between mythology and history: historical personages endeavoured to imitate their archetypes, the gods and mythical heroes.[1]

And the lives and deeds of those personages, in their turn, became paradigms for posterity. Livy had already assembled a rich array of models for young Romans to emulate, when Plutarch wrote his *Lives of Famous Men*, a veritable mine of examples for the centuries to come. The moral and civic virtues of these illustrious personages continued to provide the supreme criteria for European pedagogy, especially after the Renaissance. Right to the end of the nineteenth century European education for citizenship was still following the archetypes of classical antiquity, those models which had been made manifest *in illo tempore*, in that privileged interval of time which educated Europeans regarded as the highest point of the Greco-Latin culture.

But they did not think of assimilating the functions of mythology to the process of instruction, because they overlooked one of the chief characteristics of the myth, which is the creation of exemplary models for a whole society. In this, moreover, we recognise a very general human tendency; namely, to hold up one life-history as a paradigm and turn a historical personage into an archetype. This tendency survives even among the most eminent representatives of the modern mentality. As Gide has

[1]Upon this point, one may refer to the researches of Georges Dumézil. *Cf.* also my *The Myth of the Eternal Return*, pp. 37ff.

rightly observed, Goethe was highly conscious of a mission to lead a life that would be exemplary for the rest of humanity. In all that he did he was trying to *create an example*. In his own life he, in his turn, was imitating, if not the lives of the gods and mythical heroes, at least their behaviour. As Paul Valéry wrote in 1932: "He represents for us, *gentlemen of the human race*, one of our best attempts to render ourselves like gods."

But this imitation of model lives is promoted not only by means of school education. Concurrently with official pedagogy, and long after this has ceased to exert its authority, modern man is subjected to the influence of a potent if diffuse mythology that offers him a number of patterns for imitation. Heroes, real and imaginary, play an important part in the formation of European adolescents: the characters in tales of adventure, heroes of war, screen favourites, etc. This mythology is continually enriched with the growing years; we meet, one after another, the exemplary figures thrown up by changes of fashion, and we try to become like them. Critical writers have often pointed out modern versions of, for example, Don Juan, the political or the military hero, the hapless lover; of the cynic, the nihilist, the melancholy poet, and so forth: all these models are carrying on mythological traditions which their topical forms reveal in mythical behaviour. The copying of these archetypes betrays a certain discontent with one's own personal history; an obscure striving to transcend one's own local, provincial history and to recover some "Great Time" or other—though it be only the mythic Time of the first surrealist or existentialist manifesto.

But an adequate analysis of the diffuse mythologies of the modern world would run into volumes: for myths and mythological images are to be found everywhere, laicised, degraded or disguised; one only needs to be able to recognise them. We have referred to the mythological basis of New Year celebrations, and of the festivities that mark any "new beginning"; in which we can discern anew the nostalgia for a *renewal*, the yearning for the world to be renovated; that one might enter upon a new History, in a world reborn; that is, *created afresh*. It would be easy to multiply instances. The myth of the lost paradise still survives in the images of a paradisiac island or a land of innocence; a privileged land where laws are abolished and Time stands still. For it is important to underline this fact—that it is, above all, *by analysing the attitude of the modern man towards Time that we can penetrate the disguises of his mythological behaviour.* We must never forget that one of the essential functions of the myth is its provision of an opening into the Great Time, a periodic re-entry into Time primordial. This is shown by a tendency to a neglect of the present time, of what is called the "historic moment".

The Polynesians, when setting out upon a grandiose maritime adventure, are careful to deny its "novelty", its unprecedentedness, its spontaneity; for them, it is only a case of repeating the voyage that was made by some mythical hero *in illo tempore*, to " show men the way", to set an example. But thus to embark on a present adventure as the reiteration of a mythic saga is as much as to put the present time out of mind. Such disinclination to face historic time, together with an obscure desire to share in some glorious, primordial, *total* Time, is betrayed, in the case of modern people, by a sometimes desperate effort to break through the homogeneity of time, to "get beyond" duration and re-enter a time qualitatively different from that which creates, in its course, their own history. It is with this in mind that we can render the best account of what has become of myths in the world of today. For modern man, too, by means that are multiple, but homologous, is endeavouring to liberate himself from his "history" and to live in a qualitatively different temporal rhythm. And in so doing he is returning, without being aware of it, to the mythical style of life.

One can understand this better if one looks more closely at the two principal ways of "escape" in use by modern people— visual entertainment, and reading. We need not go into all the mythical precedents for our public spectacles; it is enough to recall the ritual origins of bull-fighting, racing and athletic contests; they all have this point in common, that they take place in a "concentrated time", time of a heightened intensity; a residuum of, or substitute for, magico-religious time. This "concentrated time" is also the specific dimension of the theatre and the cinema. Even if we take no account of the ritual origins and mythological structure of the drama or the film, there is still the important fact that these are two kinds of spectacle that make us live in time of a quality quite other than that of "secular duration", in a temporal rhythm, at once concentrated and articulated, which, apart from all æsthetic implications, evokes a profound echo in the spectator.

4

When we turn to reading, the question is of greater subtlety. It is concerned, on the one hand, with the forms and the mythical origins of literature and, on the other, with the mythological function that reading performs in the mind that feeds upon it. The successive stages of myth, legend, epic and modern literature have often been pointed out and need not detain us here. Let us merely recall the fact that the mythical archetypes survive to some degree in the great modern novels. The difficulties and trials that the novelist's hero has to pass through are prefigured in the adventures of the mythic Heroes. It has been possible also to show how the mythic themes of the primordial waters, of the isles of Paradise, of the quest of the Holy Grail, of heroic and mystical initiation, etc., still dominate modern European literature. Quite recently we have seen, in surrealism, a prodigious outburst of mythical themes and primordial symbols. As for the literature of the bookstalls, its mythological character is obvious. Every popular novel has to present the exemplary struggle between Good and Evil, the hero and the villain (modern incarnation of the Demon), and repeat one of those universal motives of folk-lore, the persecuted young woman, salvation by love, the unknown protector, etc. Even detective novels, as Roger Caillois has so well demonstrated, are full of mythological themes.

Need we recall how much lyric poetry renews and continues the myths? All poetry is an effort to *re-create* the language; in other words, to abolish current language, that of every day, and to invent a new, private and personal speech, in the last analysis *secret.* But poetic creation, like linguistic creation, implies the abolition of time—of the history concentrated in language—and tends towards the recovery of the paradisiac, primordial situation; of the days when one could *create spontaneously*, when the *past* did not exist because there was no consciousness of time, no memory of temporal duration. It is said, moreover, in our own days, that for a great poet the past does not exist: the poet discovers the world as though he were present at the cosmogonic moment, contemporaneous with the first day of the Creation. From a certain point of view, we may say that every great poet is *remaking* the world, for he is trying to see it as if there were no Time, no History. In this his attitude is strangely like that of the "primitive", of the man in traditional society.

But we are interested chiefly in the mythological function of reading in itself; for here we are dealing with a specific phenomenon of the modern world, unknown in earlier civilisations. Reading replaces not only the oral folk traditions, such as still survive in rural communities of Europe, but also the recital of the myths in the archaic societies. Now, reading, perhaps even more than visual entertainment, gives one a break in duration, and at the same time an "escape from time". Whether we are "killing time" with a detective story, or entering into another temporal universe as we do in reading any kind of novel, we are taken out of our own duration to move in other rhythms, to live in a different history. In this sense reading offers us an "easy way", it provides a modification of experience at little cost: for the modern man it is the supreme "distraction", yielding him the illusion of a *mastery of Time* which, we may well suspect, gratifies a secret desire to withdraw from the implacable becoming that leads towards death.

The defence against Time which is revealed to us in every kind of mythological attitude, but which is, in fact, inseparable from the human condition, reappears variously disguised in the modern world, but above all in its *distractions*, its amusements. It is here that one sees what a radical difference there is between modern cultures and other civilisations. In all traditional societies, every responsible action reproduced its mythical, transhuman model, and consequently took place in sacred time. Labour, handicrafts, war and love were all sacraments. The re-living of that which the Gods and Heroes had lived *in illo tempore* imparted a sacramental aspect to human existence, which was complemented by the sacramental nature ascribed to life and to the Cosmos. By thus opening out into the Great Time, this sacramental existence, poor as it might often be, was nevertheless rich in significance; at all events it was not under the tyranny of Time. The true "fall into Time" begins with the secularisation of work. It is only in modern societies that man feels himself to be the prisoner of his daily work, in which he can never escape from Time. And since he can no longer "kill" time during his working hours—that is, while he is expressing his real social identity—he strives to get away from Time in his hours of leisure: hence the bewildering number of distractions invented by modern civilisation. In other terms, it is just as though the order of things were reversed from what it is in traditional societies, for there, "distractions" hardly exist; every responsible occupation is itself an "escape from Time". It is for this reason that, as we have just seen, in the great majority of individuals who do not participate in any authentic religious experience, the mythical attitude can be discerned in their distractions, as well as in their unconscious psychic activity (dreams, fantasies, nostalgias, etc.). And this means that the "fall into Time" becomes confused with the secularisation of work and the consequent mechanisation of existence—that it brings about a scarcely disguisable loss of freedom; and the only escape that remains possible upon the collective plane is distraction.

These few observations will suffice. We cannot say that the modern world has completely eliminated mythical behaviour; but only that its field of action is changed: the myth is no longer dominant in the essential sectors of life: it has been repressed, partly into the obscurer levels of the psyche, partly into the secondary or even irresponsible activities of society. It is true that mythical behaviour persists, though disguised, in the part that is played by education, but this is almost exclusively in what concerns the very young; and, what is more, the exemplary func-

tion of education is on the way to disappearance: modern pedagogy encourages spontaneity. Except in authentically religious
life, the myth functions, as we have seen, chiefly in distractions.
But it will never disappear; in the collective life it sometimes
reasserts itself with considerable force, in the form of a political
myth.

It is no less safe to predict that the understanding of the myth
will one day be counted among the most useful discoveries of the
twentieth century. Western man is no longer the master of the
world; he is no longer managing "natives" but talking with
other men. It is as well that he should learn how to open the
conversation. It is necessary for him to realise that there is no
longer any break in the continuity between the "primitive" or
"backward" world and that of the modern West. It is not
enough, as it was half a century ago, to discover and admire the
art of Negroes or Pacific islanders: we have now to rediscover
the spiritual sources of these arts in ourselves; we must become
aware of what it is, in a modern existence, that is still "mythical",
and survives as such simply because this, too, is part and parcel of
the human condition, in that it expresses the anxiety of man
living in Time.

II

The Myth of the Noble Savage or, the Prestige of the Beginning

UNA ISOLA MUY HERMOSA...

AN EMINENT Italian writer upon folk-lore, G. Cocchiara, lately wrote that: "Before being discovered, the savage was first invented."[1] This witty observation is not without its truth. The sixteenth, seventeenth and eighteenth centuries invented a type of "noble savage" as a criterion for their moral, political and social disquisitions. Idealists and utopians seemed to be infatuated with "savages", especially their conduct in regard to family life, society and property; envying their freedom, their just and equitable division of labour, their beatific existence in the bosom of Nature. But this "invention" of a savage congenial to the sensibilities and the ideology of the seventeenth and eighteenth centuries was but a revalorisation, in radically secularised form, of a much more ancient myth—the myth of the earthly Paradise and its inhabitants in the fabulous times before History. Instead of an "invention" of the good savage, one really ought to speak of the mythicised memory of his exemplary Image.

To recall the essential records: we know that, before they constituted a dossier for an ethnography yet to be born, the journals of travellers in the newly-discovered countries were read and appreciated for a very special reason; that they described a blissful humanity which had escaped the misdeeds of civilisation and provided models for utopian societies. From Pietro Martire and Jean de Léry to Lafitau, the travellers and learned men outdid one another in praising the goodness, the purity and the

[1]Giuseppe Cocchiara, *Il Mito del Buon Selvaggio, Introduzione alla storia delle teorie etnologiche,* Messina, 1948, p. 7.

happiness of savage peoples. Pietro Martire, in his *Decades de Orbe Novo* (1511, completed in 1530), evokes the age of gold, and embellishes the Christian ideology about God and the earthly Paradise with classical reminiscences; he compares the condition of savages with the realm of beatitude sung by Virgil—the *saturnia regna*. The Jesuits likened the savages to the ancient Greeks, and Fr. Lafitau, in 1724, found among them the last living vestiges of antiquity. Las Casas had no doubt that the utopias of the sixteenth century could be realised; and the Jesuits were only putting his conclusions into practice when they founded their theocratic state in Paraguay.

It would be idle to pretend that these interpretations and apologias amounted to one consistent conclusion. There were different emphases, reservations and corrections. The subject has been sufficiently well known, since the studies of R. Allier, E. Fuetter, R. Gonnard, N. H. Fairchild, G. Cocchiara and others, to excuse us from pursuing it further. We must note, however, that these "savages" of the two Americas and of the Indian Ocean were far from being representative of "primitive culture"; far from being peoples "without history", or *Naturvölkern*, as they are still called in Germany. They were indeed highly "civilised" in the obvious sense of the term (we now know that every society constitutes a civilisation), and above all in comparison with other "primitives" such as the Australians, the Pygmies or the Fuegians. Between the latter and the Brazilians or the Hurons who were so much extolled by the explorers and the idealists, there was in fact a gulf comparable to that which divides the paleolithic from the early neolithic, or even from the chalcolithic. The true primitives, the "primitive of the primitive", have been only rather lately discovered and described; but this discovery, in the heyday of Positivism, has had no effect upon the myth of the noble savage.[1]

This "good savage", who was compared with the models of classical antiquity and even with Biblical characters, was an old acquaintance. The mythic image of a "natural man" who lived before history and civilisation had never been wholly effaced.

[1]These "true primitives" played an important part in positivist and evolutionary mythology, before they were re-evaluated by Fr. Wilhelm Schmidt, as adherents of an *Urmonotheismus*, the last believers in the primordial revelation.

During the Middle Ages it was merged with that of the earthly Paradise, which inspired the adventures of so many navigators. The memory of a Golden Age had haunted antiquity since Hesiod's time, and Horace thought he saw the purity of patriarchal life among the barbarians.[1] He suffered, even then, from the nostalgia for a simple and sane existence in the bosom of Nature.[2] The myth of the noble savage. was but a renewal and continuation of the myth of the Golden Age; that is, of *the perfection of the beginning of things*. Were we to believe the idealists and utopians of the Renaissance, the loss of the Golden Age was the fault of "civilisation". The state of innocence, and the spiritual blessedness of man before the fall, in the paradisiac myth, becomes, in the myth of the good savage, the pure, free and happy state of the exemplary man, surrounded by a maternal and generous Nature. But in that image of primordial Nature we can easily recognise the features of a paradisiac landscape.[3]

One detail that strikes one immediately, is that the "noble savage" described by the navigators and extolled by the idealists belonged, in a good many cases, to a society of cannibals. The travellers make no mystery of this. Pietro Martire encountered some cannibals in the West Indies (the Caribs) and on the coast of Venezuela, a fact which did not, however, deter him from talking about the Age of Gold. During his second voyage to Brazil (1549–1555), Hans Stades was taken prisoner nine times by the Tupinaba; and in the narrative he published in 1557 he describes in considerable detail the cannibalism of his captors: he even includes some singular wood-engravings of it. Another explorer, O. Dapper, also illustrated his book with numerous engravings representing the various procedures at cannibal feasts in Brazil.[4] As for Jean de Léry's travel-book on Brazil,[5] this was read and annotated by Montaigne, who left us his opinion about cannibalism—he thought it was more barbarous "to eat a man alive than to eat

[1]The *Odes*, II, 24, 12–29.
[2]Upon all this, see Lovejoy and Boas, *Documentary history of Primitivism and related ideas in antiquity*, Vol. I, Oxford-Baltimore, 1935.
[3]We should note also that "Nature", and especially exotic nature, never lost this paradisiac aspect and function, not even during the more obtuse of the phases of positivism.
[4]Cf. *Die Unbekannte Neue Welt*, Amsterdam, 1637.
[5]Jean de Léry, *L'Histoire d'un voyage fait en la terre de Brézil, autrement dite Amérique*, 1568.

him dead". Garcilasso de la Vega, upon the Incas, went further still. He praised the empire of the Incas as an example of the ideal State; the goodness and happiness of the natives as worthy to serve as a model to the European world.[1] It is true, added Garcilasso de la Vega, that before the domination of the Incas cannibalism was spreading all over Peru, and he dwells at length upon the passion of these natives for human flesh. (This was the statement of a well-informed man: the regions of Peru and the upper Amazon are notorious in the annals of anthropophagy, and cannibal tribes have still not ceased to be discovered there.)

But while such information was growing ever more abundant and accurate, the myth of the good savage still pursued its brilliant career through all the utopias and social theorisings of the West up to Jean-Jacques Rousseau—which, from our point of view, is highly instructive. It shows that the unconscious of Occidental man had not given up the old dream of finding contemporary men still living in an earthly Paradise. All this literature about savages is therefore precious documentation for the study of the minds of Western men: it reveals their longing for the conditions of Eden—a longing attested, furthermore, by so many other paradisiac images and attitudes—the islands and the heavenly landscapes of the tropics, the blessed nudity, the beauty of native women, sexual freedom and so forth. The list of clichés is interminable: *una isola muy hermosa . . ., tierras formosisimas . . .* One could write a fascinating study of these exemplary images; it would reveal the innumerable disguises in which the nostalgia for Paradise appears. One question is of the greatest interest to us, since the myth of the good savage is the creation of a memory: is it of Judæo-Christian origin, or is it traceable to classical reminiscences? What matters most, however, is that the men of the Renaissance, like those of the Middle Ages and the Classical period, cherished memories of a mythical time when man was good, perfect and happy; and in the aboriginals they were then discovering they expected to find contemporaries of that primordial, mythical epoch.

[1] *Cf.* Cocchiara, *op. cit.*, p. 11, upon G. de la Vega; *Commentarios reales que tratan del origen de los Incas.* 1609 and 1617.

It will not be irrelevant to pursue our enquiry by asking what the savages thought about themselves, how *they* estimated their freedom and happiness. Research into that question would have been inconceivable in the days of Montaigne and Lafitau; but modern ethnology has made it possible. So let us leave the mythologies of the Western utopians and idealists, and examine those of the newly-found "good savages".

THE CARES OF THE CANNIBAL

The savages, for their own part, were also aware of having lost a primitive Paradise. In the modern jargon, we might say that the savages regarded themselves, neither more nor less than if they had been Western Christians, as beings in a "fallen" condition, by contrast with a fabulously happy situation in the past. Their actual condition was not their original one: it had been brought about by a catastrophe that had occurred *in illo tempore*. Before that disaster, man had enjoyed a life which was not dissimilar from that of Adam before he sinned. The myths of Paradise differed, no doubt, from one culture to another, but certain common features constantly recur: at that time man was immortal and able to meet God face to face; he was happy, and did not have to work for his food; either a Tree provided him with subsistence, or else the agricultural implements worked for him of themselves, like automata. There are other and equally important elements in this paradisiac myth (the relations between Heaven and Earth, authority over the animals, etc.), but we may dispense with analysis of them here.[1] For the moment what needs to be emphasised is that the "good savage" of the travellers and theorists of the sixteenth to the eighteenth centuries already knew the Myth of the Good Savage; he was their own ancestor who had really lived a paradisiac life, enjoying every beatitude and every freedom without having to make the slightest effort. But this Good primordial Ancestor, like the Biblical Ancestor of the

[1]See below, p. 59ff.

Europeans, had lost his Paradise. For the savage, too, *perfection had existed at the beginning.*

There was, however, a difference, which is of capital importance: the savage took pains not to forget what had come to pass *in illo tempore.* Periodically he re-memorised the essential events which had placed him in the position of "fallen" man. And it must be said at once, the importance he attached to precise recollection of the mythical events did not imply any high valuation of memory for its own sake: primitive man was interested only in the *beginnings,* in what had taken place *ab origine*: to him it mattered little what had happened to himself, or to others like him, in more or less distant times. We have not space here to deal at length with this peculiar attitude towards events and to Time. But it is necessary to recognise that, for the primitive, there are two categories of events, taking place in two kinds of Time which are qualitatively irreducible: one of these comprises the events that we call mythical, which took place *ab origine* and which constitute cosmogony, anthropogony, the myths of inauguration (of institutions, civilisations and of culture), and *all this he must memorise.* The other comprises the events that follow no exemplary pattern, the facts which have merely happened and, for him, are not interesting: he forgets them; he "burns" the memory of them.

Periodically, the most important events were re-enacted, and so re-lived: thus, one recited the cosmogony, repeated the exemplary gestures of the Gods, the deeds that founded civilisation. There was a nostalgia for the *origins*; in some cases one could even speak of a nostalgia for the primordial Paradise. The real "nostalgia for Paradise" is found among the mystics of the primitive societies; during their ecstasies, they enter into the paradisiac condition of the mythic Ancestor before the "fall".[1] These ecstatic experiences are not without consequence for the whole community: all its ideas about the Gods and the nature of the soul, the mystical geographies of Heaven and the Land of the Dead, and, in general, the diverse conceptions of "spirituality", as well as the origins of lyric poetry and the epic and—partly, at all

[1]See below, p. 66.

events—the origins of music, are more or less directly derived from such ecstatic experiences of the shamanist type. One may say, then, that the nostalgia for Paradise, the longing to recover the Eden-like state of the Ancestor, were it only for the briefest space of time and only in an ecstasy, has had considerable repercussions upon the cultural creations of primitive man.

Among a great many peoples, notably the earliest cultivators of tubers (but not of cereals), the traditions about the origins of the present condition of man appear in a still more dramatic form. According to their mythology, man became what he is today— mortal, sexual and condemned to labour—in consequence of a primordial murder. *In illo tempore* a divine Being, often enough in the form of a young woman, sometimes of a child or a man, consented to be immolated in order that the tubers of the fruit-trees might grow from his or her body. This first assassination radically altered the mode of being of the human race. The immolation of the divine Being brought about the necessity for food, no less than the fatality of death, and, by way of consequence, sexuality—the only means of assuring the continuity of life. The body of the immolated divinity was transformed into nourishment; his soul descended beneath the earth, where it founded the Country of the Dead. Ad. E. Jensen who has devoted an important study to divinities of this type—whom he calls *dema* divinities —has very clearly shown us how, both in nourishing himself and in dying, man participates in the existence of the *dema*.[1]

Among all these paleo-agricultural peoples the essential duty is the periodic evocation of the primordial event which inaugurated the present condition of humanity. All their religious life is a commemoration, a re-memorising. The Remembrance, re-enacted ritually—therefore, by the repetition of the primordial assassination—plays the decisive part: one must take the greatest care not to forget what happened *in illo tempore*. The real sin is forgetfulness. The young woman who, during her first menstruation, lives for three days in a dark cabin and speaks to no one,

[1] Ad. E. Jensen, *Das Religiöse Weltbild einer frühen Kultur*, Stuttgart, 1948: the term *dema* was borrowed by Jensen from the Marind-anim of New Guinea.

does so because the mythical Young Woman who was assassin-
ated was then transformed into the Moon and remains three days
in darkness. If the young recluse breaks the tabu of silence and
speaks, she renders herself guilty of having forgotten a primordial
event. Among these paleo-agriculturists also, the personal memory
does not count: the important thing is to memorise the mythical
event, which alone is worthy of interest because it alone is
creative. To the primordial myth belongs the conservation of the
true History, the history of the human condition: it is in this that
one must seek and find again the principles and the paradigms
for all the conduct of life.

It is at this stage of culture that we meet with ritual cannibalism which, after all, is the spiritually conditioned behaviour of
the Good Savage. The greatest anxiety of the cannibal would
seem to be essentially metaphysical—lest he should ever forget
what took place *in illo tempore*. Volhardt and Jensen have clearly
shown this: by killing and devouring sows on festive occasions,
and by eating the first-fruits at the harvest of tubers, one is eating
the body of the divinity just as one does during the cannibal feasts.
The sacrifice of the sow, head-hunting and cannibalism are symbolically the same as the harvesting of the tubers or the coconuts.
It is the merit of Volhardt to have unravelled the religious meaning of anthropophagy and, at the same time, the human responsibility assumed by the cannibal.[1] The edible plant is not given by
Nature: it is the product of an assassination, because that is how it
was created at the beginning of time. Head-hunting, human
sacrifice, cannibalism—all this has been accepted by man in order
to assure the life of plants. Volhardt has rightly insisted upon this:
the cannibal assumes his responsibility in the world: cannibalism
is not a "natural" depravity of primitive man (moreover, it is not
found at the most archaic levels of culture), but a kind of cultural
behaviour based upon a religious vision of life. So that the
vegetable world may continue, man must kill and be killed; he
must, moreover, assume sexuality, even to its extreme limits—the
orgy. An Abyssinian song proclaims this: "She who has not yet
given birth, let her give birth; he who has not yet killed, let him

[1]E. Volhardt, *Kannibalismus*, Stuttgart, 1939.

kill!" It is a way of saying that the two sexes are condemned each to accept its destiny.

It should always be remembered, before passing judgment upon cannibalism, that it was founded by divine Beings. But they inaugurated it to enable human beings to take on a responsibility in the Cosmos; to put them in a position to watch over the continuation of the vegetative life. It was concerned, therefore, with responsibility of a religious nature. This is affirmed by the Uitoto cannibals: "Our traditions are always alive among us, even when we are not dancing; but we only work in order to be able to dance." The dances consist of repetitions of all the mythical events, including therefore the first assassination, followed by anthropophagy.

Whether a cannibal or not, the Good Savage praised by the Western travellers and theorists was continually preoccupied by the "origins", by the initial events which had made him, inasmuch as he was a "fallen" being, destined to death, to sexuality and labour. The more we come to know about "primitives" the more we are struck by the extraordinary importance they attach to the re-memorising of their mythical events. This singular valuation of memory merits examination.

THE GOOD SAVAGE, THE YOGI
AND THE PSYCHOANALYST

So much for the obligation, felt by archaic societies, periodically to repeat the cosmogony and all the deeds by which their institutions, customs and conduct were inaugurated.[1] That "return to the past" is susceptible of differing interpretations, but above all it is their need to recall what came to pass *ab origine* that arrests our attention. Needless to say, the values imputed to the "beginnings" vary greatly. As we have just seen, for a great many peoples, still at the earliest stages of culture, the "beginning" meant the disaster (the "loss of Paradise") and the "fall" into History: while for the paleo-agriculturists it was equated with the coming of death,

---

[1]*Cf. The Myth of the Eternal Return.*

sexuality and work (motives which also figure in the mythological stories of Paradise). But in both cases, the Remembrance of the primordial event played an impressive part; it was periodically re-enacted in the rituals, so that the event was re-lived and one became once again contemporary with the mythic *illud tempus*. Indeed, the "revival of the past" made it *present*—re-integrated one into the original plenitude.

We can still better estimate the importance of this *regressus ad originem* when we pass from the collective rituals to certain particular applications. In some widely dissimilar cultures the cosmogonic myth is re-enacted not only upon such occasions as the New Year, but also at the enthronement of a new chief, at a declaration of war, or in order to save a threatened harvest or, lastly, to cure an illness. This last is of the greatest interest to us. It has been shown that a fairly large number of peoples, ranging from the most primitive to the most civilised (the Mesopotamians, for instance), made use of solemn recitation of the cosmogonic myth as a therapeutic method. We can easily see why: by making the patient symbolically "return to the past" he was rendered contemporary with the Creation, he lived again in the initial plenitude of being. One does not *repair* a worn-out organism, it must be *re-made*; the patient needs to be born again; he needs, as it were, to recover the whole energy and potency that a being has at the moment of its birth. And such a return to the "beginning" is rendered possible by *the patient's own memory*. The cosmogonic myth is recited before him and for him; it is the sick man who, by recollecting one after another the episodes of the myth, re-lives them, and therefore becomes contemporary with them. The function of memory is not to *conserve* the memory of the primordial myth, but to transport the patient to *where that event is in process of accomplishment*—namely, to the dawn of Time, to the "commencement".

This "return to the past" by the vehicle of memory, as a means of magical cure, naturally invites us to widen our research. How can we but compare this archaic procedure with the techniques of spiritual healing, nay even with the soteriologies and philosophies elaborated in historical civilisations infinitely more complex than those we have just been considering? We are reminded first of all of one of the fundamental techniques of yoga, in use among the Buddhists as well as the Hindus: needless to add, the comparisons we shall draw do not imply the least depreciation on our part of either Greek or Indian thought; nor do we attach any undue value to archaic thinking. But modern sciences and discoveries, whatever their immediate frame of reference, can claim a certain solidarity, and the results obtained in any one field of study may invite us to make new approaches in others related to it. It seems to us that the importance allowed to Time and to History in contemporary thought, as well as the findings of depth-psychology, may shed further light upon certain spiritual dispositions of archaic humanity.[1]

According to the Buddha, as indeed in Indian thought as a whole, man's life is doomed to suffering by the very fact that it is lived in Time. Here we touch upon a vast question which could not be summarised in a few pages, but it may be said, as a simplification, that suffering in this world is based upon, and indefinitely prolonged by, *karma*, therefore by the temporal nature of existence. It is the law of *karma* which imposes the innumerable transmigrations, the eternal return to existence and therefore to suffering. To deliver oneself from the karmic law, to rend the veil of Mâyâ—this is equivalent to spiritual "cure". The Buddha is "the king of physicians" and his message is proclaimed as the "new medicine". The philosophies, the ascetic and contemplative techniques and the mystical systems of India are all directed to the same end: to cure man of the pain of existence in Time. It is by "burning up" even the very last germ of a future life that one finally breaks out of the karmic cycle and attains deliverance from Time. Now, one of the methods of "burning up" the karmic residua is a technique for "returning to the past", becoming con-

---

[1] It is scarcely fifty years since the problems of Time and History came to occupy the centre of Western philosophic thought. This, moreover, is why we have today a better understanding of the behaviour of the primitives and of the structure of Indian thought than we had in the latter half of the nineteenth century. In the one case as in the other, the key is to be found in their peculiar conceptions of temporality. It had long been known that primitives, as well as the Indians and other ancient peoples of Asia, shared a cyclic conception of Time, but that was all: we had not noticed that cyclic Time itself was periodically annulled; and that, consequently, even those who held that view of Time were manifesting their desire to escape from duration, their refusal to assume it.

scious of one's previous lives. This is a technique that is universal in India. It is attested in the *Yoga-sûtra* (III, 18), and was known to all the sages and contemplatives contemporary with the Buddha, who himself practised and recommended it.

The method is to cast off from a precise instant of time, the nearest to the present moment, and to retrace the time backwards (*pratiloman* or "against the stream") in order to arrive *ad originem*, the point where existence first "burst" into the world and unleashed Time. Then one rejoins that paradoxical instant before which Time was not, because nothing had been manifested. We can grasp the meaning and the aim of this technique: to re-ascend the stream of time would necessarily bring one back ultimately to the point of departure, which coincides with that of the cosmogony. To re-live one's past lives would also be to understand them and, to a certain degree, "burn up" one's "sins"; that is, the sum of the deeds done in the state of ignorance and capitalised from one life to the next by the law of *karma*. But there is something of even greater importance: one attains to the beginning of Time and enters the Timeless—the eternal present which preceded the temporal experience inaugurated by the "fall" into human existence. In other words, it is possible, starting from any moment of temporal duration, to exhaust that duration by retracing its course to the source and so come out into the Timeless, into eternity. But that is to transcend the human condition and to regain the non-conditioned state, which preceded the fall into Time and the wheel of existences.

We must abstain from the intricacies into which we should be led by any attempt to do justice to this technique of the yogis.[1] Our purpose here is simply to indicate the therapeutic virtue of memory as the Hindus have understood it, and, indeed, its soteriological function. For India, the knowledge which leads to salvation is founded upon memory. Ananda and other disciples of Buddha could "remember births", they were numbered among "those who remembered births" (*jatissaro*). Vâmadeva, the author of a well-known Rigvedic hymn, said of himself: "Finding

[1] *Cf.* Mircea Eliade, *Yoga, Immortality and Freedom*, Trans. by W. R. Trask, New York, 1958, p. 180ff.

myself in the womb, I knew all the births of the gods"; Krishna himself "knew all previous existences".[1] Now, he who *knows*, in this sense, is one who *can recollect the beginning*, or, more exactly, one who has become contemporaneous with the birth of the world, when existence and Time first became manifest. The radical "cure" of the suffering of existence is attained by retracing one's footsteps in the sands of memory right back to the initial *illud tempus*—which implies the abolition of profane time.

We can now see the sense in which such a soteriological philosophy is comparable to those archaic therapies which, in their way, are also intended to render the patient contemporaneous with the cosmogony. (As we need hardly protest, there can be no question of confusing the two categories of facts—of an attitude on one side and a philosophy on the other.) The man of the archaic society is trying to transport himself back to the beginning of the world in order to re-absorb the initial plenitude and recover, intact, the reserves of energy in the new-born babe. The Buddha, like most of the yogis, will have nothing to do with "origins"; he regards any search for first causes as futile: he is simply seeking to neutralise the consequences that those first causes have brought upon every individual in particular. His aim is to sever the succession of transmigrations; and one of the methods is this retracing of the course of one's previous lives, through the memory of them, back to the moment when the Cosmos came into existence. In this respect, therefore, there is an equivalence between the two methods: in both cases, the "cure" and, consequently, the solution of the problem of existence, becomes possible by the Remembrance of the primordial deed, of that which came to pass *at the beginning*.

Another parallelism is evident in the *anamnesis*. Without stopping to analyse the famous Platonic doctrine and its probably Pythagorean origin, let us note, incidentally, the way in which an archaic attitude has been developed to philosophic advantage. We know very little about Pythagoras, but the surest thing we do know is that he believed in metempsychosis and remembered his

[1] *Rig Veda*, IV, 27, 1 and *Bhagavad-Gîtâ*, IV, 5.

previous lives. Xenophon and Empedocles[1] described him as "a man of an extraordinary knowledge", for "when he put forth all the powers of his mind he could easily see what he had been in ten, or twenty, human lives". Tradition is insistent upon the importance given to memory training in the Pythagorean brotherhoods.[2] The Buddha and the yogis were not alone, then, in being able to remember their previous lives: and the same kind of prestige was accorded to the shamans; which need not surprise us, since the shamans were "those who had memory of the beginnings". In their ecstasies they re-entered the primordial *illud tempus*.[3]

It is now generally agreed that the Platonic doctrine of *anamnesis* was derived from the Pythagorean tradition. But with Plato it is no longer a matter of personal recollection of personal lives, but of a kind of "impersonal memory" buried deep in each individual, made up of memories of the time when the soul was directly contemplating the Ideas. There can be nothing personal in these recollections: if there were, there would be a thousand ways of understanding the triangle, which obviously would be absurd. We remember only the Ideas; and the differences between individuals are due solely to the imperfections of their *anamnesis*.

It is in the Platonic doctrine of the Remembrance of impersonal realities that we find the most astonishing persistence of archaic thought. The distance between Plato and the primitive world is too obvious for words; but that distance does not imply a break in continuity. In this Platonic doctrine of Ideas, Greek philosophy renewed and re-valorised the archaic and universal myth of a fabulous, pleromatic *illud tempus*, which man has to remember if he is to know the *truth* and participate in *Being*. The

---

[1] Xenophon, *frag.* 7 and Empedocles, *frag.* 129.

[2] Diodorus, X, 5; and Iamblichus, *Vita Pyth*, 78ff.

[3] I hope this comparison with the shamans will not annoy classicists. Only lately, two eminent hellenists devoted two long chapters to shamanism in their works on the history of Greek thought: *cf.* E. R. Dodds, *The Greeks and the Irrational*, Berkeley, 1951, pp. 135–178; F. M. Cornford, *Principium Sapientiae*, Cambridge, 1952; pp. 88–106. One could, moreover, extend these researches, notably by studying the "shamanic" images and symbols used by Plato to illustrate the "flight of the soul"; the ecstasy evoked by beauty, and the *anamnesis*. *Cf.* the "unaccustomed warmth" at the sight of Beauty, which causes "the feathers of the soul" to grow; indeed, "in former times the soul was feathered all over". *Phaedra*, 251a, etc. But this magic warmth, and this ascension by means of plumage like that of birds, are found among the most ancient elements of shamanism.

primitive, just like Plato in his theory of *anamnesis*, does not attach importance to *personal* memories: only the myth, the exemplary History is of importance to him. One might even say that Plato comes nearer than Pythagoras to traditional thinking: the latter, with his personal recollections of ten or twenty previous lives, is more nearly in line with the "elect"—with Buddha, the yogis and the shamans. In Plato it is only the pre-existence of the soul in the timeless universe of Ideas that matters; and the *truth* (*aletheia*) is the remembrance of that impersonal situation.

We cannot refrain from thinking of the significance that the "return to the past" has acquired in modern therapeutics. Psychoanalysis especially has found out how to use, as its chief curative method, the memory, the recollection of the "primordial events". But, within the horizons of modern spirituality, and in conformity with the Judæo-Christian conception of historic and irreversible Time, the "primordial" could mean only one's earliest childhood, the true individual *initium*. Psychoanalysis, therefore, introduces historical and individual time into therapeutics. The patient is no longer seen as an individual who is suffering only because of contemporary and objective events (accidents, bacteria, etc.) or by the fault of others (heredity), as he was supposed to be in the pre-psychoanalytic age; he is also suffering the after-effects of a shock sustained in his own temporal duration, some personal trauma that occurred in the *illud tempus* of childhood—a trauma that has been forgotten or, more exactly, has never come to consciousness. And the cure consists precisely in a "return to the past"; a re-tracing of one's steps in order to re-enact the crisis, to re-live the psychic shock and bring it back into consciousness. We might translate the operative procedure into terms of archaic thought, by saying that the cure is to begin living all over again; that is, to repeat the birth, to make oneself contemporary with "the beginning": and this is no less than an imitation of the supreme beginning, the cosmogony. At the level of archaic thought, owing to its cyclic conception of Time, the repetition of the cosmogony presented no difficulty: but for the modern man, personal experience that is "primordial" can be no other than that of infancy. When the psyche comes to a crisis, it is to infancy that he must return in order to re-live, and confront anew, the event from which that crisis originated.

Freud's was a most audacious undertaking: it introduced Time and History into a category of phenomena that had previously been approached from without, rather in the way that a naturalist treats his subject. One of Freud's discoveries above all has had portentous consequences, namely, that for man there is a "primordial" epoch in which all is decided—the very earliest childhood—and that the course of this infancy is exemplary for the rest of life. Restating this in terms of archaic thinking, one might say that there was once a "paradise" (which for psychoanalysis is the pre-natal period, or the time before weaning), ending with a "break" or "catastrophe" (the infantile trauma), and that whatever the adult's attitude may be towards these primordial circumstances, they are none the less constitutive of his being. One would be tempted to extend these observations to take in Jung's discovery of the collective unconscious, of the series of psychic structures prior to those of the individual psyche, which cannot be said to have been forgotten since they were not constituted by individual experiences. The world of the archetypes of Jung is like the Platonic world of Ideas, in that the archetypes are impersonal and do not participate in the historical Time of the individual life, but in the Time of the species—even of organic Life itself.

Certainly all this calls for further development and definition. But it already enables us to clarify a general attitude to what happened "in the beginning", *ab origine*. "Paradise" and "the Fall", or the catastrophic overturning of the previous régime, involving cannibalism, death and sexuality, as the primitive traditions see it; or a primordial rupture in the interior of Being, as Indian thought would explain it—these are so many images of a mythical event which, in happening, laid the foundations of the human condition. Whatever the differences between these images and formulæ, in the final reckoning they all mean the same thing: that *the essential human condition precedes the actual human condition*, that the decisive deed took place before us, and even before our parents: that decisive deed having been done by the mythic Ancestor (Adam, in the Judæo-Christian context). Better still, man is obliged to return to the actions of this Ancestor, either to confront or else repeat them; in short, never to forget them, whatever way he may choose to perform this *regressus ad originem*. Never to forget the essential deed—that was, in effect, to make it present, to re-live it. As we have seen, that was the attitude of the Good Savage. But Christopher Columbus, too, suffered from a nostalgia—namely, for the earthly Paradise: he had sought it everywhere and he believed he had found it during his third voyage. Mythical geography still obsessed the man who had just opened up the way to so many real discoveries. Good Christian as he was, Columbus felt himself to be, essentially, constituted by the history of the Ancestors. If he believed, to the end of his days, that Haiti was the Biblical Ophir, this was because, to him, this world could be no other than the exemplary world whose history is written in the Bible.

To recognise that one is constituted by what took place *in illo tempore* is not, moreover, a peculiarity of primitive thought and of the Judæo-Christian tradition. We have found an analogous tendency of the spirit in yoga and psychoanalysis. One might go further still, and examine the innovations added to this traditional dogma which affirms that the essential human condition precedes the actual. Above all it is historicism that has tried to innovate, by postulating that man is no longer constituted by his origins alone, but also by his own history and by the entire history of mankind. It is historicism that definitely secularises Time, by refusing to admit the distinction between a fabulous Time of the *beginnings*, and the time that has succeeded it. No magic any longer illuminates the *illud tempus* of the "beginnings": there was no primordial "fall" or "break", but only an infinite series of events, *all* of which have made us what we are today. There is no "qualitative" difference between these events; all deserve to be re-memorised and continually revalued by the historiographic *anamnesis*. There are neither events nor persons that are privileged: in studying the epoch of Alexander the Great or the message of the Buddha, one is no nearer to God than in studying the history of a Montenegrin village or the biography of some forgotten pirate. Before God, all historical events are equal. Or, if one no longer believes in God—before History . . .

One cannot be unmoved by this grandiose asceticism that the European mind has thus imposed upon itself; by this frightful humiliation, self-inflicted, as if in atonement for its innumerable sins of pride.

ARCHAIC
REALITIES

III

Nostalgia for Paradise
in the Primitive Traditions

BAUMANN SUMS up African myths relating to the primordial paradisiac epoch, in this way: in those days men knew nothing of death; they understood the language of animals and lived at peace with them; they did no work at all, they found abundant food within their reach. Following upon a certain mythical event —the study of which we will not now undertake—this paradisiac stage came to an end, and humanity became such as we know it today.[1]

In more or less complex forms, the *paradisiac myth* occurs here and there all over the world. It always includes a certain number of characteristic features, besides the supreme *paradisiac* element, immortality. One could classify these myths into two main categories; first, those that speak of an extremely close proximity that existed primordially between Heaven and Earth; and, secondly, those that refer to a concrete means of communication between Heaven and Earth. There can be no question, here, of analysing the many variant forms of each type, nor of defining their respective areas of diffusion, or their chronology. The one thing of interest for our present purpose is that, in describing the primordial situation, the myths express its paradisiac character simply by depicting Heaven as, *in illo tempore*, very close to the Earth, or as easily accessible, either by climbing a tree or a tropical creeper or a ladder, or by scaling a mountain. When Heaven had been abruptly *separated* from the earth, that is, when it had become *remote*, as in our days; when the tree or the liana connecting Earth

[1] Herman Baumann, *Schöpfung und Urzeit des Menschen im Mythos afrikanischer Völker*, Berlin, 1936, pp. 267ff. In Africa, a certain number of *paradisiac myths* have ended by becoming *myths of origin*: they explain, indeed, the origin of death. *Cf.* Hans Abrahamsson, *The Origin of Death: Studies in African Mythology*. Upsala, 1951.

to Heaven had been cut; or the mountain which used to touch the
sky had been flattened out—then the paradisiac stage was over,
and man entered into his present condition.

In effect, all these myths show us primordial man enjoying a
beatitude, a spontaneity and freedom, which he has unfortunately
lost in consequence of the *fall*—that is, of what followed upon the
mythical event that caused the *rupture* between Heaven and
Earth. *In illo tempore*, in the paradisiac age, the gods came down
to earth and mingled with men; and men, for their part, could go
up to Heaven by climbing the mountain, the tree, creeper or
ladder, or might even be taken up by birds.

A careful ethnological analysis will bring to light the cultural
context of each of these types of myth. One could show, for
instance, that the myths of the primordially close proximity of
Heaven to Earth, which are chiefly diffused over Oceania and
South-east Asia, are in some sense connected with a matriarchal
ideology.[1] Similarly, one could show that the mythic image of an
axis mundi—mountain, tree or creeper—to be found at the *centre
of the world*, connecting Earth with Heaven, an image attested
already among the most primitive of tribes (Australian, Pygmy
and Arctic), had been elaborated above all by the pastoral and
sedentary cultures and transmitted right down to the great urban
cultures of Oriental antiquity.[2] But the ethnological analysis must
not detain us here: for the purpose of this chapter, the typology
of the myths will suffice.

Let us enumerate the specific marks of the men of the paradisiac epoch, irrespective of their respective contexts. These marks
are immortality, spontaneity, freedom; the possibility of ascension into Heaven and *easily meeting* with the gods; friendship with
the animals and knowledge of their language. These freedoms
and abilities have been lost, as the result of a primordial event—the
"fall" of man, expressed as an ontological mutation of his own
condition, as well as a cosmic schism.

But it is not without interest to note that, by means of special

[1]*Cf.* H. Th. Fischer, *Indonesische Paradiesmythen*, in *Zeitschrift für Ethnologie*, LXIV,
1932, pp. 204–245; Franz Kiichi Numazawa, *Die Weltanfänge in der japonischen Mythologie*,
Paris–Lucerne, 1946.
[2]Mircea Eliade, *The Myth of the Eternal Return*, pp. 6ff.

techniques, the shamans endeavour to rise above the present condition of man—that of *man corrupted*—and to re-enter the state of the primordial man described to us in the paradisiac myths. We know that, among all the other mediators of the sacred in archaic societies, the shaman is above all the specialist in ecstasy. It is owing to his capacity for ecstasies—that is, because he is able, at will, to pass out of his body and undertake mystical journeys through all the cosmic regions—that the shaman is a healer, and a director of souls[1] as well as a mystic and visionary. Only the shaman is able to pursue the wandering soul of the sick person, capture it and bring it back into the body: it is the shaman who accompanies the souls of the dead to their new dwelling-places, and he, again, who embarks on long, ecstatic journeys in Heaven to present the soul of the sacrificed animal to the gods, and implore their divine benediction. In a word, the shaman is the great specialist in *spiritual questions*, it is he who knows better than anyone else the numerous dramas, the risks and dangers of the soul. The shamanist complex represents, in the "primitive" societies, that which is usually known in the more highly developed religions as *mysticism* and *mystical experience*.

A shamanic session generally consists of the following items: first, an appeal to the auxiliary spirits, which, more often than not, are those of animals, and a dialogue with them in a *secret language*; secondly, drum-playing and a dance, preparatory to the mystic journey; and thirdly, the trance (real or simulated) during which the shaman's soul is believed to have left his body. The objective of every shamanic session is to obtain the ecstasy, for it is only in ecstasy that the shaman can *fly* through the air or *descend into Hell*, that is, fulfil his mission of curing illness and shepherding souls.

Now, it is significant that, in preparing himself for the trance, the shaman uses the secret language, or, as it is called in some other regions, the *language of the animals*. The shaman imitates, on the one hand, the behaviour of the animals and, on the other, he endeavours to copy their cries, especially those of birds.

---

[1] "Psychopomp "—a title of Hermes, meaning a guide of souls to the place of the Dead. (Trans.)

Shieroszewski says of the Yakut shamans: "Sometimes up above, sometimes below, or before, or behind him, the shaman produces mysterious sounds ... You think you are hearing the plaintive cry of the peewit, mingled with the croaking of a hawk, interrupted by the whistle of a woodcock: it is the shaman who is making these noises by varying the intonation of his voice ... you hear the raucous cry of eagles, and mingling with it the plaintive call of lapwings, the piercing notes of the woodcock and the refrain of the cuckoo."[1] Castagné describes the Kirghiz-Tartar *baqça*, "imitating with remarkable accuracy the cries of animals, the songs of birds and the whirrings of their flight".[2] As Lehtisalo has observed, a good many of the words used during a shamanic session have their origin in imitations of the cries of birds and other animals. This is true especially of the refrains and the yodelling, which are mostly onomatopoeic, made up of phonemes and trills, the origins of which it is not hard to guess: imitations of the cries and songs of birds.[3] As a rule the shaman speaks during the session in a high voice, in "head notes" or falsetto, meaning thereby to indicate that it is not he who is speaking, but a spirit or a god. But it should be noted that the same high voice is generally used for chanting magical formulæ. *Magic* and *chanting*—especially singing in a bird-like manner—are often expressed by the same term. The Germanic vocable for a magic formula is *galdr*, which is used with the verb *galan*, "to sing", a term that is especially applied to the cries of birds.

If we take account of the fact that, during his initiation, the shaman is supposed to meet with an animal who reveals to him certain secrets of the craft, or teaches him the *language of the animals*, or who becomes his *familiar spirit*, we can still better understand the relationship of friendship and familiarity that is established between the animals and the shaman; the latter speaks their language and becomes their friend and master. We should note at once that to win the friendship and spontaneous mastery

[1] W. Shieroszewski, *Du chamanisme d'après les croyances des Yakoutes*, in the *Revue de l'Histoire des Religions*, XLVI, 1902.

[2] J. Castagné, *Magie et exorcisme chez les Kazak-Kirghizes et autres peuples turcs orientaux*, in the *Revue des Etudes Islamiques*, 1930, pp. 53-51 and 93.

[3] T. Lehtisalo, *Beobachtungen über die Jodler*, in the *Journal de la Société Finno-Ougrienne*, XLVIII, 1936-1937, 2, pp. 1-34.

of the animals does not signify, within the horizons of an archaic mind, any regression to a lower biological level. For, on the one hand, animals are charged with a symbolism and a mythology of great importance for the religious life;. so that to communicate with animals, to speak their language and become their friend and master is to appropriate a spiritual life much richer than the merely human life of ordinary mortals. And, on the other hand, the prestige of animals in the eyes of the "primitive" is very considerable; they know secrets of Life and Nature, they even know the secrets of longevity and immortality. By entering into the condition of the animals, the shaman shares their secrets and enjoys their plenitude of life.

Let us underline this—that friendship with the animals and knowledge of their language belong to the paradisiac syndrome. *In illo tempore*, before the "fall", this friendship was constitutive of the primordial human condition. The shaman returns, in some degree, to the paradisiac situation of primordial man, and this by recovering the animals' spontaneity (imitation of their behaviour) and the language of animals (imitation of their cries). It is important, however, to observe that this conversation with the animals, or their *incorporation* in the shaman (a mystical phenomenon that we must take care not to confuse with *possession*), constitutes the pre-ecstatic phase of the session. The shaman cannot leave his body and set out on his mystical journey until after he has recovered, by intimacy with the animals, a bliss and a spontaneity that would be unattainable in his profane, everyday situation. The vital experience of this friendship with the animals takes him out of the general condition of "fallen" humanity and enables him to re-enter the *illud tempus* described to us by the paradisiac myths.

To turn to the ecstasy itself: this includes, as we saw, the leaving of the body and the mystical journey to Heaven or to Hell. For our purpose, one point is of special interest—the fact that the celestial ascension of the shaman is contrived by means of a tree or a post, which symbolises the cosmic Tree or Pillar. It is thus, for instance, that the Altaic shaman uses, for his ceremony, a young birch tree stripped of its lower branches, on the trunk of which seven, nine or twelve footholds are contrived. The birch is the symbol of the Tree of the World; the seven, nine or twelve notches represent the corresponding number of heavens, that is, the different celestial levels. After having sacrificed a horse, the shaman avails himself of these notches to ascend as far as into the ninth Heaven inhabited by Bai Ulgän, the supreme God: he describes to his audience, in endless detail, all that he sees and all that is happening in each of the heavens. Finally, at the ninth Heaven, he prostrates himself before Bai Ulgän and offers him the soul of the horse that was sacrificed. This marks the culminating point of the ecstatic ascension of the shaman: he collapses exhausted and, after a little while, rubs his eyes, appears to wake up from a deep sleep, and greets those who are present as though he had returned after a long absence.[1]

The symbolism of the ascension into heaven by means of a tree is no less clearly illustrated by the ceremony of initiation of the Buriat shamans. The candidate climbs up a post in the middle of the yourt, reaches the summit and goes out by the smoke-hole. But we know that this opening, made to let out the smoke, is likened to the "hole" made by the Pole Star in the vault of Heaven. (Among other peoples, the tent-pole is called the *Pillar of the Sky* and is compared to the Pole Star, which is also the hub of the celestial pavilion and is named, elsewhere, the *Nail of the Sky*.) Thus, the ritual post set up in the middle of the yourt is an image of the Cosmic Tree which is found at the *Centre of the World*, with the Pole Star shining directly above it. By ascending it, the candidate enters into Heaven; that is why, as soon as he comes out of the smoke-hole of the tent he gives a loud cry, invoking the help of the gods: up there, he finds himself in their presence.

A similar symbolism is the explanation of the important part played by the shamanic drum. Emsheimer has shown that the dreams or ecstasies that accompany the initiation of the future shamans include a mystical journey to the Cosmic Tree at the top of which is found the Lord of the World. It is from one of the branches of this Tree, which the Lord lets fall for the purpose,

[1]Mircea Eliade, *Le Chamanisme et les techniques archaïques de l'extase*, pp. 175ff.

that the shaman fashions the barrel of his drum. But we know that the Cosmic Tree is supposed to be situated at the Centre of the World and that it connects Earth with Heaven: the frame of his drum being made of the actual wood of the Cosmic Tree, the shaman's drumming transports him magically near to the Tree; that is, to the Centre of the World, the place where there is a possibility of passing from one cosmic level to another.

Thus, whether he is climbing up the seven or nine notches of the ceremonial birch-tree or is at work on his drum, the shaman is on a journey to Heaven. In the former case he is laboriously imitating the ascent of the Cosmic Tree; in the latter, he is *flying* around the Tree by the magic of his drum. The shaman's *flight*, moreover, takes place quite frequently; often it is confused with the ecstasy itself. Among the numerous varieties of the shamanic flight, the flight to the Centre of the World is that which interests us most: for it is there that one finds the Tree, the Mountain or the Cosmic Pillar connecting Earth to Heaven; there, also, is to be found the "hole" made by the Pole Star. By scaling the Mountain, or climbing the Tree, by flying up to and through the "hole" at the zenith of the celestial vault, the shaman completes his ascension to Heaven.

Now, we know that, *in illo tempore*, in the mythic time of Paradise, a Mountain, a Tree or a Pillar or a liana connected Earth with Heaven, so that primordial man could easily go up into Heaven by climbing it. Communication with Heaven *in illo tempore* was simple, and meetings with the gods took place *in concreto*. The remembrance of this paradisiac period is still vividly present to these primitives. The Koryaks remember the mythical era of their hero Great Raven, when men could go up to Heaven without any difficulty: in our days, they add, it is only the shamans who are still capable of this. The Bakairi of Brazil think that, for the shaman, Heaven is no higher than a house, so that he reaches it in the twinkling of an eye.[1]

This again is as much as to say that the shaman, during his journey, returns to the paradisiac condition. He re-establishes the *communications* that used to exist *in illo tempore* between Heaven

[1] M. Eliade, *Le Chamanisme . . .*, pp. 235ff., 419ff.; *cf.* also *ibid.* pp. 227–295.

and Earth: for him, the cosmic Mountain or Tree becomes again a concrete means of access to Heaven, just as they were before the Fall. For the shaman Heaven once again draws near to Earth; it is no higher than the top of a house, just as it used to be before the primordial schism. Lastly, the shaman renews the friendship with the animals. In other words, the ecstasy reactualises, provisionally and for a limited number of persons—the mystics—what was the original state of all mankind. In this respect, the mystical experience of primitives is equivalent to a *journey back to the origins*, a regression into the mythical time of the Paradise lost. For the shaman in ecstasy, this present world, our fallen world—which, according to modern terminology, is under the laws of Time and of History—is done away with. There is, it is true, a great difference between the situation of primordial man and that which the shaman recovers during an ecstasy: the shaman bridges only temporarily the gulf dividing Heaven from Earth; he goes up to Heaven in the spirit but no longer, like the primordial man, *in concreto*; nor does he annul death (all the notions about immortality that one can collect among primitives imply previous death, just as do those of civilised peoples; the "immortality" in question is always post mortem, *spiritual*).

To sum up: the most representative mystical experience of the archaic societies, that of shamanism, betrays the *Nostalgia for Paradise*, the desire to recover the state of freedom and beatitude before "the Fall", the will to restore communication between Earth and Heaven; in a word, to abolish all the changes made in the very structure of the Cosmos and in the human mode of being by that primordial disruption. The shaman's ecstasy restores a great deal of the paradisiac condition: it renews the friendship with the animals; by his *flight* or ascension, the shaman reconnects Earth with Heaven; up there, in Heaven, he once more meets the God of Heaven face to face and speaks directly to him, as man sometimes did *in illo tempore*.

Now, an analogous situation can be studied in the latest and most highly elaborated mysticism of all: that of Christianity. Christianity is ruled by the longing for Paradise. "Praying towards the East re-connects us with the paradisiac themes . . . To turn towards the East appears to be an expression of the nostalgia for Paradise."[1] The same paradisiac symbolism is attested in the rites of baptism: "instead of Adam, falling under the domination of Satan and being expelled from Paradise, the catechumen appears as though set free by the New Adam from the power of Satan and re-admitted into Paradise."[2] "Christianity thus seems to be the realisation of Paradise. The Christ is the Tree of Life (Ambrose, *De Isaac*, 5, 43) or the fountain of Paradise" (Ambrose, *De Paradiso*, III, 272, 10). But this realisation of Paradise takes place in three successive phases. Baptism is the entry into Paradise (Cyril of Jerusalem, *Procatech.*, P.G. XXXIII, 357A); the mystical life is a deeper entry into Paradise (Ambrose, *De Paradiso*, I, 1); and finally, death introduces the martyrs into Paradise (*Passio Perpet.* I, P.L. III, 28A). It is remarkable indeed to have found the paradisiac language applied to all these three aspects of the Christian life.[3]

Naturally, it is mysticism that best exemplifies the restoration of the life of Paradise. The first syndrome of that restoration is the recovery of dominion over the animals. As we know, in the beginning Adam was enjoined to provide the animals with names (*Genesis*, II, 19); for to name the animals was equivalent to ruling over them. St Thomas explains Adam's power over the non-rational creation, as follows: "The soul, by its commandment, rules over the sensitive powers, such as the appetites of anger and concupiscence, which, in a manner, are obedient to reason. *Whence*, in the state of innocence, man by his commandment ruled over the other animals."[4] But "the fact of giving names or changing them plays a similarly important part in eschatological pronouncements . . . the messianic kingdom brings about a moral conversion of humanity, and even a transformation of the animals . . . which characterises the world fresh from the hand of God."[5] And, in the mystical state, the animals are sometimes

[1] Jean Daniélou S.J., *Bible et Liturgie*, Paris, 1951, p. 46.
[2] Jean Daniélou S.J., *ibid*, p. 47.
[3] Jean Daniélou S.J., *Sacramentum futuri*, Paris, 1950, p. 16.
[4] Dom Anselme Stolz, *Théologie de la Mystique* (Fr. trans.) 2nd edn. Editions des Bénédictins d'Amay, Chevetogne, 1947. p. 104.
[5] J. Daniélou S.J., *Sacramentum futuri*, p. 6.

obedient to the saints, as they were to Adam. "The tales about the ancient fathers of monasticism show them—and this is not a rare happening—being obeyed by wild animals which they feed just like domestic animals."[1] St Francis of Assisi does what the desert Fathers did before him. Friendship with the wild animals, and their spontaneous acceptance of man's authority, are manifest signs of the recovery of a paradisiac situation.

One might also take account of the paradisiac symbolism of churches and of monastery gardens. The landscape that surrounds the monk reflects the earthly Paradise and, in some sort, anticipates it. But it is above all the mystical experience as such that interests us. And, as Dom Stolz has so well demonstrated, the exemplary Christian mystical experience is the ascension into heaven of St Paul: "I know a man in Christ who, fourteen years ago, was caught up to the third heaven—whether in the body or out of the body I do not know, God knows. And I know that this man was caught up into Paradise—whether in the body or out of the body I do not know, God knows—and he heard things that cannot be told, which a man may not utter" (*II Corinthians*, XII, 1–4). We need not here insist upon the ascensional symbolism of Christian mysticism, in which the Ladder of Paradise plays a leading part. The successive steps of contemplation denote the stages of the ascension of the soul towards God. But St Paul definitely avers that the mystical ascension bears man up to Paradise: "The things which a man may not utter" he had heard there, were they not those of God himself? For Adam, when in Paradise, "usually enjoyed conversation with God"—as St Gregory assures us.[2]

Thus, although Christianity may be ruled by the nostalgia for Paradise, it is only the mystics who obtain, in part, the restoration of that state: friendship with the animals, ascent to Heaven and meeting with God. The same situation obtains in the archaic religions: a certain longing for Paradise is attested at every level of the religious life,[3] but it is manifested above all in mystical experience; that is, in the ecstasies of the shamans. And the specific

[1]Dom Stolz, *op. cit.*, p. 31.　　[2]Dom Stolz, *op. cit.*, p. 111.
[3]Mircea Eliade, *Patterns in Comparative Religion* (trans. by Rosemary Sheed), London and New York, 1958; pp. 374ff.

marks of the restoration of *illud tempus* are the same: friendship with animals, ascension to Heaven, and converse with the God of Heaven. As with the Christian saint, the recovery of Paradise by the shaman in ecstasy is only provisional, for neither the one nor the other succeeds in annihilating death; neither succeeds in completely re-establishing the situation of primordial man.

Lastly, one might also remember that, in the Christian tradition, Paradise has been rendered inaccessible by the fire that surrounds it, or, what comes to the same thing, its entrance is guarded by angels with *flaming* swords. "God," says Lactantius (*Divin. Institut.* II, 12), "has expelled man from Paradise, which he has surrounded with fire so that man can have no access thereto." St Thomas is alluding to this when he explains that Paradise is beyond our reach, most of all by reason of "the heat which keeps it far from our countries".[1] Thus it is, that whosoever wishes to enter into Paradise must first go through the fire that rings it round. "In other words, only he who has been purified by fire can thenceforth enter into Paradise. For the way of purgation comes before the mystical union, and the mystics do not hesitate to put the purification of the soul on the same plane as the purifying fire on the way to Paradise."[2]

These few texts should suffice; they sum up and justify a whole doctrine about the purifying fire that guards the approach to Paradise. We are not entering here into discussion of the symbolism of fire in mysticism and Christian theology. But it is worth noting that a similar symbolism can be discerned in a whole group of shamanic techniques: those concerned with the well-known *mastery of fire*.[3] Indeed, all over the world the shamans are reputedly *masters of fire*; during their sessions they swallow live coals, touch red-hot iron and walk upon fire. This mastery of fire has been attested among shamans of the most archaic societies; it is constitutive of shamanism to the same degree as the ecstasy, the ascension to Heaven or the language of animals. The ideology implied in this mastery of fire is not difficult to make out: in the primitive world (and moreover in the popular imagination in general) *spirits* are distinguished from men by their *incombust-*

[1] Dom Stolz, *op. cit.*, p. 24.   [2] Dom Stolz, *op. cit.*, p. 32.   [3] *Cf.* below, pp. 92ff.

ibility; that is, by their capacity to endure the temperature of live coals: the shamans are thought to have passed beyond the human condition and to partake of the condition of *spirits*; just like spirits, they become invisible, they fly in the air, they mount up to Heaven, go down to Hell and, finally, they enjoy incombustibility. The mastery of fire expresses in sensory terms a *transcendence of the human condition*; here again, the shaman is demonstrating that he is raised to a *spiritual condition*, that he has become—or can become during the session—*a spirit*.

If we compare the purifying fire surrounding Paradise in the Christian traditions, with the shamanic mastery of fire, we see that they have at least one point in common. In the one case as in the other, to pass through fire with impunity is a sign that one has transcended the human condition. But in Christianity, as in the archaic traditions, the present condition of man is the consequence of the "Fall". It follows that, to overcome this condition, even provisionally, is equivalent to a re-entry into the situation of primordial man; in other words, to the annulment of Time, a going back to, and recovery of, the paradisiac *illud tempus*. How precarious it is, this renewal of the primordial situation, is shown above all by the fact that the shaman attains it by imitating the condition of *spirits*. We have already noted this in speaking of other shamanic techniques; during the trance, it is not the shaman who flies up to Heaven, but only his *spirit*. Christian mysticism presents an analogous situation: it is only the *soul* which, purified by fire, enters into Paradise.

The analogies we have been drawing here seem to us important: they imply that there is no break in continuity between the ideology of primitive mystical experience and Judæo-Christian mysticism. Among primitives, as among Christian saints and theologians, mystical ecstasy is a return to Paradise; that is, it is expressed as an annulment of Time and History (of the Fall), and a recovery of the situation of primordial man.

But let us be rightly understood: in drawing these analogies we are making no pretensions to pronounce value-judgments upon the content of the different mystical experiences, primitive or otherwise. We are content to have observed that their ideologies have, as their centre and kernel, the nostalgia for Paradise. That does not, of course, exclude the numerous differences that exist not only between the primitive mystics and the mystics of Judæo-Christianity, but between different schools of Christian mysticism. On the other hand, we have expressly chosen to compare the Christian with the most archaic type of mystical experience, leaving aside the great Oriental traditions—although the *going out of Time* and the abolition of History constitute the essential element of all mystical experience, and consequently of Oriental mysticisms also. But it seems to us that the paradisiac theme is better preserved in the archaic mysticisms. In a sense, comparisons between types of primitive and of Christian mysticism are better warranted than comparisons between the latter and Indian, Chinese or Japanese mysticism.

Yet though we were not presuming to outline, in these few pages, a comparative study of mysticism, it is important to underline the principal result of our enquiry: the clear ideological continuity between the most elementary mystical experience and Christianity. At the *commencement* as at the *end* of the religious history of humanity, we find again the same nostalgia for Paradise. If we take account of the fact that this nostalgia for Paradise was similarly discernible in the general religious conduct of men in the archaic societies, we are justified in supposing that the mythical remembrance of a non-historical happiness has haunted humanity from the moment when man first became aware of his situation in the Cosmos. A new perspective is opened up, therefore, in the study of archaic anthropology. Not that this is the place to enter upon such a study. Suffice it to say that, in the light of all the observations we have been making, certain aspects of primitive spirituality that were considered to be *aberrations* are nothing of the kind. The imitation of the cries of animals by the shamans, which has not failed to impress observers, and which ethnologists have often supposed to be the manifestation of a pathological *possession*, actually betokens the desire to recover friendship with the animals and thus enter into the primordial Paradise. The ecstatic trance, whatever its phenomenology may be, only appears as an aberration if we lose sight of its spiritual significance. In reality, as we saw, the shaman tries to re-establish the communications between Earth and Heaven that were interrupted by "the Fall". The mastery of fire, too, is no mere superstition of savages; on the contrary, it is a demonstration that the shaman partakes of the nature of *spirits*.

Considered from its own point of view, all the strange behaviour of the shaman reveals the highest spirituality; it is, in fact, expressive of an ideology which is coherent and of great nobility. The myths by which this ideology is constituted are among the most beautiful and profound in existence: they are the myths of Paradise and the Fall, of the immortality of primordial man and his conversation with God, of the origin of death and the discovery of the *spirit* (in every sense of the word). Nor is this without consequences for the understanding and evaluation of the behaviour of the primitive and, in general, of non-European man: all too often the Occidental allows himself to be impressed by the *manifestation* of an ideology, when he is ignorant of the one thing it is important above all others to know: the ideology itself, that is, the myths. But the manifestations depend, in the first place, upon local fashions and cultural styles, and these may or may not be immediately accessible. One then judges according to the impression: a ceremony is *beautiful*, a certain dance is *sinister*, a rite of initiation is *savage* or an *aberration*. Yet if one takes the trouble to understand the ideology that underlies all these manifestations, if we study the myths and the symbols that condition them, we can free ourselves from the subjectivity of impressions and obtain a more objective view. Sometimes an understanding of the ideology is enough to re-establish the "normality" of a kind of behaviour. To recall just one example: the imitation of the animals' cries. For more than a century it was thought that the strange cries of the shaman were a proof of his mental disequilibrium. But they were signs of something very different: of the nostalgia for Paradise which had haunted Isaiah and Virgil, which had nourished the saintliness of the Fathers of the Church, and that blossomed anew, victorious, in the life of St Francis of Assisi.

IV

Sense-Experience and
Mystical Experience among Primitives

PRELIMINARY REMARKS

IN SOCIETIES still at the ethnographic stage, mystical experience is generally the prerogative of a class of individuals who, by whatever name they are called, are *specialists in ecstasy*. The shamans, the medicine-men, magicians, healers, the ecstatic and the inspired of every description, are distinguished from the rest of the community by the intensity of their religious experience. They live the sacred side of life in a profounder and more personal manner than other people. In most cases they attract attention by some unusual behaviour, by the possession of occult powers, by having personal and secret relations with divine or demonic beings, by a style of life, or dress, by insignia and ways of speaking, which are theirs alone. By general agreement, these individuals are regarded as the equivalents, among "primitives", of the religious élites and the mystics in other and more highly evolved cultures.

If it be true that the shamans and the medicine-men represent the richest and most authentic mystical experience of humanity at the ethnographic stage, we have a keen interest in finding out what function they ascribe to sensory activity in their quest for sanctity. In other words, it would be interesting to know how far sense-experience as such can be charged with religious meaning or value; or to what degree, among "primitives", the attainment of a condition regarded as superhuman may be reflected in the senses.

Let us begin with two observations about method.

(1) Our having decided here to enlarge upon the various

73

forms of shamanism and upon the techniques of ecstasy, does not at all imply that these privileged beings are the only ones in whom sensory activity is capable of taking on religious value or significance. On the contrary; among primitives as well as among the civilised, religious life brings about, in one way and another, a religious use of "sensibility". Broadly speaking, there can be no religious experience without the intervention of the senses; all hierophany represents a new incursion of the sacred into the cosmic environment, but hierophany in no way interferes with the normality of sense-experience. When the collective religious life is centred in a "sensory experience"—such as, for instance, the communion of the first-fruits, which lifts the tabus on food-stuffs and makes it possible to eat the new harvest—the act in question is at once a sacrament and a physiological action. Moreover, among "primitives" every responsible action is charged with a magico-religious value and meaning: one need only recall the cosmological implications and, in the last analysis, the mystiques, of sex-activity, of fishing and agriculture; nutrition, like sexuality and work, is at one and the same time a physiological activity and a sacrament. In short, throughout religious history, sensory activity has been used as a means of participating in the sacred and attaining to the divine. If we have chosen to speak only of the "mystics" of primitive societies, it is because their experiences more readily afford us glimpses of the processes which lead up to the transformation of sensory activities in contact with the sacred.

(2) Our second observation bears upon the actual experience of the mystics. When we speak of their "sensory activity" we are using this term in its widest and least technical sense; not implying any judgment at all about the actual nature of that activity. The "sensibility" is always and continually integral with a kind of behaviour, and consequently participates in the collective psychology, as well as in the underlying ideology, in any society, at whatever stage of evolution. Needless to add that, in taking our stand upon the plane of the history of religions, we do not mean to pursue the analysis of the psychological facts further than their magico-religious significance. We are only seeking to find out to

what extent, among the "primitives", sensory experience comes to assume religious values—that and nothing more.

ILLNESS AND INITIATION

One becomes a shaman (*a*) by spontaneous vocation—the "call" or "election"; (*b*) by hereditary transmission from the shamanist profession; and (*c*) by personal decision or, more rarely, by the will of the clan. But whatever the method of his selection, a shaman is only recognised as such at the end of a twofold instruction: first, of the ecstatic order (dreams, visions, trances, etc.) and, secondly, of the traditional order (shamanic techniques, names and functions of the spirits, mythology and genealogy of the clan, secret language, etc.). This dual instruction, for which the spirits and the old master-shamans are held responsible, is equivalent to an initiation. The initiation may be public, and constitute an autonomous ritual in itself. But lack of a ritual of this kind does not at all imply lack of the initiation; for this may very well be brought about in dreams or in the ecstatic experience of the neophyte.

It is, above all, the syndrome of the mystical vocation with which we are concerned. The future shaman marks himself off progressively by some strange behaviour: he seeks solitude, becomes a dreamer, loves to wander in woods or desert places, has visions, sings in his sleep, etc.[1] Sometimes this period of incubation is characterised by rather grave symptoms; among the Yakuts, the young man occasionally becomes violent and easily loses consciousness, takes refuge in the forests, feeds upon the bark of trees, throws himself into the water or the fire or wounds himself with knives. According to Shirokogorov, the future shamans of Tonga undergo a hysteric or hysteroid crisis at the approach of maturity, but the vocation may declare itself in more tender years: the boy may flee into the mountains, remaining there for seven days or more, living upon animals "that he

[1] See the examples given in our book *Le Chamanisme et les techniques archaïques de l'extase*, Paris, 1951, pp. 26ff.; 30ff.

catches directly with his teeth" and then returning to the village, dirty, blood-stained, with his clothes torn and his hair dishevelled "like a savage". It is only after about another ten days that the neophyte begins to stammer some incoherent words.

Even when the office is hereditary, the election of a new shaman is preceded by a change of behaviour: the souls of shaman ancestors choose a young man out of the family; he becomes absent-minded or dreamy, is seized with a desire for solitude, he has prophetic visions and, in some cases, attacks that leave him unconscious. During that time, as the Buriats think, his soul is carried away by spirits, is welcomed in the palace of the gods, and receives instruction from ancestor shamans in the secrets of the craft, the forms and names of the gods, the cult and the names of spirits, etc. It is only after this first initiation that the soul re-enters the body. Among the Altaians, the future *kam* manifests himself from infancy by a frail constitution, by solitary and contemplative inclinations. If, in a family, one young man is subject to fits of epilepsy, the Altaians are convinced that one of his ancestors was a shaman.

One may also become a shaman in consequence of an accident, or of some unusual event: thus, among the Buriats, the Soyotes and the Eskimos, if one has been touched by lightning, or has fallen from a tree, or if one has undergone with impunity any trial comparable to an initiatory ordeal (such an Eskimo, for instance, spent five days in ice-cold water without wetting his garments, etc.).

The strange behaviour of future shamans has not failed to attract the attention of the learned, and several times since the middle of last century they have tried to explain the phenomena of Arctic and Siberian shamanism as a mental ailment (Krivoshapkin, 1861; Bogoraz, 1910; Vitashevskij, 1911; Czaplicka, 1914). The last advocate of this theory that shamanism was an Arctic hysteria, A. Ohlmarks, went so far as to distinguish an Arctic from a sub-Arctic shamanism, by the degree of neuropathic disturbance in their representatives. According to this author, shamanism was normally an exclusively Arctic phenomenon, essentially related to the influence of the geographical situation upon the nervous instability of the inhabitants of Polar regions. The excessive cold, the long nights, the desert solitudes, shortage of vitamins, etc., took their toll of the nervous constitution of the Arctic populations, producing either mental illnesses (Arctic hysteria, the *meryak*, the *menerik*, etc.) or the shamanic trance. The only difference between a shaman and an epileptic was that the latter could not bring about a trance at will.[1]

But the hypothesis "shamanism is an Arctic phenomenon" will not stand up to more careful analysis. There are no special geographical zones where the shamanic trance is a spontaneous and organic phenomenon; we find shamans here and there all over the world, and everywhere observers have noted the same relationship between their mystical vocation and nervous instability; shamanism cannot, therefore, be a consequence of Polar physical surroundings. G. A. Wilken asserted, more than sixty years ago, that Indonesian shamanism had originally been a real illness, and it was only later that people began to make dramatic representations of the genuine trance.[2]

This problem, in our view, has been wrongly stated. In the first place, it is not correct to say that shamans are, or must *always* be, neuropaths: on the contrary, a great many of them are perfectly sound in mind. Moreover, those who had previously been ill have *become shamans just because they succeeded in getting well*. Very often, when the vocation reveals itself in the course of an illness or an attack of epilepsy, the initiation is also a cure. The acquisition of the shamanic gifts indeed presupposes the resolution of the psychic crisis brought on by the first signs of this vocation. The initiation is manifested by—among other things— a new psychic integration.

This explains, furthermore, the social prestige of the shaman and his considerable status in the cultural life of the tribe. Far from being neuropaths or degenerates, shamans are, from the intellectual point of view, evidently superior to those around

---

[1]Ake Ohlmarks, *Studien zum Problem des Schamanismus*, Lund-Kopenhagen, 1939, pp. 1, 100ff., 122ff. and *passim*. See the criticisms of the methods of Ohlmarks in our *Chamanisme*, pp. 36ff.

[2]G. A. Wilken, *Het Shamanisme bij de volken van den Indischen Archipel* ('s Gravenhage, 1887), *passim*. But later researches into Indonesian shamanism have not confirmed this hypothesis; the phenomenon is infinitely more complex. *Cf. Le Chamanisme*, pp. 304ff.

them. They are the principal custodians of the rich oral literature: the poetic vocabulary of a Yakut shaman comprises some 12,000 words, whilst his ordinary speech—all that is known to the rest of the community—consists of only 4,000. Among the Kasakh-Kirghizes the *baqça*, "singer, poet, musician, seer, priest and doctor, seems to be the guardian of the popular religious traditions, the custodian of legends several centuries old". The shamans exhibit powers of memory and of self-control well above the average. They can perform their ecstatic dance in the very restricted space in the middle of a yourt crowded with spectators; and this without touching or hurting anyone, though they are wearing costumes loaded with from thirty to forty pounds of iron in the form of discs and other objects.

There have been analogous observations about the shamans of other regions. According to Koch-Grünberg, "The Taulipang shamans are, as a general rule, intelligent individuals, sometimes artful, but always of a great force of character; for in their training, and in the exercise of their functions, they are obliged to give proof of energy and self-mastery." And A. Métraux writes of the shamans of the Amazon, that "No physical or physiological anomaly or peculiarity would seem to have been chosen as the symptom of a special predisposition to the exercise of shamanism."[1] As for the Sudanese tribes studied by Nadel, "there can be no shaman who, in his everyday life, is an 'abnormal' individual, a neurasthenic or a paranoiac; if he were, he would be numbered among the fools, not respected as a priest. All things considered, shamanism cannot be put down to abnormality, nascent or latent; I cannot remember a single shaman whose professional hysteria degenerated into serious mental disorder." One cannot, then, say that "shamanism absorbs the mental abnormality diffused throughout the community, nor that it is founded upon a marked and prevalent psychopathic predisposition. Beyond all question, shamanism is not to be explained simply as a cultural mechanism designed to deal with abnormality or to exploit a hereditary psychopathological predisposition."[2]

---

[1]For all this, see *Le Chamanisme*, pp. 41ff.
[2]Nadel, quoted in *Le Chamanisme*, pp. 42ff.

THE MORPHOLOGY OF "ELECTION"

But though we cannot ascribe shamanism to psychopathology, it remains true that this mystical vocation often enough involves a profound crisis, sometimes touching the borderline of "madness". And since one cannot become a shaman until one has resolved it, this crisis evidently plays the part of a *mystic initiation*. Indeed, as we have shown in detail in a previous work, the shaman is consecrated by a long and often difficult initiation centred in the experience of the mystical death and resurrection. Now, every initiation, of whatever order, includes a period of isolation and a certain number of trials and ordeals. The illness produced in the future shaman by the agonising feeling that he has been "chosen" is, by that very fact, turned to advantage as an "initiatory illness". The precarious state and the solitude incident to every illness are, in this special case, aggravated by the symbolism of the mystical death: for to assume the supernatural "election" is to be filled with the sense of being abandoned to the divine or demonic powers; that is, doomed to imminent death.

Very often, the syndrome of the "illness"—that is, as we have just seen, of the psychopathology exhibited by the future shaman —closely follows the classic ritual of initiation. The sufferings of the "elect" are in every way similar to the tortures of initiation; just as the candidate was slain by the demons—"masters of the initiation"—so the future shaman sees himself being cut to pieces by the "demons of the illness". The specific rites of shamanic initiation include a symbolic ascent to Heaven by means of a tree or a post[1]; the sick man "chosen" by the gods or the demons[2] sees himself, in a dream or in a series of dreams, upon his celestial journey right to the foot of the Tree of the World. The ritual death, without which no initiation is possible, is passed through

[1] *Cf.* our *Le Chamanisme*, pp. 116ff., 125ff., etc.

[2] Within the spiritual horizons of shamanism, this term does not necessarily imply a negative value-judgment. Demons, more often than not, are shaman-ancestors and, therefore, the Masters of Initiation. Their "demonic" character is due to the fact that they torture the neophyte and put him to death; but these sufferings and this "death" are those of initiation, leading to the transmutation of the profane condition into the superhuman.

by the "patient" in the form of a descent into Hell. He is present, in a dream, at his own dismemberment, sees the demons cut off his head, tear out his eyes, etc.

This whole set of procedures is highly important for a correct understanding of the shamanic psychopathology: these "crises", these "trances" and this "madness" are not anarchic; in other words, not "profane", they do not belong to ordinary symptomatology; *they are of an initiatory pattern and meaning.* The future shaman sometimes takes the risk of being mistaken for a "madman"—that is often the case among the Malays—but in reality his "madness" fulfils a mystic function; it reveals certain aspects of reality to him that are inaccessible to other mortals, and it is only after having experienced and entered into these hidden dimensions of reality that the "madman" becomes a shaman.

In studying the symptomatology of the "divine election" we are struck by the pattern of all these pathological experiences; their structure is always the same, and the symbolism is always that of initiation. Too much has been made of the psychopathological character of the first symptoms of being "chosen": we are presented, in effect, with a total crisis, very often leading to disintegration of the personality. The "psychic chaos" has its value, within the horizon of archaic spirituality, as a replica of the "pre-cosmogonic chaos", the amorphous and indescribable state which precedes all cosmogony. But we know that, for the archaic and traditional cultures, the *symbolic return to chaos is indispensable to any new Creation,* upon whatever plane of manifestation it may be: every new sowing and every new reaping is preceded by a collective orgy which symbolises the re-integration of the "pre-cosmogonic chaos"; every New Year brings with it a number of ceremonies which signify the repetition of the primordial chaos and of the cosmogony. The "return to chaos" is, for a man of the archaic culture, equivalent to the preparation for a new "Creation".[1] Now, *the same symbolism is discernible in the "madness" of the future shamans, in their "psychic chaos"; it is a sign that the profane man is on the way to dissolution, and that a new*

---

[1] Upon this symbolism, see our *Patterns in Comparative Religion*, pp. 358ff., 398ff., and *The Myth of the Eternal Return*, pp. 17ff.

personality is about to be born. All the tortures, trances or initiatory rites that accompany and prolong this "return to chaos" represent, as we have seen, stages in a mystical death and resurrection—in the last analysis, the birth of a new personality.

For our purpose, we want to know to what extent the shamanic vocation and initiation give an additional value to sensory experience, by rendering it capable of more directly apprehending the sacred. Broadly speaking, one might say that the process to which we have just been referring—that of the "illness" as an *initiation*—leads to a change of sensibility, a qualitative alteration in the sensitivity: from being "profane" it becomes "chosen". During his initiation the shaman learns how to penetrate into other dimensions of reality and maintain himself there; his trials, whatever the nature of them, endow him with a sensitivity that can perceive and integrate these new experiences. The psychopathological crisis registers the break-up of normal, profane experience. "Chosen" by supernatural powers, the future shaman no longer resists, with his previous "sensibility", the initiatory experience. One might almost say that, thanks to all these trials, the sensory activity of the "elect" tends to become a hierophany: through the strangely sharpened senses of the shaman, the sacred manifests itself.

ILLUMINATION AND INTERIOR VISION

Sometimes, the change of organisation of sensory experience brought about by supernatural "election" is easily understandable. The man who has survived being struck by lightning acquires a "sensibility" not attainable at the level of ordinary experience; the revelation of the divine "choice" is manifested by the destruction of all the anterior structures: the "elect" becomes "another"; he feels himself to be not only dead and re-born, but *born into existence* which, while it is lived to all appearances in this world of ours, is framed in other existential dimensions. In terms of traditional shamanic ideology, this experience is expressed as the combustion of the flesh and the breaking-up of the skeleton. Struck by lightning, the Yakut Bükes Ullejeen is shattered and scattered in a thousand fragments; his companion hurries to the village and returns with several men to collect the remains for burial; but finds Bükes Ullejeen safe and sound. "The God of Thunder came down from Heaven and cut me into little pieces," Bükes tells them. "Now I have come back to life, a shaman; and I can see what is happening all around to a distance of thirty versts."[1]

Bükes passed in the space of an instant through the initiatory experience which, for others, takes a fairly long time, and includes the cutting up of the body, the reduction to a skeleton and the renewal of the flesh. No less does initiation by lightning modify the sensory experience. Bükes is straightway gifted with clairvoyance. To "see at a distance of thirty versts" is the traditional term for clairvoyance in Siberian shamanism: during a séance, when the shaman begins his ecstatic journey, he announces that he can see "at thirty versts".

Now, this modification of the sensibility, acquired spontaneously by the shock of an extraordinary event, is what is laboriously sought for during the apprenticeship of those who are working to obtain the shamanic gift. Among the Iglulik Eskimos, the young men or women who aspire to become shamans present themselves before a master they have chosen, declaring: "I come to you because I want to see." Instructed by the master, the apprentice passes many hours in solitude: he rubs one stone against another, or remains seated in his cabin of snow, meditating. But *he has to have the experience of the mystical death and resurrection;* he falls down "dead" and remains inanimate three days and three nights; or he is devoured by an enormous white bear, etc. "Then the bear from the lake or from the glacier in the interior will come forth, he will eat all the flesh and make a skeleton of you, and you will die. But you will find your flesh again, you will awaken and your garments will fly towards you."[2]

The neophyte ends by obtaining the "flash" or "illumination"

---

[1] G. W. Ksenofontov, *Legendy i raskazy o shamanach u jakutov, burjat i tungusov,* 2nd edn., Moscow, 1930, pp. 76ff.

[2] The "flight" of the garments is a characteristic feature of the séances of Eskimo shamans; see our book, *Le Chamanisme . . .,* pp. 267ff.

(*qaumaneq*), and this mystical experience both lays the foundation of a new "sensibility" and reveals to him capacities of extra-sensory perception. The *qaumaneq* consists of "a mysterious light that the shaman suddenly feels in his body, in the interior of his head, at the very centre of the brain, an inexplicable guiding light, a luminous fire which makes him able to see in the dark, literally as well as figuratively, for now he is able, even with eyes closed, to see through the darkness and see things and events of the future, hidden from other human beings. In this way he can see into the future as well as into the secrets of others." When the candidate experiences this "illumination" for the first time, it is "as though the house in which he is were suddenly lifted up; he can see very far in front of him, right through the mountains, exactly as if the earth were one great plain and his sight reached to the ends of the earth. Nothing is now hidden before him. Not only is he now able to see a long way, but he can also discover the stolen souls, whether they are guarded, hidden in strange distant places, or whether they have been carried away up on high, or down below into the land of the dead."[1]

This mystical experience is related to the *contemplation of his own skeleton*, a spiritual exercise of great importance in Eskimo shamanism, but which is also found in Central Asia and in Indo-Tibetan Tantrism. The ability to see oneself as a skeleton implies, evidently, the symbolism of death and resurrection; for, as we shall not be slow to see, the "reduction to a skeleton" constitutes, for the hunting peoples, a symbolico-ritual complex centred in the notion of life as perpetual renewal. Unfortunately, the information that we have about this spiritual exercise of the Eskimo shamans is rather lacking in precision. Here is what Rasmussen reports of it: "Although no shaman can explain how or why, he can, nevertheless, by the power that his thought receives from the supernatural, divest his body of flesh and blood, so that nothing of it remains but the bones. He then has to name all the parts of his body, mentioning each bone by name; and for this he must not use ordinary human language, but only the special and sacred language of the shamans that he has learned from his

[1]K. Rasmussen, quoted in *Le Chamanisme* . . ., p. 69.

instructor. While seeing himself thus, naked and completely delivered from the perishable and ephemeral flesh and blood, he dedicates himself, still in the sacred language, to his great task, through that part of his body which is destined to resist, for the longest time, the action of sun, wind and weather." (*Cf. Le Chamanisme*, p. 71.)

Such a spiritual exercise implies the "exit from time", for not only is the shaman, by means of an interior vision, anticipating his physical death, but he is finding again what one might call the non-temporal source of Life, the *bone*. Indeed, for the hunting peoples the bone symbolises the ultimate root of animal Life, the matrix from which the flesh is continually renewed. It is starting with the *bones* that animals and men are re-born; they maintain themselves awhile in carnal existence, and when they die their "life" is reduced to the essence concentrated in the skeleton, whence they will be born anew according to an uninterrupted cycle that constitutes an eternal return. It is duration alone, *time*, which breaks and separates, by the intervals of carnal existence, the timeless unity represented by the quintessence of Life concentrated in the bones. By contemplating himself as a skeleton, the shaman does away with time and stands in the presence of the eternal source of Life. So true is this, that in the ascetic technique of mysticisms as highly developed as Tantric Buddhism and Lamaism, meditation upon the image of one's skeleton, or divers spiritual exercises done in the presence of corpses, skeletons or skulls, still play an important part; such meditations, among others, reveal the evanescence of temporal duration and, consequently, the vanity of all incarnate existence. But evidently this "going out of time" by means of the contemplation of one's own skeleton is differently evaluated among the shamans of hunting and pastoral peoples, and among the Indo-Tibetan ascetics; for the former, its aim is to re-discover the ultimate source of animal life and thence to participate in Being; while, for the Indo-Tibetan monks, it is to contemplate the eternal cycle of existences ruled by *karma*; and hence to dispel the Great Illusion (*mâyâ*) of Cosmic Life, striving to transcend it by placing oneself in the unconditioned, symbolised by Nirvâna.

THE CHANGE IN THE ORGANISATION
OF SENSORY EXPERIENCE

As we have just seen, the attainment of a state higher than "profane sensibility" is preceded by the experience of the initiatory death. Spontaneously, as in the case of the shaman "elected" by lightning, or laboriously as among the Eskimo shaman-apprentices, one comes out upon a level of experience where clairvoyance, clairaudience and other kinds of extra-sensory perception become possible. Sometimes the symbolism of the mystical agony, death and resurrection is conveyed in a brutal manner, aiming directly at the "change of sensibility": certain operations of the shaman-apprentices disclose the aim of "changing the skin" or of radically modifying the sensibility by innumerable tortures and intoxications. Thus, the Yagan neophytes of Tierra del Fuego rub their faces until the second or even the third skin appears, "the new skin" visible only to initiates. "The old skin must disappear and give place to a new, delicate and translucent layer. If the first weeks of friction and painting have at last rendered this apparent—at least to the imagination and the hallucinations of the *yékamush* (medicine-man)—the old initiates have no longer any doubt about the capacities of the candidate. From that moment, he must go on, with redoubled zeal, delicately rubbing his cheeks until a third skin, still more fine and delicate, is revealed; it is so sensitive that it cannot be touched without causing the most acute pain. When the learner has at last reached this stage, the regular instruction is ended."[1]

Among the Caribs of Dutch Guiana, the apprentice shamans undergo a progressive intoxication by tobacco-juice and the cigarettes which they smoke quite incessantly. Instructresses massage their bodies every evening with a red liquid; they listen to their masters' lessons after their eyes have been well rubbed with pimento-juice; and, lastly, they dance in turn upon tight-

[1]Gusinde, quoted in *Le Chamanisme*, p. 63 Note 3.

ropes at various heights, or swing suspended in the air by their hands. They finally attain the ecstasy upon a platform "suspended from the roof of the hut by several cords twisted together, which, as they untwine, make the platform revolve more and more rapidly."[1]

The aberrant and infantile side of these operations is of no interest to us; it is their end and aim that we find revealing. The symbolism of the mystical death—which, moreover, is attested, among the same peoples, in other rites of shamanic initiation—expresses itself in the cases we have cited as a *will to change the sensibility*. Now, as we have already said, such a change seeks, in effect, to "hierophanise" all sensory experience: through the senses themselves the shaman discovers a dimension of reality which remains inaccessible to the uninitiated. To obtain such a "mystic sensitivity" is equivalent to surpassing the human condition. All the traditional shamanic practices pursue this same end: to destroy the "profane" kinds of sensibility; the monotonous chants, the endlessly repeated refrains, the fatigue, the fasting, dancing, the narcotics, etc., end by creating a sensory condition that is wide-open to the "supernatural". This is not only, of course, a matter of physiological techniques: the traditional ideology directs and imparts values to all these efforts intended to break the frame of profane sensibility. What is above all indispensable, is the absolute belief of the subject in the spiritual universe which he desires to enter; nothing can be attained without the "faith". In the cases of apprentices who have no vocation—that is, of those who have not had the experience of "election"—the voluntary quest for shamanic powers implies formidable efforts and tortures.

But whatever the point of departure—supernatural election or a voluntary quest for magico-religious powers—the personal labour which precedes and follows initiation leads of necessity to a change of sensibility: *the apprentice endeavours to "die" to profane sensibility so as to be "re-born" with a mystical sensibility.* This is manifested by a considerable expansion of the sensory capacities, as well as by the acquisition of paranormal extra-sensory faculties.

[1] A. Métraux, quoted in *Le Chamanisme*, p. 128.

The Eskimos call the shaman *elik*, "he who has eyes",[1] thereby emphasising his clairvoyance. The shamanic visual power is described, among the Selk'nam of Tierra del Fuego, as "an eye which, stretching out of the magician's body, goes in a straight line towards the object that it has to observe while still remaining united with the magician". This occult power, say the Fuegians, stretches out like "a thread of gum",[2] and the image corresponds to a genuine ability to see at a distance; and of this the neophyte has to give proof by describing, without moving from his place, objects hidden some distance away from him.[3]

EXTRA-SENSORY PERCEPTION
AND PARANORMAL POWERS

We now touch upon a problem of the greatest importance, one which cannot be altogether avoided although it exceeds the range of the present study—that is, the question of the *reality* of the extra-sensory capacities and paranormal powers ascribed to the shamans and medicine-men. Although research into this question is still at its beginning, a fairly large number of ethnographic documents has already put the authenticity of such phenomena beyond doubt. Recently, an ethnologist who is also a philosopher, Ernesto de Martino, subjected the testimonies of explorers concerning extra-sensory perception to a searching criticism and concluded that they were real.[4] From among the best-observed cases, let us recall those of clairvoyance and thought-reading among the shamans of Tonga, recorded by Shirokogorov: some

[1] Knud Rasmussen, *Intellectual Culture of the Copper Eskimos* (Report of the Fifth Thule Expedition, 1921–1924, IX, Copenhagen, 1932), p. 27.
[2] M. Gusinde, *Die Feuerland Indianern*, Band. I, *Die Selk'nam*, Modling bei Wien, 1937, p. 751.
[3] M. Gusinde, *op. cit.*, pp. 784ff.
[4] Ernesto de Martino, "Percezione extrasensoriale e Magismo etnologico" in *Studi e Materiale di Storia delle Religione*, 18, 1942, pp. 1–19; 19–20, 1943–1946, pp. 31–84. The same author's *Il Mondo Magico. Prolegomeni a una storia del Magismo*, Turin, 1948. *Cf.* also O. Leroy, *La raison primitive*, Paris, 1927, pp. 141ff.; Betty M. Humphrey, "Paranormal occurrences among pre-literate peoples" in the *Journal of Parapsychology VIII*, 1944, pp. 214–229. There is a bibliography of recent works on paranormal psychology in the volume of writings edited by Rhine, Greenwood *et al.*, *Extra-Sensory Perception after Sixty Years*, New York, 1940; and in R. A. Madou, *La Parapsychologie*, Paris, 1954.

strange cases of prophetic clairvoyance in dreams among the
Pygmies, as well as cases of the discovery of thieves with the aid
of a magic mirror; some very concrete instances concerning the
results of the chase, also aided by a mirror; examples of the
understanding, among these same Pygmies, of unknown languages[1]; cases of clairvoyance among the Zulus;[2] and, lastly—
attested by a number of authors and by documents that guarantee
its authenticity—the collective ceremony of fire-walking in Fiji.[3]
Several other paranormal phenomena have been noted among the
Chukchee by W. Bogoraz, who has even made disc-records of
the "voices of the spirits" of the shamans; these sounds had previously been ascribed to ventriloquism, but this seems improbable,
for the voices clearly came from a source far from the apparatus
in front of the shaman.[4] Rasmussen, among the Iglulik Eskimos,
and Gusinde, among the Selk'nam, have collected many cases of
premonitions, clairvoyance, etc., and this list could easily be
extended.[5]

This problem belongs to parapsychology; hence it cannot
usefully be discussed in the perspective of the history of religions,
to which we have adhered from the beginning of this study.
Parapsychology examines the conditions under which certain
paranormal phenomena occur, and endeavours to understand,
and even to explain them; whereas the historian of religions is
concerned with the *meanings* of such phenomena, and seeks to
reconstitute the ideology in which they are assumed and given
value. To confine ourselves to a single instance: parapsychology
seeks primarily to establish the authenticity of the concrete case,
such as one of levitation, and studies the conditions of its manifestation; the history of religions tries to elucidate the symbolism of
ascension and of the magical flight, in order to understand the

---

[1] R. G. Trilles, *Les Pygmées de la forêt équatoriale*, Paris, 1932, pp. 193, 180ff., 144ff.:
E. de Martino, *op. cit.*, pp. 25ff.

[2] D. Leslie, *Among the Zulu and the Amatongos*, 2nd edn., Edinburgh, 1875, quoted by
A. Lang, *The Making of Religion*, 2nd edn., London, 1909, pp. 68ff.; E. de Martino, *op.
cit.*, p. 28.

[3] The essential documentation is reproduced in de Martino, *op. cit.*, pp. 29–35.

[4] Waldemar G. Bogoraz, *The Chukchee* (The Jesup North Pacific Expedition, Vol. VII,
1907; Memoirs of the American Museum of Natural History, Vol. XI), pp. 435ff. De
Martino, *op. cit.*, pp. 46ff.: see also *Le Chamanisme*, pp. 229ff.

[5] De Martino, *op. cit.*, pp. 71ff. Other examples of "shamanist prowess" are recorded in
our book *Le Chamanisme*.

relations between the ascensional myths and rituals and, finally, to define the ideology which gave them their value and justification.

To succeed in his task, the historian of religions is not bound to pronounce upon the authenticity of this or that particular case of levitation, nor to limit his enquiry to study of the conditions under which such a case may really occur. Every belief in the "magical flight", every ritual of ascension, every myth containing the motif of a possible communication between Earth and Heaven, is equally of importance for the historian of religions: each one represents a spiritual document of very great value, for these myths, rites and beliefs express existential predicaments of man in the Cosmos, and at the same time disclose his obscure desires and longings. In one sense, all these things are *real* for such a historian, for each represents an authentic spiritual experience in which the human soul has found itself profoundly involved.

For our purpose, what is important is to underline the perfect *continuity of paranormal experience* from the primitive right up to the most highly evolved religions. There is not a single shamanic "miracle" which is not also well attested in the traditions of the Oriental religions and in Christian tradition. This is true, above all, of those most shamanic of all such experiences, the "magical flight" and the "mastery of fire". The essential difference between the archaic world and certain religions of Asia, to say nothing of Christianity, has to do with the *value that one attaches to such paranormal powers*. Buddhism and classical yoga, just like Christianity, are careful never in any way to encourage the quest for "marvellous powers" (*siddhi* or, in Pali, *iddhi*). Patañjali, although he speaks at length about the *siddhi*, allows them no importance for the attainment of deliverance. (*Yoga Sutra* III, 35 *et seq.*) The Buddha knew them, too, and his description of them follows the pan-Indian magical tradition, as well as the immemorial tradition of the shamans and primitive "sorcerers". The *bhikku*, Buddha tells us, "enjoys marvellous power (*iddhi*) in its different modalities: from being one, he becomes several; having become several, he again becomes one; he becomes visible or invisible; he passes,

without feeling any resistance, through a wall, a rampart or a hill
as if it were air: he dives from on high down through the solid
earth as through water; he walks upon water without sinking in
it, as though upon firm land. With his legs crossed and folded
under him, he voyages in the heavens as do birds upon the wing.
The Moon itself and the Sun, strong and powerful though they
are, he touches, he feels them with his hand; while remaining
in the body, he attains even unto the heaven of Brahma . . ."
"With that clear, celestial hearing that surpasses the hearing of
men, he senses both human and heavenly sounds, either far or
near . . ." "Penetrating the hearts of other men by his own, he
knows them . . . With his heart thus tranquil, etc., he directs
and inclines his attention to the knowledge of his previous
lives."[1]

There is not a single one of these *siddhi* evoked by the Buddha
that we do not meet with in the shamanic traditions; even the
knowledge of previous lives, a specifically Indian "mystical
exercise", has been reported among the shamans of North
America.[2] But Buddha is very well aware of the vanity of such
acts of magical prowess, and most of all of the dangers they may
portend in minds that are ill-advised. After an exhibition of such
siddhi, the unbeliever might retort that they were not obtained
through the excellence of Buddhist teaching and practice, but
were gained by mere magic; that is, by a vulgar and useless
fakirism. "If a believer (a Buddhist) claimed the possession of
mystical powers (*iddhi*) whilst in a state of multiform becoming,
the unbeliever would say to him, 'Why, yes, sir, there is a certain
charm called the *gandharva* charm. That is the power by which he
does all this!' Indeed, Kevaddha! It is just because I see the danger
of performing mystical marvels (*iddhi*) that I execrate, abominate
and am ashamed of them!"[3]

However, for Buddha, as well as for Patañjali, the *siddhi* are
paranormal powers *the possession of which cannot be avoided*. In the

[1] *Samañña Phalla Sutta*, 87 et seq.; *Dîghanikâya*, I, p. 78ff. *Cf.* M. Eliade, *Yoga, Immortality and Freedom*, p. 178.
[2] *Cf.* p. ex. Ake Hultkrantz, *Conceptions of Soul among North American Indians*, Stockholm, 1953, p. 418ff.
[3] *Kevaddha Sutta*, 4 et seq., *Dîghanikâya*, I, 212ff., *Yoga*, pp. 179ff.

course of their ascetic and contemplative labours the yogi and the *bhikku* necessarily come to a plane of experience on which extra-sensory experience and all the other "wonderful powers" are *given* to them. Buddha, Patañjali and others drew attention not only to the danger of "exhibiting" such "marvellous powers" but to the dangers that they present to their possessor; for the yogi is in danger of yielding to the temptation of magic; of being content to enjoy the marvellous powers instead of sticking to his spiritual work and obtaining the final liberation.

Let us remember this fact: that the *siddhi* follow automatically from success in the ascetic and mystical techniques undertaken. If we take account that, in yoga as in Buddhism, liberation amounts to an actual surpassing of the human condition—in other words, that one has to "die" to the profane "natural" existence constituted by the law of endless "conditionings" (*karma*) and be re-born into an "unconditioned", that is, a perfectly free and autonomous existence—we recognise here again the same archaic and universal symbolism of an *ontological mutation through the experience of death and resurrection*. Yoga and Buddhism, with the ascetic and mystical practices related to them, are continuations—although of course on another plane and directed to quite a different end—of the immemorial ideologies and techniques which endeavoured to change the condition of man by a change in his psychosomatic structures. At the end of long and painful exercises in mystical physiology, the Indian apprentice attains a radical modification of his "sensibility". If one reads the yoga texts attentively one can follow the successive stages leading up to this final ontological mutation. We cannot analyse them here; but we know that, from beginning of the apprenticeship, one is trying to break down the structures of the "profane sensibility", to make way for extra-sensory perception (clairvoyance, clair-audience, etc.) as well as for an almost unbelievable control over the body. The exercises of Hatha yoga, in the first place those of rhythmic respiration (*prânâyâma*), refine the sensory experience and introduce it to planes inaccessible under normal behaviour. And in other ways, one undergoes a progressive "reversal" of normal behaviour: in the words of the texts, the senses are made

to "withdraw themselves from objects" (*pratyâharâ*) and to turn
in upon themselves. The ordinary profane condition being characterised by movement, disordered breathing, mental dispersion,
etc., the yogi sets himself to reverse it by practising just the
opposite: immobility (*âsana*), controlled breathing (*prânâyâma*),
concentration of the psycho-mental flux upon a single point
(*ekâgratâ*), etc. This aim, of "reversing" the natural behaviour, can
be seen even in the Tantric-yoga practice of erotic mysticism: the
normal sensitivity is progressively abolished; the yogi transforms
himself into a god and his partner into a goddess; the sexual union
becomes a ritual and all the normal physiological reactions are
"inverted": not only is the seminal emission arrested, but the
texts emphasise the importance of the "return of the semen"[1].
Once again: all these efforts are directed to "the death of the
profane man", and the symbolism of yogi or Tantric initiation
continues the symbolism of the shamanic death and resurrection,
even though the aim of yoga is quite other than that of a "primitive" mystic or magician.

THE "MAGICAL HEAT" AND THE "MASTERY OF FIRE"

Since it would be impossible to study all the "wonderful powers"
(*siddhi*) which are as prominent in the Indian—and the general
Asiatic—traditions as they are in the primitive, let us be content
to observe one type only: the class of paranormal powers which
includes the "magical heat" and the "mastery of fire". Their
study is instructive, because the documents available derive from
every cultural level, from the most archaic to the most highly
developed.

One of the initiatory ordeals of shamanism demands a capacity to endure extreme cold, as well as the heat of embers.
Among the Manchurians, for instance, the future shaman has to
undergo the following trial: in the winter, nine holes are made in
the ice; the candidate has to plunge into one of these holes, swim

---

[1] *Cf. Le Yoga*, pp. 270ff.

under the ice and come out at the next one, and so on to the ninth hole.[1] And there are certain Indo-Tibetan initiatory ordeals which consist precisely in testing a disciple's progress by his ability, during a winter night and under falling snow, to dry both his naked body and a number of wet sheets. This "psychic heat" is called in Tibetan *gtûm-mo* (pronounced *tumo*). "Sheets are dipped in icy water, each man wraps himself up in one of them and must dry it on his body. As soon as the sheet has become dry, it is again dipped in the water and placed on the novice's body to be dried as before. The operation goes on in that way until daybreak. Then he who has dried the largest number of sheets is acknowledged the winner of the competition."[2]

This *gtûm-mo* is an exercise of Tantric yoga well known in the Indian ascetic tradition. As we shall see in another connection (p. 146, the awakening of the *kundalini* is accompanied by a sensation of great warmth. That discovery is not to be credited to the Tantric yogis: as early as the *Rig Veda* the ascetic effort in general (*tapas*) was regarded as productive of "heat". Here we are in the presence of a very ancient mystical experience; for a number of primitive traditions represent the magico-religious power as "burning". Moreover, this magico-religious power is not a monopoly of the mystics and magicians; it is also obtained in the "excitement" of initiatory military combats; as we shall also see later (pp. 147-148).

The "magical heat" is related to another technique that may be called the "mastery of fire", that which renders its practitioners insensible to the heat of live embers. From almost everywhere in the shamanic world we have accounts of such exploits, reminding us of those of the fakirs. In preparation for his trance, the shaman may play with live coals, swallow them, handle red-hot iron, etc. During the festivities at the "ordination" of an Araucanian shaman, the masters and the novices walk barefoot over fire, without burning themselves or setting fire to their clothes. Throughout Northern Asia the shamans gash their bodies, and they are able to swallow burning coals or to touch red- or

[1]Shirokogorov, quoted in *Le Chamanisme*, p. 114.
[2]Alexandra David-Neel, *With Mystics and Magicians in Tibet*, Chap. VI.

white-hot iron. The same feats are attested among the shamans of North America. Among the Zuni, for example, the shamans play all kinds of tricks with fire: they are able to swallow glowing coals, to walk upon fire, touch red-hot iron, etc. Matilda Coxe Stevenson relates, among her personal observations, that a shaman kept hot embers in his mouth for up to sixty seconds. The *wâbêne* of Ojibwa are called "handlers of fire", and they manipulate blazing coals with impunity.[1]

Such exploits are sometimes collective. Thus, in China, the *sai-kong* leads the march over the fire: the ceremony is called "walking on a road of fire", and takes place in front of a temple; the *sai-kong* is the first to step out upon the embers, followed by his younger colleagues, and even by the public (see *Le Chamanisme*, p. 400). The most striking example, which has also been the best observed, of collective walking upon white-hot stones, is the well-known ceremony of Fiji. Certain families possess this "power" and pass it on to their posterity. During the ceremony a great number of the non-initiated, and even of strangers, walk over the glowing embers with impunity: but for this, it should be noted, a degree of "faith" and respect for a particular ritual symbolism are necessary: at Rarotonga, one of the Europeans, who had turned back after starting on the walk, had his feet burned.[2] Similar ceremonies occur sporadically in India. At Madras, a yogi made this fire-walk possible for a considerable number of spectators who were not only unprepared, but some of them frankly sceptical; among them the Bishop of Madras and his attendants.[3]

The "mastery of fire" is attested, together with other shamanic marvels—ascension, magical flight, disappearances, walking upon water, etc.—among the mystics of Islam. One tradition of the dervishes tells us that "the séyyd, while listening to the teachings of the sheik and understanding the mysteries of them, became so excited that he put both feet into the hearth, and took pieces of

[1] *Le Chamanisme*, pp. 63, 285ff.
[2] Upon this ceremony at Rarotonga, see W. E. Gudgeon, "The Umu-ti, or Fire-walking Ceremony", in the *Journal of the Polynesian Society*, VIII, 1899. *Cf.* also E. de Martino, *Il Mondo Magico*, pp. 29ff.
[3] *Cf.* the detailed report in the book of Olivier Leroy, *Les Hommes Salamandres. Sur l'incombustibilité du corps humain.* Paris, 1931.

glowing coal out of it with his hand . . ."[1] Lastly, let us remember that a collective ritual of walking on fire still survives in some places in Greece: although integrated with popular Christian devotion, this rite is incontestably archaic; not only pre-Christian, but perhaps pre-Indo-European. One point of importance to us is that the insensibility to heat and the incombustibility are obtained by prayer and fasting: "faith" plays the essential part, and sometimes the walk over the embers is achieved in ecstasy.[2]

Thus there exists a perfect continuity of these mystical techniques, from cultures at the paleolithic stage right up to the modern religions. The true meaning of the "magical heat" and the "mastery of fire" is not difficult to guess: these "marvellous powers" indicate the attainment of a known condition of ecstasy, or, upon other cultural levels (in India, for instance), access to a non-conditioned state of perfect spiritual freedom. The "mastery of fire" and the insensibility both to extreme cold and to the temperature of live embers are material expressions of the idea that the shaman or the yogi has surpassed the human condition and already participates in the condition of the "spirits".[3]

THE SENSES, ECSTASY AND PARADISE

Upon the plane of the archaic religions, participation in the condition of the "spirits" is what endows the mystics and the magicians with their highest prestige. No less than the spirits, the shamans are "fireproof", they fly through the air and become invisible. Here we must direct attention to the important fact that the supreme experience of the shaman ends in the ecstasy, in the "trance". It is during his ecstasy that the shaman undertakes, *in the spirit*, long and dangerous mystical journeys even up to the highest Heaven to meet the God, or up to the Moon or down into Hell, etc. In other words, the supreme experience of the shaman, the ecstasy, is reached *beyond the realm of the sensorial*; it is

[1] Cl. Huart, quoted in *Le Chamanisme*, p. 361.
[2] C. A. Romaios, *Cultes populaires de la Thrace*, Athens, 1945, pp. 84ff.; *Revue Métapsychique*, No. 23, May–June, 1953, pp. 9–19.
[3] See also above, p. 72.

an experience that brings into play and engages only his "soul", not the whole of his being, body and soul; his ecstasy manifests the separation of the soul; that is, it anticipates the experience of death.

This is no more than we might expect: having already, in his initiation, passed through death and resurrection, the shaman is able to enter into the discarnate condition with impunity; he can exist, in his capacity as a "soul", without its separation from the body being fatal to him. Every "trance" is another "death" during which the soul leaves the body and voyages into all the cosmic regions. Yet, although the shamanic ecstasy is universally regarded as the conclusive proof of "sanctity", it represents, none the less, in the eyes of the primitive, a *decadence compared with the primordial status of the shamans*. Indeed, the traditions speak of a time when the shamans set out on their travels to Heaven *in concreto;* they claim remembrance of an epoch when shamans *really* flew up above the clouds. Moreover the ecstasy, that mystical ecstasy realised only in the spirit, is regarded as inferior to his earlier situation, when the shaman *in his own body* realised all his miracles—magic flight, ascension to Heaven and descent into Hell. The mastery of fire remains one of the rare concrete proofs of a "real" miracle worked in our carnal condition—which, moreover, is why such great importance is attributed to this phenomenon in all shamanic circles. *It is the proof that the shaman participates in the condition of the "spirits" while still continuing to exist in the flesh:* the proof that the "sensibility" can be transmuted without being abolished; that the human condition has been surpassed without being destroyed, that is, that it has been "restored" to its primordial perfection. (We shall shortly return to this mythic motive of a primordial perfection.)

But even the "mastery of fire" is alleged to be decadent in comparison with earlier manifestations. The Maoris declare that their ancestors could traverse a great trench full of burning coals: but in our days this ritual has disappeared. At Mbenga, it is said that the trench used to be much wider, and that the crossing was repeated three or four times.[1] The Buriats say that "in the old times" the blacksmith shaman touched the fire with his tongue and held melted iron in his hand. But Sandschejev, when he attended a ceremony, did not himself see anyone do more than touch red-hot iron with the feet.[1] The Paviotso still speak of the "old shamans" who put burning coals in their mouths and handled red-hot iron with impunity. The Chukchee, the Koryak and the Tongans, as well as the Selk'nam of Tierra del Fuego are all agreed that the "old shamans" had much greater powers and that the shamanism of today is in decline. The Yakuts recall with nostalgia the time when the shaman flew right up to heaven upon his courser; one could see him, dressed all in iron, soaring through the clouds, followed by his drum.[2]

The decadence of the shamanism of today is a historical phenomenon to be explained partly by the religious and cultural history of the archaic peoples. But in the tradition to which we have just been alluding, something else is in question; namely, a myth *about* the decline of the shaman; since they claim to know there was a time when the shaman did not fly to heaven in ecstasy but in physical fact. *In illo tempore* this ascension was not made "in the spirit" but bodily. The "spiritual" state therefore signifies a fall in comparison with the earlier situation, in which the ecstasy was not necessary because no separation between body and soul was possible; which means that there was no death. It was the appearance of Death that broke up the unity of the whole man by separating the soul from the body, and limiting survival to the "spiritual" principle. To put it another way: for primitive ideology present-day *mystical experience* is inferior to the *sensory experience of primordial man.*

Indeed, according to the myths, as we have already seen (p. 59ff), the Ancestor or primordial Man knew nothing of death, suffering or work: he lived at peace with the animals and had easy access to Heaven for direct encounter with God. A catastrophe occurred and interrupted communications between Heaven and Earth; and that was the beginning of the present condition of man, limited by temporality, suffering and death.

So, during his trance, the shaman seeks to *abolish this human*

[1] *Cf. Le Chamanisme . . .*, p. 410.   [2] *Ibid.*, pp. 271, 227, 231ff. and p. 212.

condition—that is, the consequences of the "fall"—and to *enter
again into the condition of primordial man* as it is described in the
paradisiac myths. The ecstasy re-actualises, for a time, what was
the initial state of mankind as a whole—except that the shaman
no longer mounts up to Heaven in flesh and blood as the primordial man used to do, but only *in the spirit*, in the state of ecstasy.

We can understand, then, why the shaman's ecstasy is looked
upon as something decadent; it is a purely "spiritual" experience,
not to be compared with the powers of the "shamans of old"
who, though they did not manage completely to surpass the
human condition, were nevertheless capable of working "miracles" and, in particular, were able to fly up to Heaven *in concreto*.
Thus, the "shamans of old" themselves were already representatives of a decadent humanity, striving to get back into the paradisiac state of things before "the fall".

This depreciation of the ecstasy accompanied by a high
esteem for the "powers" does not, in our view, signify disrespect
for "spirituality" nor the wondering fear aroused by "magic",
but the nostalgia for a lost paradise, the longing to know Divinity,
as well as the unattainable realms of reality, *with our very senses*.
In other terms, one might say that primitive man longs once
more to meet with the sacred in the body and therefore *easily
accessible*, and this it is that explains his view of the Cosmos as a
hierophany, the fact that any and every object may become an
embodiment of the sacred. We have no right to infer from this
any "mental inferiority" on the part of the primitive, whose
powers of abstraction and speculation have now been attested by
so many observers. The "nostalgia for Paradise" belongs, rather,
to those profound emotions that arise in man when, longing to
participate in the sacred with *the whole of his being*, he discovers
that this wholeness is only apparent, and that in reality the very
constitution of his being is a consequence of its dividedness.

V

Symbolisms of Ascension and "Waking Dreams"

THE MAGIC FLIGHT

IN CONFORMITY with his theories about Sovereignty, A. M. Hocart regarded the ideology of the "magical flight" as inseparable from and, indeed, contributory to the institution of the god-kings. The kings of South-East Asia and Oceania were carried shoulder-high because, being ranked with the gods, they must never touch the earth; like gods, they "flew through the air".[1] Although expressed with a rigidity characteristic of the great English anthropologist, this hypothesis is by no means uninteresting. The royal ideology does imply, in one way or another, the ascent to Heaven. In an impressive study, which ought to initiate a whole literature, E. Bickerman has shown that the apotheosis of the Roman Emperor included an ascension of this nature.[2] The imperial apotheosis has a long history, one might say pre-history, in the Oriental world. Recently, when studying the ideas of royalty and the ritual pattern of sovereignty in the Middle East of antiquity, G. Widengren brilliantly elucidated this ascensional complex: despite the inevitable divergences due to varieties of culture and the modifications imposed by history, the symbolism and the scenario of the Sovereign's ascension remained much the same for thousands of years. What is more, the same *pattern* was maintained in the exemplary images and the mythical biographies of the divine Messenger, of the Elect and of the Prophet.[3]

---

[1]A. M. Hocart, "Flying through the air" in the *Indian Antiquary*, 1923, pp. 80–82; republished in the volume *The Life-giving Myth*, London, 1952, pp. 28–32.

[2]E. Bickerman, "Die romische Kaiserapotheose" in the *Archiv. f. Religionsgewissenschaft*, 27, 1929, pp. 1–34, esp. 9–13.

[3]*Cf.* G. Widengren, *The Ascension of the Apostle of God and the Heavenly Book*, Upsala-Leipzig, 1950; and the same author's *Muhammad the Apostle of God and his Ascension*, Upsala-Wiesbaden, 1955; esp. pp. 204ff.

We find an analogous situation in China. The first of the Sovereigns who, according to tradition, succeeded in flying was the Emperor Shun (2258–2208, in Chinese chronology); the two daughters of the Emperor Yao, who seem to have been redoubtable magicians, revealed to Shun the art of "flying like a bird". There are other examples of emperors flying through the air. B. Laufer has abundantly proved that, in China, the "magical flight" was an obsession which also found expression in innumerable legends relating to chariots and other flying apparatus.[1] There were even examples of "apotheosis by abduction": the Yellow Emperor Hoang-ti was caught up to Heaven, with his wives and counsellors to the number of seventy persons, by a bearded dragon.

But already, from the circumstance that the Emperor Shun learned the art of flying from two lady magicians, we are entitled to presume that this mythico-ritual complex was not a creation of the ideology of royalty. Indeed, the terms "feathered sage" or "feathered visitor" denoted a Taoist priest. To "mount up to heaven in flight" is expressed in Chinese as follows: "by means of the feathers of birds he has been transformed and has gone up like an immortal."[2] The Taoists and the alchemists had the power of rising up into the air.[3] As for the plumage of birds, this is one of the symbols of the "shamanic flight" that is most commonly met with, and it is abundantly exemplified in the most ancient Chinese iconography.[4]

It is not necessary for our purpose in this chapter to show in detail and for each of the cultural areas under consideration, that this celestial flight is not the monopoly of the Sovereigns, but is also a feat performed by magicians, sages and mystics of every kind. We need only prove that the magical flight transcends the sphere of sovereignty and has chronological precedence to the formation of the ideology of kingship. If the Sovereigns are able

[1]B. Laufer, *The Prehistory of Aviation*, Chicago, 1928.   [2]B. Laufer, *op. cit.*, p. 16.
[3]Several examples are given in Laufer, pp. 26ff. and in our book *Le Chamanisme et les techniques archaïques de l'extase*, pp. 369ff. *Cf.* also A. Waley, *Nine Chinese Songs*, London, 1954.
[4]*Cf.* Hentze, *Sakralbronzen und ihre Bedeutung in den frühchinesischen Kulturen*, Antwerp, 1941, pp. 100ff., 115ff.

to go up to Heaven, it is because they no longer participate in the merely human condition. Nor are they the only, nor the first, human beings to have realised such a change of being. We propose, then, to examine and describe the existential situation in which the formation of this vast assemblage of myths, rites and legends relating to the "magic flight" became possible.

Let us observe at once that the surpassing of the human condition does not necessarily imply that "divinisation" which is an essential concept in the ideology of divine Kingship. The Chinese and Indian alchemists, the yogis, the sages and the mystics as well as the sorcerers and the shamans, although all capable of flying, do not therefore claim to be gods. Their behaviour proves, above all, that they participate in the condition of "spirits"; and we shall see presently how important this participation can be for the understanding of archaic anthropology.

First, when taking our bearings in the immense documentation of the "magical flight", it is convenient to distinguish two main categories of facts: first, the group of myths and legends about the aerial adventures of the mythic Ancestors, the *Märchen* of the *Magische Flucht* type, with, in general, all the legends relating to bird-men (or feathered men); and, secondly, the category of rites and beliefs that imply experience of "flight" or ascent to Heaven. Now, the ecstatic character of the ascension is in no doubt. As we know, techniques of ecstasy are constitutive of the phenomenon generally known by the name of shamanism. Having devoted a whole volume to analysis of this phenomenon, we will limit ourselves here to summarising those findings which are directly to our purpose. The "flight" expresses in spatial terms the ability of certain individuals to leave their bodies at will, and to travel "in the spirit" through the three cosmic regions. One commits oneself to "flight"—that is, one induces ecstasy (not necessarily involving a trance)—either to bring the soul of a sacrificial animal to the highest heaven and offer it to the God of Heaven, or to go in search of the soul of a sick person which is supposed to have been decoyed or ravished away by the demons—in which case the journey is as likely to be made horizontally into distant regions as vertically down into Hell—or, finally, in order to guide the soul of a dead person to his new dwelling-place. Naturally, apart from these ecstatic voyages undertaken for collective religious reasons, the shaman sometimes undergoes ecstasy, or may seek it, for spiritual reasons of his own. Whatever socio-religious system it may be that rules and legalises the functions of the shaman, the shaman-apprentice has to go through the ordeals of an initiation that includes the experience of a symbolic "death" and "resurrection". During his initiation the soul of an apprentice is believed to travel to Heaven and to Hell. Evidently, the shamanic flight is equivalent to a ritual "death". The soul abandons the body and flies away into regions inaccessible to the living. By his ecstasy the shaman renders himself equal to the gods, to the dead and to the spirits: the ability to "die" and come to life again—that is, voluntarily to leave and to re-enter the body —denotes that he has surpassed the human condition.

This is not the place to enlarge upon the means whereby the shamans seek ecstasy: let us simply note that they claim equally to take flight like birds, or mounted upon a horse or a bird, or to fly away upon their drum.[1] This specifically shamanic instrument plays an important part in the preparation for the trance: the shamans both of Siberia and of Central Asia say that they travel through the air seated upon their drums. We find the same ecstatic technique again among the Bon-po priests of Tibet:[2] we meet with it even in cultures where shamanism, in the strict sense of the term, is less common, in Africa, for example.[3]

Thus it is in the ecstatic experience of ascension that we must look for the existential situation responsible for the symbols and images relating to the "magical flight". It would be profitless to identify the "origin" of such a complex of symbols in a certain cultural cycle or in a certain moment in the history of mankind. Although specific of shamanism *stricto sensu*, the ecstasy, the rituals, the beliefs and symbols that are integral with it have been widely reported in all the other archaic cultures. Very likely, the ecstatic

---

[1] *Cf.* Eliade, *Le Chamanisme*, pp. 180, 186, 193 (the shamans mounted on birds), 185ff. (on a horse), 51ff., 212ff., 222ff., 415ff. (flying like birds), 160ff. (flying on their drums).

[2] *Cf.* Helmut Hoffmann, *Quellen zur Geschichte der Tibetischen Bon-Religion*, Wiesbaden, 1950, p. 203.

[3] Adolf Friedrich, *Afrikanische Priestertumer*, Stuttgart, 1939, pp. 193ff.

experience in its innumerable aspects is co-existent with the human condition, in the sense that it is an integral feature of what is called man's becoming aware of his specific situation in the Cosmos.

All this stands out still more clearly when we consider another set of facts relating to the myths and the legends of the "flight". For our purpose, it is a matter of indifference whether the epic content of such myths and legends depends directly upon a real ecstatic experience (a trance of the shamanic type) or whether it is an oneiric creation or a product of pure imagination. From a certain point of view, the oneiric and the imaginary participate in the magic of ecstasy; we shall see presently what meaning we should attach to this participation. For the moment, let us remember that the depth-psychologies have recognised the dimension of the imaginary as one of vital value, as of primordial importance to the human being as a whole. Imaginary experience is constitutive of man, no less certainly than everyday experience and practical activities. Although its structure is not homologous with the structures of "objective" realities, the world of the imaginary is not "unreal". We shall see in a moment the importance of its creations for philosophical anthropology.

What strikes us first about the mythology and folk-lore of the "magical flight" are their primitivity and their universal diffusion. It is agreed that the theme of the *Magische Flucht* is one of the most ancient motifs in folklore: it is found everywhere, and in the most archaic of cultural strata.[1] Strictly speaking, what is in question is not a "flight" but a dizzy trajectory, mostly in a horizontal direction, as one would expect if, as the students of folk-lore think, the fundamental point of the story is the escape of a young hero from the kingdom of death, pursued by a terrifying figure who personifies Death itself. It would be interesting to analyse the structure of the space in which the magical flight takes place at greater length than we can do here: we should find in it all the elements of anxiety, of the supreme effort to escape from an imminent danger, to free oneself from a dreaded presence. The

[1] *Cf.* Dr Marie Pancritius, "Die magische Flucht, ein Nachhall uralter Jenseitsvorstellungen" in *Anthropos*, 8, 1913, pp. 854–879; 929–943; Antti Aarne, *Die Magische Flucht. Eine Märchenstudie*, (FFC, No. 92), Helsinki, 1930.

hero flees more quickly than magic coursers, faster than the wind, as quick as thought—and yet it is not until the end that he manages to shake off his pursuer. Note, moreover, that he does not fly away towards Heaven; he is not escaping upwards, or not vertically only. The spatial universe of the *Magische Flucht* remains that of man and of death, it is never transcended. The speed rises to a fantastic pitch, yet there is no change of dimension. Divinity does not intervene in this nightmare, this rout of man before Death; it is only friendly animals or fairies who help the fugitive, and it is by the magical objects that he throws over his shoulder, and which transform themselves into grandiose natural obstacles (mountains, forests, seas), that he is at last enabled to escape. This has nothing in common with the "flight". But in this universe of anxiety and vertiginous speeds it is important to distinguish one essential element: the desperate effort to *be rid of* a monstrous presence, to *free oneself.*

Space takes on quite a different aspect in the countless myths, tales and legends concerning human or superhuman beings who fly away into Heaven and travel freely between Earth and Heaven, whether they do so with the aid of birds' feathers or by any other means. It is not the speed with which they fly, nor the dramatic intensity of the aerial voyage that characterise this complex of myth and folk-lore; it is the fact that *weight is abolished*, that an ontological mutation has occurred in the human being himself. It is not possible here to pass in review all the species and varieties of this "flight" and of the communications between Earth and Heaven. Let it suffice to say that the motif is of universal distribution,[1] and is integral to a whole group of myths concerned both with the celestial origin of the first human beings and with the paradisiac situation during the primordial *illud tempus* when Heaven was very near to Earth and the mythical Ancestor could attain to it easily enough by climbing a mountain, a tree or a creeper.[2]

One fact of outstanding importance for our purpose is that the motifs of flight and of ascension to Heaven are attested at every

---

[1] *Cf.* Gudmund Hatt, *Asiatic influences in American folk-lore*, Copenhagen, 1949, pp. 56ff.
[2] See above, pp. 59ff.

level of the archaic cultures, as much in the rituals and mythologies of the shamans and the ecstatics as in the myths and folk-lore
of other members of the society who make no pretence to be
distinguished by the intensity of their religious experience. In
short, the ascension and the "flight" belong to an experience
common to all primitive humanity. That this experience constitutes a profound dimension of spirituality is shown by the
subsequent history of the symbolism of ascension. Let us remember the importance assumed by the symbols of the soul as a bird,
of the "wings of the soul", etc., and the images which point to
the spiritual life as an "elevation", the mystical experience as an
ascension, etc. The amount of documentation now at the disposal
of the historian of religions is such, that any enumeration of these
motifs and these symbols would be likely to be incomplete. So
we must resign ourselves to a few allusions bearing upon the
symbolism of the bird.[1] It is probable that the mythico-ritual
theme "bird—soul—ecstatic flight" was already extant in the
paleolithic epoch; one can, indeed, interpret in this sense some
of the designs at Altamira (man with the mask of a bird), and the
famous relief of Lascaux (man with a bird's head), in which Horst
Kirchner sees the representation of a shamanic trance.[2] As for the
mythical conceptions of the soul as a bird and as a spirit-guide
(psychopomp), they have been studied enough for us to content
ourselves here with a mere allusion. A great many symbols and
significations to do with the spiritual life and, above all, with the
power of intelligence, are connected with the images of "flight"
and "wings". The "flight" signifies intelligence, the understanding of secret things and metaphysical truths. "Intelligence (*manas*)
is the swiftest of birds", says the *Rig Veda* (VI, 9, 5); and the
Pañcaviṃça Brâhmana (IV. 1, 13), states that "he who understands
has wings". We can see how the archaic and exemplary image of
"flight" becomes charged with new meanings, discovered in the
course of new awakenings of consciousness. We shall return
presently to consideration of this process of revalorisation.

The extreme archaism and the universal diffusion of the

[1]*Cf. Le Chamanisme*, pp. 415ff.
[2]Horst Kirchner, "Ein archäologischer Beitrag zur Urgeschichte des Schamanismus"
in *Anthropos*, 47, 1952, pp. 244–286, esp. 271ff.; *cf*. pp. 258ff. upon the symbolism of birds

symbols, myths and legends relating to the "flight" present a problem which extends beyond the sphere of the historian of religions into that of philosophic anthropology. We cannot however neglect it; and it was, indeed, part of our intention to show that the documents of ethnography and of the history of religions, inasmuch as they deal with the original spiritual situations, are of interest to the phenomenologist and the philosopher. Now, if we consider the "flight" and all the related symbolisms as a whole, their significance is at once apparent: they all express a break with the universe of everyday experience; and a dual purposiveness is evident in this rupture: both *transcendence* and, at the same time, *freedom* are to be obtained through the "flight". Needless to add, terms denoting "transcendence" or "freedom" are not to be found at the archaic levels of culture in question—but the experience is present, a fact that has its importance. On the one hand, it proves that the roots of freedom are to be sought in the depths of the psyche, and not in conditions brought about by certain historical moments; in other words, that the desire for absolute freedom ranks among the essential longings of man, irrespective of the stage his culture has reached and of its forms of social organisation. The creation, repeated to infinity, of these countless imaginary universes in which space is·transcended and weight is abolished, speaks volumes upon the true nature of the human being. The longing to break the ties that hold him in bondage to the earth is not a result of cosmic pressures or of economic insecurity—it is constitutive of man, in that he is a being who enjoys a mode of existence unique in the world. Such a desire to free himself from his limitations, which he feels to be a kind of degradation, and to regain spontaneity and freedom— the desire expressed, in the example here discussed, by symbols of the "flight"—must be ranked among the specific marks of man.

The breaking of the plane effected by the "flight" signifies, on the other hand, an act of transcendence. It is no small matter to find already, at the most archaic stage of culture, the longing to go beyond and "above" the human condition, to transmute it by an excess of "spiritualisation". For one can only interpret all the myths, rites and legends to which we have been referring, by a longing to see the human body behaving like a "spirit", to transmute the corporeal modality of man into a spiritual modality.

Long analyses would be required to define and extend these few observations. There is no room here to enter upon them. But certain conclusions seem to us to have been gained already, and we will limit ourselves to an outline of these. The first is of a general character, and of interest for the history of religion as a whole. We have remarked elsewhere that, even where religious belief is not dominated by the "ouranian" gods (those of the sky), the symbolism of the ascent to heaven still exists, and always expresses the *transcendent*.[1] It seems to us, therefore, that the description of a religion exclusively upon the basis of its specific institutions and of its dominant mythological themes is not exhaustive; it would be like the description of a man founded only upon his public behaviour and leaving out of account his secret passions, his nostalgias, his existential contradictions and the whole universe of his imagination, which are more essential to him than the ready-made opinions that he utters. If, before proceeding to the description of this or that religion, we took equal account of all the implicit symbolisms of the myths, legends and stories that make up the oral tradition, as well as of the symbolisms legible in the structure of dwellings and in the various customs—we would open up a whole dimension of religious experience which had seemed to be absent, or barely suggested, in public worship and the official mythologies. Whether this set of implicit beliefs be "repressed" or camouflaged by the religious life, or simply its "decay", is another problem which we will not stop to examine here. Enough to have said why one cannot know and describe a religion without reckoning with the implicit religious contents, signified by the symbols.

To return to our present question—it is important to specify that, despite the many and various revalorisations that the symbols of "flight" and of ascension have undergone in the course of history, their structural solidarity remains still discernible. In other terms, whatever be the content and the value ascribed to

[1] *Cf.* our *Patterns in Comparative Religion*, pp. 110ff.

ascensional experience by the many religions in which "flight" and ascension play their parts, there remain always the two essential motifs we have emphasised—transcendence and freedom, both the one and the other obtained by a rupture of the plane of experience, and expressive of an ontological mutation of the human being. It is because they no longer partake of the human condition, and in so far as they are "free", that the Sovereigns are supposed to be able to fly through the air. It is for the same reason that the yogis, the alchemists, the *arhat*, are able to transport themselves at will, to fly, or to disappear. One has only to analyse the Indian data attentively to realise what considerable innovations, deriving from successive spiritual experiences and fresh awakenings of consciousness, have taken place in the long history of India. Some of these developments are to be found in our previous writings;[1] we content ourselves here with a few indications only. Let us recall that the "flight" is so characteristic of the Buddhist *arhat*, that *arahant* is the basis of the Sinhalese verb *rahatve*, "to disappear, to pass instantaneously from one place to another". In this case we are evidently dealing with a theme of folk-lore (the flying sage and magician) which has so struck the popular imagination as to find expression in a linguistic creation. But one must also take into consideration the special meaning of the "flight" of an *arhat*, a meaning bound up with that spiritual experience which is supposed to transcend the human condition. As a general rule, one can say that the *arhat*—like all the *jñanin* and the yogis—are *kamacarin*—beings who can "transport themselves at will". As Coomaraswamy expresses it, what is implied by *kamacarin* is "the condition of one who, being in the Spirit, no longer needs to move at all in order to be anywhere".[2] Ananda Coomaraswamy reminds us that the usual Sanskrit expression for "to disappear" is *antar-dhânam gam*—literally, "to go into an interior position". In the *Kâlingabodhi Jâtaka*, the flight through the air depends upon one's having "clothed the body with the raiment of contemplation" (*jhâna vethanena*).[3] What all this amounts to is that, at the level of pure metaphysical knowledge,

[1] *Cf. Le Chamanisme*, pp. 362ff., and *Yoga . . .*, 318ff.
[2] Ananda Coomaraswamy, *Figures of Speech or Figures of Thought*, London, 1946, p. 184.
[3] Coomaraswamy, *op. cit.*, pp. 183–184.

the "flight" and the "ascension" become mere traditional formulæ, no longer expressive of any corporal locomotion, but of a sort of spatial simultaneity granted to one by the intelligence.

Still more interesting from our point of view are the images which signify transcendence of the human condition owing to the ability of the *arhat* to fly over the roofs of houses. The Buddhist texts speak of *arhat* who "fly through the air breaking through the roof of the palace "[1]; or who, "flying at their own will, break and pass through the roof of the house and rise up into the air"[2]: the *arhat* Moggalâna, for instance, "breaking the dome, plunges into the air".[3] This symbolism is susceptible of a dual interpretation; upon the plane of subtle physiology and mystical experience it refers to an "ecstasy", and therefore to the flight of the soul through the *brahmarandhra*[4]; while on the metaphysical plane it is a case of the abolition of the conditioned world. For the "house" stands for the Universe; to "break the roof of the house" means that the *arhat* has transcended the world or risen above it. However wide the gulf that divides the archaic mythology and folklore about the "flight" from India's world-transcending techniques and metaphysical knowledge, it remains true that one can homologise the different images they bring into play.

A whole study has yet to be made of the phenomenology of levitation and ascensional ecstasy among "magicians"—that is, among those who claim to have acquired the power of autonomous translocation—and among the mystics. When that has been done, we may know better what precisions and distinctions are required for the description of each type, not to mention their innumerable variants. One need only refer to the ascensional ecstasy of Zoroaster[5] and to the *mirâj* of Mohammed[6] to convince oneself that, in the history of religions as everywhere else, to

---

[1] *Jâtaka*, III, p. 472.

[2] *Dhammapada Atthakathâ*, III, p. 66; Ananda Coomaraswamy, "Symbolism of the Dome", in the *Indian Historical Quarterly*, 14, 1938, pp. 1–56, p. 54.

[3] *Dhammapada Atthakathâ*, III, p. 66; Coomaraswamy, *ibid.*

[4] A term denoting the "opening" at the summit of the cranium, which plays a leading part in the techniques of Tantric yoga.

[5] Upon the "shamanic" structure of Zoroaster, see *Le Chamanisme*, pp. 356ff.; G. Widengren, "Stand und aufgaben der Iranischer Religionsgeschichte", II, in *Numen* 2, 1955, pp. 66ff.

[6] See, lastly, G. Widengren, *Muhammad the Apostle of God*, pp. 96ff.

compare is not to confuse. It would be absurd to minimise the differences of content that diversify examples of "flight", "ecstasy" and "ascension". But it would be just as absurd not to recognise the correspondence of structure which emerges from such comparisons. And, in the history of religions, as in other mental disciplines, it is knowledge of structure which makes it possible to understand meanings. It is only after we have clarified, as a whole, the structure of the symbolism of the "flight" that we can arrive at its first meaning; the way is then open for us to understand each case separately. It is important, then, not to forget that, at every level of culture and in spite of their widely different historical and religious contexts, the symbolism of the "flight" invariably expresses the abolition of the human condition, transcendence and freedom.

THE SEVEN STEPS OF THE BUDDHA

Let us now examine another set of images and symbols which we have already pointed out in connexion with the symbolism of the flight—the ascension to Heaven by means of steps. First, here is a Buddhist text of particular interest, which shows us the extent to which these traditional images are susceptible of metaphysical re-valorisation.

"As soon as he is born, the Bodhisattva places his feet flat on the ground and, turning towards the North, takes seven strides, sheltering under a white parasol. He looks at the regions all around and says, with his voice like that of a bull: 'I am at the top of the world, I am the best in the world; this is my last birth; for me, there will never again be another existence.'" (*Majjhima-Nikâya*, III, p. 123.) This mythical feature of the Nativity of the Buddha is repeated, with certain variations, in the subsequent literature of the Nikâya-Agama, of the Vinaya, and in biographies of the Buddha. In a long note to his translation of the *Mahâprajñâpâra-mitâsastra* of Nâgârjuna, Mr Etienne Lamotte has grouped together the most important texts: the Buddha takes seven steps in a single direction, to the North or in four, six or ten directions;

he takes these steps with feet placed flat on the ground, or placed upon a lotus, or at a height of four inches.[1] The frequent appearance of the first motif—the seven steps taken exclusively to the North—persuades us that the other, variant forms (the four, six or ten directions) are of later date, due perhaps to the integration of this theme into a more complicated symbolism.

Let us, for the moment, leave on one side the analysis of the different ways in which the Buddha reaches the North (upon "flatly-placed" feet, or upon a lotus, or in a gliding attitude), and confine our attention to the central symbolism of the seven steps. Mr Paul Mus, in his study of this mythic theme, has well brought out its cosmological structure and metaphysical significance.[2] In effect, the seven steps bring the Buddha to the summit of the cosmic system. The expression, "I am the highest in the world" (*aggo'ham asmi lokassa*) means no other thing than that the Buddha *has transcended space*. He reaches "the summit of the world" (*lokkagge*) by passing through the seven cosmic stages which, as we know, correspond to the seven planetary heavens. On the other hand, the monument known by the name of the "*seven-storied prâsâda*" symbolises the world culminating in the cosmic North: from its summit one reaches the supernal land of the Buddha.[3]

What the myth of his Nativity expresses with perfect precision, is that as soon as the Buddha is born he transcends the Cosmos and abolishes space and time (he becomes the "highest" and the "oldest" in the world). A great deal of light is shed on the symbolism of this transcendence by the different ways in which the Buddha takes the seven steps. Either he does not touch the ground, or lotuses spring up under his feet, or he glides along—he is undefiled by any direct contact with this world of ours. Concerning the symbolism of the feet placed parallel with the ground, Burnouf had already quoted a Buddhist text to which Paul Mus refers, with the comment that: "Wherever the master of the

[1] Etienne Lamotte, *Le Traité de la Grande Vertu de Sagesse, de Nâgârjuna*, Vol. I, Louvain, 1944, pp. 6ff. For the representations of the *sapta padâni*, see A. Foucher, *L'Art gréco-bouddhique du Gandhâra*, Paris, 1905-1922, figs. 154-155; *cf.* also *Images et Symboles*, pp. 98ff.

[2] Paul Mus, *Barabudur. Esquisse d'une histoire du Bouddhisme*, Hanoï, 1935, I, pp. 476-575; and the same author's *La notion du temps réversible dans la mythologie bouddhique*, Melun, 1939.

[3] P. Mus, *Barabudur*, p. 95ff., p. 320ff.

World goes, the hollow places are filled up, and the raised places become level, etc." Under the feet of the Buddha the Earth becomes "smooth"—meaning thereby that mass is reduced and the third dimension abolished; an image expressive of spatial transcendence.[1]

The metaphysical significance of this symbolism of spatial transcendence is carried to its extreme limits in Buddhist speculation. But this symbolism is evidently not a Buddhist creation. The transcendence of the World by elevation into Heaven was already known in pre-Buddhist times. "The sacrifice, in its entirety, that is the ship that sails to Heaven" (*Çatapatha Brâhmana*, IV, 2, 5, 10). The pattern of the rite is a *dûrohana*—a "difficult ascension". The celebrant mounts the steps (*âkramana*) to the sacrificial stake and, arriving at the summit, he stretches out his hands (as a bird spreads its wings!) and cries out, "I have attained to Heaven, to the Gods; I have become immortal!" (*Taittirîya Samhita*, I, 7, 9.) "Verily, the celebrant makes himself a ladder and a bridge in order to reach the celestial world". (*Ibid.* VI, 6, 4, 2.[2]) In this case we are evidently dealing with a belief in the magico-religious efficacy of the Vedic sacrifice; not yet with the "transcension" of the Cosmos that is the theme of the Buddhist Nativity. Nevertheless, it is important to note the analogy between the steps of the Buddha and the "stairs" of the sacrificial stake which the celebrant ascends to the summit. The effects in the two cases are homologous: attainment of the supreme summit of the universe, equated with the cosmic North, or "Centre of the World".

The Buddha's passing through the seven heavens to attain the "highest point"—that is, his ascension through the cosmic stages which correspond to the seven planetary heavens—is a theme belonging to a symbolic-ritual complex which is common to India, Central Asia and to the Middle East. We have studied this system of beliefs and rites in our *Le Chamanisme* (pp. 237ff., 423ff. and *passim*). Let us mention only that the "seven steps of the Buddha" are analogous to the Siberian shaman's ascent to Heaven

---

[1] P. Mus, *Barabudur*, p. 484.
[2] *Cf.* also *Images et Symboles*, p. 57, and *Le Chamanisme*, pp. 362ff.

by means of the steps cut in the ceremonial birch-tree (seven, nine
or sixteen notches corresponding to the same numbers of Heavens),
or to the ladder with seven rungs which is mounted by the initiate
in the mysteries of Mithra. All these rites and myths are of a
common structure: the universe is conceived as having seven
stages, one above another—that is, the seven planetary heavens;
the summit is located either in the cosmic North, or in the Pole
Star, or in the Empyrean, equivalents for the same symbolism of
the "Centre of the World". Elevation into the supreme Heaven,
that is, the act of transcending the world, takes place near to a
"Centre" (a temple, or a royal city, or it may be a sacred tree,
homologised with the Cosmic Tree, the stake of sacrifice assimilated to the *Axis Mundi*, etc.) because it is in a "Centre" that the
"break" occurs from one plane to another, and, therefore, the
passage from Earth to Heaven.[1]

To return to the theme of the Buddha's nativity: here we are
certainly confronted by a re-interpretation of the archaic symbolism of transcendence. The principal difference between the
Seven Steps of the Buddha and the Brahmanic, Siberian or Mith-
raic rituals consists in their religious orientation and their different
metaphysical implications. The myth of the Nativity reveals to us
the transcendence, by the Buddha, of this soiled and sorrowful
world. The Brahmanic and shamanic rituals point to a heavenly
ascension that is to make one a partaker in the world of the Gods
and assure one of a privileged condition after death, or to obtain
some service from the Supreme Deity. The initiate in the mysteries of Mithra undertakes a symbolic journey through the seven
heavens in order to "purify" himself from the influences of the
tutelary planets and uplift himself to the Empyrean. But the
structure of all these "motifs" is identical: one *transcends the
world by passing through the seven heavens and attaining the summit of
the Cosmos, the Pole.*

As Paul Mus remarks of the Indian cosmology, the point
from which the Creation starts is the summit. "The creation was
effected gradually, thence downwards by successive stages." The
Pole is not only the axis of the cosmic movements; it is also the

[1] *Cf. Images et Symboles*, pp. 52ff.

"oldest" place, because it is from there that the World has come into existence. That is why the Buddha cries out: "It is I who am at the peak of the World . . . it is I who am the Eldest." For, upon attaining to the summit of the Cosmos, Buddha *becomes contemporary with the commencement of the world.* He has abolished Time and the Creation, and finds himself in the a-temporal instant that precedes the cosmogony. What happens is a "return to the past" in order to reproduce the primordial situation "pure" and uncorrupted because not yet involved in Time. To "come back again", until one reaches the "oldest" place in the World, is equivalent to abolishing duration, annihilating the work of Time. By declaring himself the "Eldest of the World" the Buddha proclaims his transcendence in relation to Time, just as he declares that he has transcended Space by reaching "the peak of the World". Both images express a complete surpassing of the World and re-entry into an "absolute" and paradoxical state beyond Time and Space.

Let us note that the Indian cosmology is not alone in making Creation begin from the summit. According to Semite traditions, the world was created beginning from the navel (image of the Centre) and the same ideas are found elsewhere.[1] The "centre of the World" is necessarily the "oldest" part of the Universe. But we must not forget that, from the point of view of the symbolisms we are considering, this "agedness" is a formula for primordial Time, for the "first" time. The "old age" (*jyeshta*) of the Buddha is a figure of speech, meaning that he was already present before the birth of the World, that he saw the World's coming into existence and the first appearance of Time.

On the other hand, we know that ritual ascensions to Heaven always take place in a "centre". The shamanic tree is supposed to be at the "centre of the World", since it is assimilated to the Cosmic Tree: and, in India, the sacrificial stake (*yûpa*) corresponds to the *Axis mundi*. But an analogous symbolism is attested in the very structure of the temples and human habitations. From the

[1] *Cf. The Myth of the Eternal Return,* pp. 16ff.; *Patterns in Comparative Religion,* pp. 377ff.

fact that all the sanctuaries, palaces and royal cities, and, by extension, all the houses are situated, symbolically, at the "Centre of the World", it follows that, in no matter which of these buildings, a rupture of planes is possible; that is, it may be possible to transcend space (by elevation into Heaven) and at the same moment to transcend Time (by re-entering the primordial instant before the World had yet come into existence). This ought not to surprise us, since we know that every habitation is an *imago mundi* and every building of a new house is a repetition of the cosmogony. Altogether, these mutually confirming and complementary symbols present, each in its own special perspective, one and the same meaning: that there does exist, for man, a possibility of transcending the World; spatially, by going "upward", and temporally by a "reversal", or "going backwards". By transcending this world of ours, one re-enters into a primordial situation; the plenary condition of the World's beginning, the perfection of the "first instant", before anything had been defiled and when nothing was faded or worn, because the World had only just been born.

By many ways and starting from different points of view, religious man has always been trying to regenerate or renew himself by periodically re-entering into "the perfection of the beginnings"; that is, by rediscovering the primal source of Life as it was when Life, like the whole of Creation, was still *sacred* because it was still new from the hands of the Creator.

DÛROHANA AND THE "WAKING DREAM"

Now, we know that flight, elevation, and ascension by the mounting of stairs are themes of fairly frequent occurrence in dreams. Sometimes, indeed, one of these themes becomes a dominant factor in the oneiric or imaginative activity. Let us again refer to an example we have already mentioned upon an earlier occasion.[1] Julien Green noted in his *Journal* of 4 April 1933: "In all my books, the idea of fear, or of any other strong emotion,

[1] *Cf. Images et Symboles*, pp. 64ff.

seems linked in some inexplicable way with a staircase. I realised this yesterday, when I passed in review all the novels I have written . . . (the references follow). I wonder how I can have so often repeated this motif without noticing it. As a child, I used to dream that I was being chased down a staircase. My mother had the same fears in her young days; perhaps something of them has remained in me . . ."

After all that we have been saying about the "Seven Steps of the Buddha" we can understand why the staircase is linked, in the novels of Julien Green, to "the thought of fear or of any other strong emotion". The staircase is pre-eminently the symbol of a passage from one mode of being to another. The ontological mutation can take place only by a rite of passage; and, indeed, birth, initiation, sexuality, marriage and death constitute, in traditional societies, so many rites of passage. Modality can be changed only as a consequence of a rupture—and this releases ambivalent feelings of fear and of joy, of attraction and repulsion. That is why the mounting of stairs symbolises not only, as we have seen, access to the sacred—the pre-eminent "breaking of the plane"—but also death. Many are the traditions in which the soul of the dead man ascends the paths of a mountain or climbs a tree. The verb "to die" in Assyrian could also mean "to clutch at the mountain", and in Egyptian "to clutch" is a euphemism for "to die".[1] In the work of Julien Green, as he himself observed with surprise, all the most dramatic events—death, crime, revelations of love, or the appearance of a ghost—had taken place upon a staircase. The writer's imagination spontaneously produced the same typical image of the staircase whenever one of his characters was confronting some decisive experience by which he was about to become "another".

Freud interpreted the ascent of a staircase as a disguised expression of sexual desire—a one-sided and somewhat over-simplified view, which the psychologists have since corrected and amplified.[2] But even the purely sexual signification that Freud discovered does not contradict the more comprehensive symbolism of the

[1] *Ibid.* p. 62.
[2] *Cf. e.g.*, R. Desoille, *Le rêve éveillé en psychothérapie*, Paris, 1945, pp. 294ff.

staircase; for the sexual act itself constitutes a "rite of passage". To infer that the patient who is mounting a staircase in a dream is thereby gratifying a sexual desire buried in his unconscious—this is still a way of saying that, in the depths of his being, the patient is struggling to get out of a situation in which he is "stuck"—a negative, sterile situation. If it is a case of a psyche in crisis the dream in question—still according to the purely sexual meaning Freud attached to it—indicates that the psychic disequilibrium might be resolved through the desired sexual activity; that is, by such a profound modification of the patient's situation that it would be homologous with a change of behaviour, even of a mode of being. In other words, the Freudian interpretation of this image of the staircase as symptomatic of unconscious sexual desire, is perfectly compatible with the multiple meanings of "passage" illustrated by stairs, ladders, etc., in the rites and myths.

It remains to be seen whether the reductive method of Freudian psychoanalysis does justice to the function of the symbol. The problem is too complex for us to tackle in these few pages devoted to the symbols of flight and ascension. Let us, however, remember how successfully R. Desoille has used the technique of the "waking dream", and obtained curative effects even where psychoanalytic treatment had produced no noticeable improvement. Now, the type of "waking dream" that Desoille most frequently requires of his patients is precisely that of ascending a staircase or climbing a mountain. To put it another way, he obtains psychic cures by re-animating, in active imagination, certain symbols which comprise, in their own structure, the ideas of "passage" and of "ontological mutation". In the frame of reference in which they were known to the historian of religions, these symbols express the *attitudes* taken up by man and, at the same time, the *realities* he is confronting, and these are always sacred realities, for, at the archaic level of culture, the *sacred* is the pre-eminently *real*. Thus, one may say, the simple repetition, aided by an active imagination, of certain symbols which are religious (or which, more exactly, are abundantly attested in innumerable religions), brings about a psychological improvement and leads ultimately to a recovery. In other terms, the psychagogy of the "waking dream" of ascension is the application of a spiritual technique in the domain of unconscious psychic activity.

This appears still more clearly when we learn that R. Desoille not only induces his patients to imagine themselves going up stairways and mountains, but also "flying".[1] Gaston Bachelard has justly defined the technique of the waking dream as a form of the "imagination of movement"[2]: "The elevation of the soul is in proportion to its serenity. In light and in elevation a dynamic unity is formed." We have already clarified the meanings of flight and ascension, in folk-lore, in the history of religions and in mysticism; and we were able to show that the imagery in question was always that of transcendence and freedom. If we wish to avoid the over-simplified causality implied in the reductive method, we are obliged to come to this conclusion: that, upon the different but interconnected planes of the oneiric, of active imagination, of mythological creation and folk-lore, of ritual and of metaphysical speculation, and, finally, upon the plane of ecstatic experience, the symbolism of ascension always refers to a breaking-out from a situation that has become "blocked" or "petrified", a rupture of the plane which makes it possible to pass from one mode of being into another—in short, liberty "of movement", freedom to change the situation, to abolish a conditioning system. And it will be noticed that, in a number of different contexts—oneiric, ecstatic, ritual, mythological, etc.—we find complementary, but structurally indissoluble meanings which fall into a *pattern*. Furthermore, we do not manage to decipher everything that such a pattern presents, as it were in cryptography, until, after having "decoded" its particular meanings one by one, each in its own frame of reference, we take the trouble to integrate them all into a whole. For each symbolism is a "system" and can only be really understood so far as we study it in the totality of its particular applications.

All this admitted, one cannot refrain from affirming that the symbolism of ascension reveals its deepest meanings when it is examined in relation to the most "pure" activity of the spirit. It

[1]R. Desoille, *op. cit.*, pp. 29ff., 146ff. and *passim*.
[2]Gaston Bachelard, *L'air et les songes*, Paris, 1943, pp. 129ff. (lines quoted from p. 139).

may be said to deliver its "true message" upon the planes of metaphysics and mysticism. One might also say that it is thanks to the values that ascension stands for in the spiritual life (the lifting-up of the soul to God, mystic ecstasy, etc.) that its other significances, discernible on the levels of ritual, myth, dream-life or psychagogy, become fully intelligible and disclose to us their secret purport. In effect, the ascent of a stairway or a mountain in a dream or a waking dream signifies, at the deepest psychic level, an experience of "regeneration" (the solution of a crisis, psychic re-integration). Now, as we have seen, Mâhâyana metaphysics interprets the ascension of the Buddha as an event at the Centre of the World, and therefore one that signifies transcendence of both Space and Time. A great many traditions trace the creation of the World to a central point (navel) from which it is supposed to have spread out in the four cardinal directions. To attain to the centre of the World means, therefore, to arrive at the "point of departure" of the Cosmos at the "beginning of Time"; in short, to have abolished Time. We can now better understand the regenerative effect produced in the deep psyche by the imagery of ascension and flight *because we know* that—upon the planes of ritual, ecstasy and metaphysics—ascension is capable, among other things, of abolishing Time and Space and of "projecting" man into the mythical instant of the Creation of the World, whereby he is in some sense "born again", being rendered contemporary with the birth of the World.[1] Briefly, the "regeneration" which is effected in the depth of the psyche is not to be completely explained until the moment when we realise that the images and symbols that have evoked it express—in religions and mysticisms—the doing away with Time.

The problem is not so simple as might appear. The depth-psychologists are agreed, it is true, that the dynamisms of the unconscious are not governed by the categories of Space and Time as we know them in conscious experience. C. G. Jung even expressly declares that it is on account of the a-temporal character of the collective unconscious that, at the least touch of its contents, one has an "experience of the eternal", and that it is precisely the re-

[1] See above, p. 47ff.

activation of these contents which is felt as a complete regeneration of the psychic life. That is doubtless true. But a difficulty
remains. There is continuity between the functions fulfilled and
the messages transmitted by certain symbolisms to the deepest
layers of the unconscious and the meanings that they reveal upon
the plane of the "purest" spiritual activity. Now, such continuity
is at least unexpected, for psychiatrists generally record opposition
and conflict between the values of the unconscious and those of the
conscious, and the philosophers often oppose Spirit to Life or to
living Matter.

Of course, one could always fall back upon the materialist
hypothesis, the explanation by reduction to the "first form", in
whatever perspective one may situate the appearance of that "first
form". The temptation is great, to look for the "origin" of a
custom, or a mode of being, or of a category of Spirit, etc., in an
antecedent, or in some sense embryonic, situation. We know
what a number of causal explanations have been proposed by
materialists of every kind, seeking to reduce the activity and the
creations of the Spirit to some instinct, some gland or some infantile trauma. And in some respects, these explanations of complex
realities by reducing them to elementary "origins" are instructive;
but they do not, properly speaking, amount to explanations; they
are only re-statements that everything in creation has a beginning
in Time, which nobody dreams of denying. But it is obvious that
the embryonic state does not account for the mode of being of
the adult; an embryo only acquires significance in so far as it is
related to, and compared with, the adult. It is not the "foetus"
which explains man, for the specific mode of being of man in the
world emerges just inasmuch as he is no longer leading a foetal
existence. Psychoanalysts speak of psychic regressions to the
foetal state, but that is an "intrapolation". No doubt, "regressions"
are always possible; but to say so does not really mean anything
more than to say, for instance, that living matter is returning—by
death—to the state of mere matter; or that a piece of sculpture is
"regressing" to its previous state of crude material by being
broken into fragments. The real question is: from what moment
can a structure or a mode of being be said to be constituted as

such? There is no mystification involved in neglecting what has preceded the moment of its constitution. It is a mistake to suppose that we effect a de-mystification by demonstrating that, for example, this or that value of the Spirit has a (perhaps painful) "prehistory". One might as well say about an elephant that once it was an embryo.

To return to our own question—it would be useless to try to explain the function of symbols by reference to their "germinal" phases. On the contrary, the ultimate meaning of certain symbols is not revealed until their "maturity"—that is, until their function is studied in the most complex strivings of the Spirit. And, once again, this always raises the problem of the relationship between Substance, or living Matter, and the Spirit; we find ourselves, after all, on the plane of philosophy.

It is not without interest to recall that this paradoxical relationship has tormented Indian philosophic thought from the beginning. Well enough known in the West is one representative solution (notably as it is given in the Vedânta) which cuts the question short by declaring it to be "illusory" (*mâyâ*). Less well known is the other solution, proposed by the Sâmkhya and yoga philosophies, which may one day tempt some author to explain the collective unconscious of Jung. The Sâmkhya presupposes two principles, Substance (*prakriti*) and Spirit (*purusha*); the latter being always in the individual mode: that is, the Sâmkhya and yoga deny the identity of the individual spirit (*âtman*) with the universal Spirit (*Brahman*) that the Vedânta postulates. Now, although no real relation can exist between Nature and Spirit, although *prakriti* is in its own mode of being "unconscious" and "blind"; and although, moreover, she keeps man in bondage to the numberless illusions of existence and in continual suffering, *prakriti* is working, in reality, for the deliverance of the Spirit (*purusha*). Unable herself to "understand", she tries to make the Spirit do so: she who, by definition, is condemned to a conditioned being, helps the Spirit to liberate—that is, to de-condition —itself.[1] (One remembers that, for Aristotle too, Matter, which was in itself unintelligible, nevertheless pointed towards an "end"

[1] *Cf. Yoga, Immortality and Freedom*, pp. 31ff. and *passim*.

—that of service to Form.) In India a whole literature has been devoted to explanations of this paradoxical relationship between what is pre-eminently unconscious—Matter—and pure "consciousness", the Spirit, which by its own mode of being is a-temporal, free, uninvolved in the becoming. And one of the most unexpected results of this philosophic labour has been its conclusion that the Unconscious (*i.e. prakriti*), moving by a kind of "teleological instinct", imitates the behaviour of the Spirit; that the Unconscious behaves in such a way that its activity seems to *prefigure* the mode of being of the Spirit.

It would be interesting to consider the symbolism of ascension in this Indian perspective: we do indeed find, in the activity of the Unconscious (*prakriti*), certain "intentions" which can deliver their ultimate message only upon the plane of pure consciousness (*purusha*). The images of "flight" and of "ascension", so frequently appearing in the worlds of dream and imagination, become perfectly intelligible only at the level of mysticism and metaphysics, where they clearly express the ideas of *freedom* and *transcendence*. But at all the other, "lower" levels of the psychic life, these images still stand for procedures that are homologous, in their tendency, to acts of "freedom" and "transcendence".

VI

Power and Holiness
in the History of Religions

THE HIEROPHANIES

In 1917, when Rudolf Otto, Professor at the University of Marburg, published his little book entitled *Das Heilige* ("The Holy"), he was far from dreaming that he had given the public a "best seller" and a work destined to have world repercussions.[1] Since then, more than twenty editions have been sold out in Germany, and this small volume, which so rapidly grew famous, has been translated into a dozen languages. How are we to account for its unprecedented success?

It is due, no doubt, to the novelty and originality of the perspective taken by the author. Instead of studying the *ideas* of God and of religion, Rudolf Otto set to work to analyse the modalities of *religious experience*. Gifted with great psychological discrimination and fortified by training both as a theologian and as a historian of religions, he succeeded in isolating the content and the specific character of that experience. Neglecting the rational and speculative aspects of religion, he concentrated especially upon its non-rational side. For—as he has somewhere explicitly avowed—Otto had read Luther, and understood what "the living God" means to a believer, and that this is not the God of the philosophers, the God of Erasmus, for example; not an idea, an abstract notion, nor simply a moral allegory. He was, on the contrary, a terrible *power*, manifested in the "wrath" of God and in the fear of it. And in his book on "The Holy", Rudolf Otto sets himself to distinguish the characteristics of this terrifying

[1]Rudolf Otto, *Das Heilige*, Breslau, 1917; see also the same author's *Aufsätze, das Numinose betreffend*, Gotha, 1923; English trans. of the former work, by J. W. Harvey—*The Idea of the Holy*, O.U.P., 1923.

and irrational experience. He discloses the feelings of fear before what is sacred, before the *mysterium tremendum*, this *majesty* that betokens an overwhelming superiority of power: he reveals the religious fear before the *mysterium fascinans*, radiating the perfect plenitude of being. Otto designates all these experiences *numinous*, for they are evoked by some aspect of the divine *power*: the "numinous" is distinguished by its being something "wholly other" (*ganz andere*); radically and totally different; it resembles nothing either human or cosmic. In relation to it, man has the feeling of his utter "nothingness", the feeling of being "no more than a creature"; that is, to use the words in which Abraham addressed the Lord, of being no more "than dust and ashes" (*Genesis*, XVIII, 27).

From the penetrating analysis of Rudolf Otto, let us retain this observation: that the sacred always manifests itself as a power of quite another order than that of the forces of nature. It is true that human language naïvely expresses the *tremendum*, the *majestas* or the *mysterium fascinans* in terms borrowed from the realms of nature or the profane consciousness of man. But we know that this terminology is analogical, and simply due to the inability of man to express what is *ganz andere*; language is obliged to try to suggest whatever surpasses natural experience in terms that are borrowed from that experience.

The sacred, then, manifests itself equally as a force or as a power. To denote the act of manifestation of the sacred, we propose to use the term *hierophany*. This word is convenient because it requires no additional specification; it means nothing more than is implied by its etymological content—namely, that something sacred is shown to us, manifests itself. One may say that the history of religions—from the most elementary to the most developed—is constituted by a number of important hierophanies, manifestations of sacred realities. Beginning from the most elementary hierophany—for example, the manifestation of the sacred in any object whatever, say a stone or a tree—and ending in the supreme hierophany, the incarnation of God in Jesus Christ, there is no real break in the continuity. In regard to structure, we find ourselves confronted by the same mysterious

action—the manifestation of something that is "wholly other"—
of a reality that does not belong to our world—in things which
are part and parcel of this same "natural", or "profane" world.

Modern Western man feels ill at ease before many forms of
manifestation of the sacred: he finds it difficult, for instance, to
accept the fact that, for certain human beings, the sacred may
manifest itself in stones or trees. It should never be forgotten,
however, that what is in question here is not a veneration of the
stone in itself, nor a worship of the tree *as a tree*. Sacred stones or
trees are not adored in their natural capacity, but only because
they are *hierophanies*, because they "show forth" something which
is no longer mineral or vegetable but *sacred*—"wholly other".

The forms and the means of manifestation of the sacred vary
from one people to another and from one civilisation to another.
But there remains always this paradoxical—that is, incomprehensible—fact that it is the *sacred* that is manifesting, and thereby
limiting itself and ceasing to be *absolute*. This is most important for
our understanding of the specific character of religious experience:
if we admit that all manifestations of the sacred are equivalent as
such, in that the humblest hierophany and the most terrifying
theophany present the same structure and are to be explained by
the same dialectic of the sacred, we then realise that there is no
essential discontinuity in the religious life of mankind. To look
more closely at a single example: the hierophany that is attributed
to a stone, compared with the supreme theophany, the Incarnation. The great mystery consists in *the very fact that the sacred is
made manifest*; for, as we have seen above, in making itself manifest
the sacred *limits* and "historicises" itself. We realise how greatly
the sacred limits itself by taking the form of a stone: but we are
prone to forget that God himself was accepting limitation and
historicisation by incarnating in Jesus Christ. This, let us repeat it,
is the great mystery, the *mysterium tremendum*: the fact that the
sacred accepted self-limitation. Jesus Christ spoke Aramaic; he
did not speak Sanskrit or Chinese. He had accepted limitation by
life and by history. Although he continued to be God, he was no
longer the all-powerful—just as, upon quite another plane, when
the sacred manifests in a rock or a tree, it gives up being Every-

thing and limits itself. There are, of course, great differences between the innumerable hierophanies; but one should never lose sight of the fact that their structure and dialectic are always the same.

MANA AND THE KRATOPHANIES

Having now established this solidarity of structure among manifestations of the sacred in general, let us more closely examine their *power* and their dynamism. Every hierophany is a kratophany, a *manifestation of force*. So strikingly is this the case that there have been attempts to find the origin of religion in the idea of an impersonal and universal force called, after its Melanesian name, *mana*.[1] This hypothetical identification of the earliest religious experience with the experience of mana was a rather hasty generalisation and, scientifically, somewhat ill-founded. But since the concept of mana is of some importance in the history of religions and is still believed, at least in certain circles, to cover the purest and most original human experience of the sacred, we shall have to give some little attention to it.

Let us recall the precise nature of mana. Towards the end of the nineteenth century, the English missionary Codrington observed that the Melanesians spoke of a force, or influence, that was not physical. This force, wrote Codrington, "is in a way supernatural; but it shews itself in physical force, or in any kind of power or excellence which a man possesses. This mana is not fixed in anything, and can be conveyed in almost anything; but spirits, whether disembodied souls or supernatural beings, have it and can impart it".[2] It followed—still according to Codrington's informants—that the immense achievement of the creation of the Cosmos was possible only by the mana of the divinity. The chief of a clan, too, possesses mana; but the British made the Maoris their subjects because their mana was the stronger; and the office of the Christian missionary possessed a mana stronger

[1] Upon this question, see our *Patterns in Comparative Religion*, pp. 19ff.
[2] R. H. Codrington, *The Melanesians*, Oxford, 1891, pp. 118–119, especially the footnote from which we quote above.

than that of the autochthonous rites. A canoe will go swiftly only if it has mana; and the same is true of a trawl-net to catch fish, or an arrow shot to inflict a deadly wound.[1] In short, whatever pre-eminently *is* or *does*, by that fact has mana; that is, everything which impresses man as effectual, creative or perfect.

In reliance upon the fact that mana might manifest itself in any thing or any action whatsoever, it was supposed that the force in question was something impersonal, diffused throughout the Cosmos. This hypothesis was encouraged by the discovery of notions similar to that of mana, current in other primitive cultures. It was observed, *e.g.*, that the *orenda* of the Iroquois, the *oki* of the Hurons, the *megbe* of the African Pygmies, etc., repre-sent, on the whole, the same sacred *force* that is expressed by the Melanesian term *mana*.[2] From this certain theorists drew the conclusion that belief in mana preceded every other form of religion, that mana represents the pre-animistic phase of religion. We know that animism presupposes belief in the existence of the *soul*—in souls of the dead, spirits, demons—which manifests itself under various aspects. And one remembers how Tylor used to identify animism with the first phase of religion: in that author's opinion the most ancient of all religious beliefs was precisely that which regarded the Universe as *animated*, indwelt and dynamised by an infinite number of souls. But now, one had just discovered the existence of an *impersonal force*, mana, manifested here and there throughout the Universe. One was almost ready to infer that the first phase of religion was pre-animistic.

It is not our business here to discuss the origin of religion or to decide what was the most ancient religious belief of mankind. But with regard to these theories founded upon the primordial and universal character of mana, we must say without delay that they have been invalidated by later research. Also it is not without interest to note that even by the end of the century, when Codrington introduced the concept of mana to the learned world, it could have been demonstrated that this mysterious force was not impersonal. More exactly it could have been

[1] Codrington, *op. cit.*, p. 120.
[2] *Cf. Patterns in Comparative Religion*, pp. 20ff.; Hutton Webster, *Magic, a Sociological Study*, Stanford, 1948, pp. 3ff.

shown that, among the Melanesians, as among all other archaic peoples, the notions of personal and impersonal are devoid of meaning.

"PERSONAL" AND "IMPERSONAL"

Let us look at them more closely. Codrington says: "If a stone is found to have a supernatural power, it is because a spirit has associated itself with it; a dead man's bone has with it mana, because the ghost is with the bone; a man may have so close a connexion with a spirit or ghost that he has mana in himself also, and can so direct it as to effect what he desires."[1] This is as much as to say that things and men have mana *because they have received it* from certain superior beings; or, in other words, because they participate mystically in the sacred, and in the degree that they do so. Moreover, Codrington takes the trouble to specify that "this power, though itself impersonal, is always connected with some person who directs it; all spirits have it, ghosts generally, some men" (*loc. cit.*). It is clear from these few quotations that Codrington did not conceive mana to be a force hypostatised, apart from things and beings.

The later researches of Hocart, Hogbin, Williamson, Capell and others have yet more clearly defined the essence and structure of mana.[2] "How can mana be impersonal if it is always attached to personal beings?" asks Hocart ironically. At Guadalcanal and Malaita, for instance, it is exclusively the spirits and the souls of the dead who possess the *namana*, although it is within their power to use this force to the profit of man. "A man," writes Hogbin, "may work hard, but unless he obtains the approval of the spirits, who exercise the power to his profit, he will never become rich" . . . "Every effort is made to ensure the favour of the spirits so that mana may always be available. Sacrifices are the most usual

[1] Codrington, *op. cit.*, p. 119-120.
[2] *Cf.* H. Ian Hogbin, "Mana" in *Oceania*, Vol. VI, 1936, pp.241-274; A. Capell, "The word Mana; a linguistic study", *ibid.*, Vol. IX, 1938, pp. 89-96; R. W. Williamson, *Essays in Polynesian Ethnology*, Cambridge, 1939, pp. 264ff. See also the bibliographical notes in our *Patterns of Comparative Religion*, pp. 36-37, and Paul Radin, *Die Religiöse Erfahrung der Naturvölker*, Rhein-Verlag, Zurich, 1951, pp. 12-19.

method of gaining their approbation, but certain other ceremonies are thought to be equally pleasing to them" (pp. 257 and 264 of the article cited).

The same corrections have been rendered necessary by the more exact analyses of similar notions, such as the *wakanda* and *manito* of the Sioux and the Algonquins, for example. Paul Radin observes, in this connexion, that the terms in question signify "sacred", "strange", "important", "marvellous", "extraordinary" or "strong", but without implying the least idea of "inherent force".[1] "What appears to attract their attention," writes Radin, "is, in the first place, the question of 'real existence'" (*op. cit.*, p. 352). Another student of the Americas, Raphael Karsten, said, for his part, that "whether an object is to be conceived as the habitation of a spiritual being, or as possessing only an impersonal magic power—this is an entirely superfluous question, to which the Indian himself would very probably be unable to give any exact answer. It is evident that, for him, no clear distinction exists between the personal and the impersonal."[2]

It follows that the question must be put in ontological terms: that which *exists*, what is *real* on the one hand, and that which *does not exist* on the other—not in terms of the *personal or impersonal*, nor of the *corporeal or non-corporeal*, concepts which, for the consciousness of the "primitives", have none of the precision they have acquired in more highly-evolved cultures. Anything filled with mana exists on the ontological plane and is therefore efficacious, fecund, fertile. One cannot ascribe "impersonality" to mana, for that attribute is without meaning within the archaic spiritual horizon.

But there is still more to be said of this. The notion of mana is not met with everywhere; it is not a notion universally known to the history of religions. Mana is not even a pan-Melanesian concept: in many of the Melanesian islands it is unknown.[3]

[1] P. Radin, "Religion of the North American Indians", in the *Journal of American Folklore*, Vol. 28, 1914, pp. 335–373.

[2] Raphael Karsten, *The Civilization of the South American Indians*, London, 1926, p. 375.

[3] For instance, it is unknown in Otang (N.E. of the Solomons), in Wogeo (one of the New Guinea isles); *cf.* Hogbin, *Mana*, pp. 268ff., or in Wagawaga, Tubetube, etc. See C. G. Seligman, *Melanesians of British New Guinea*, Cambridge, 1910, p. 576; Capell, *op. cit.*, p. 92.

Hogbin is obliged to conclude that: "mana is by no means universal and, consequently, to adopt it as a basis on which to build up a general theory of primitive religion is not only erroneous but indeed fallacious" (*op. cit.*, p. 274).

What conclusion can be drawn, then, from all these new observations and from the analyses provided by experienced ethnologists? So many invalid hypotheses warn us to be prudent. We will limit ourselves to the statement that, among the "primitives" as among the moderns, the sacred is manifested in a multitude of forms and variants, but that all these hierophanies are charged with *power*. The sacred is strong, powerful, because it is *real*; it is efficacious and durable. The opposition between sacred and profane is often expressed as an opposition between the *real* and the *unreal* or pseudo-real.[1] Power means *reality* and, at the same time, *lastingness* and *efficiency*. But one must always reckon with the fact that the sacred discloses itself under many modalities and upon different levels. We saw, a little while ago, that mana may impregnate any object or any action whatever, and that the magico-religious force it designates derives from a number of sources—souls of the dead, spirits of nature or gods. This amounts to saying that the Melanesians implicitly acknowledge several modalities of the sacred—gods, spirits, ghosts, etc. A simple analysis of the few examples quoted will verify this. But the religious life of the Melanesians is not confined to belief in the mana conferred by gods or spirits. It consists also of cosmologies, mythologies, complex rituals and even theologies also; which means that there are different modalities of the sacred, and that various magico-religious powers correspond to these multiple modalities. It is natural that the power manifested by a canoe endowed with mana should be of quite another quality than the power that emanates from a symbol, from a myth or a divine figure. The power of mana manifests itself directly: one sees or feels it, one can verify it in this or that object or in an efficacious action. The power of a heavenly Creator-Being—such Beings are

[1]One must not, of course, expect to find in the archaic languages the pretentious terminology of the philosophers: *Real-Unreal*, etc.—but we do encounter *the thing*. For the consciousness of the archaic peoples, the *strong*, the *sacred*, is an expression of the *supremely real*.

attested more or less everywhere in Melanesia[1]—is only indirectly experienced: the Melanesian is not unaware that the Creator must have disposed of vast power to have made the world, but he does not feel that power *immediately* by his senses. Consequently, these Creator-Beings are hardly worshipped at all. They have become gods who are remote, inactive, and we shall presently see the importance of this phenomenon for the history of religions.

We feel, therefore, differences of plane between the many manifestations of the sacred. Certain hierophanies attract immediate attention; certain others, as we see from their structure itself, are more veiled, discreet; certain hierophanies appear with more frequency than we can well cope with, whilst some others are much more rare. This is important, for it helps us to understand what is the fundamental defect in a mistaken view about the religious life of "primitive" populations. Observers have allowed themselves to be over-impressed by the violence and the frequency of certain hierophanies. Observing that the Melanesians believed in an infinity of objects and actions charged with mana, they concluded that their religion was limited to an exclusive belief in this sacred and mysterious power; so that many other aspects of their religious life passed unperceived.

VARIETIES OF RELIGIOUS EXPERIENCE

It is easy for the student of religious ethnology to make this mistake, and it is not hard to see why. The standpoint taken up for the observation of a phenomenon plays a considerable part in the phenomenon itself. "It is the scale that constitutes the phenomenon" is a principle of modern science—the "scale", that is, the perspective. Henri Poincaré once asked whether "a naturalist who had never studied the elephant except by means of the microscope would think he knew enough about that animal?" Here is a striking case in point. An old Indian Civil Servant, J. Abbott, published a large volume of over 500 pages entitled *The Keys of*

[1]Upon the Supreme Beings of Melanesia and their "history", see W. Schmidt, *Der Ursprung der Gottesidee*, Vol. I, Münster in Westphalia, 1912, pp. 412ff., 480ff., Upon the ouranian Beings in Melanesia, see R. Pettazzoni, *Dio*, Rome, pp. 139ff.

Power: a study of Indian ritual and beliefs. In this book he set out to demonstrate that the rites and beliefs in question, taken as a whole, imply the conception of a magico-religious *power* or *force*. This had been well known long before; what was so much less known was the enormous number of things and beings, of gestures, actions, signs and ideas which, to the Indian mind, may embody this power. Indeed, if one perseveres to the end of the book, one is unable to say what, in the eyes of an Indian, is capable of *not* having this power. For Abbott, with an admirable industry, has shown us that man, like woman and indeed like iron and other metals, like the firmament, stones, colours, vegetation, the various gestures and signs, the successive periods of the year, the month and the day and the night, etc., etc.—that all these, as the Indians see them, are charged with *power*.

But is one justified therefore, after reading this book, in concluding that the religious life of certain peoples of modern India is limited to belief in a holy force which they call *sakti* or *barkat* or *pîr* or *balisth*, and so on? Assuredly not! There are other elements besides this belief, which combine together to make up a religion: there are gods, symbols, myths, and moral and theological conceptions—of which indeed the author himself speaks from time to time, though he adds that all these gods, myths, symbols and so forth are venerated to the degree that they are charged with *power*. This is certainly true—but what is the power in question? We must be allowed to think that the *sakti* or the *barkat* of a cake or a candied fruit[1] would not be of the same potency—nor perhaps quality—as the *power* attained through asceticism, by worship of the great gods, or by mystical contemplation.

For a better grasp of the data of this problem, let us look at the religious life of a European village. There we find, no doubt, a considerable number of beliefs—in the power of certain holy places, of certain trees and plants; a great many superstitions (about the weather, numbers, signs, demonic beings, life beyond the grave, etc.); a mythology barely camouflaged under a hagiography; a cosmology that is half Biblical and half pagan, etc.

[1] J. Abbott, *The Keys of Power*, London, 1932, pp. 310ff.

Would it be right to infer that all this mass of beliefs and super-stitions constitutes, *of itself alone*, the religion of a European village? By no means: for along with these beliefs and superstitions there is also Christian living and the Christian conscience. It may be true—at least of some localities—that belief in the saints is manifested with greater fervour and frequency than faith in God and in Jesus Christ; it still remains that this specifically Christian faith exists here too; and though not always active, it is never absent.

These two examples—Abbott's researches among the Indian peasants and our imaginary enquiry in a European village—show how we must frame the problem of the sacred and the powerful in the history of religions. Admittedly, the sacred invariably manifests itself as a *power*, but there are wide differences of degree and of frequency between these manifestations. And let no one tell us that the "primitives" are incapable of conceiving any but elementary, or direct and immediate manifestations of the sacred force! On the contrary, they are perfectly well aware that, for instance, *thought* itself can be a considerable source of energy. Many "primitive" peoples believe that the gods created the world "out of nothing", solely by thinking; that is, by self-concentration.[1] All the celestial gods of the "primitives" possess attributes and powers that denote intelligence, knowledge and "wisdom". The celestial god *sees* everything and therefore knows everything, and this knowledge, being of a supernatural order, is in itself a force.[2] Iho (Io), the supreme god of the Polynesians, is eternal and omniscient; he is great and strong, the originator of all things, the source of all sacred and occult knowledge, etc.[3] We find this also in the highly-evolved religions: intelligence, omniscience and wisdom are not only attributes of the heavenly divinity, they are

[1]The shamans also "create" through asceticism and contemplation. R. Pettazzoni assumes that the image of the creative beings, among the primitives, is built up from their observations of the behaviour of the shamans; see his paper on "Myths of the Origins and Myths of the Creation" in the *Proceedings of the VIIth Congress for the History of Religions*, Amsterdam, 1951, pp. 75ff. We believe the truth is the reverse of this; for in what they do, the shamans are trying to copy the mythic models, and these mythic examples depend, in their turn, upon the image of the celestial Being. *Cf.* our book *Le Chamanisme . . .* Paris, 1951. See also later in the present volume, p. 161.

[2]See our *Patterns in Comparative Religion*, pp. 62ff.

[3]*Cf.* R. Pettazzoni, *Dio*, pp. 173ff. and the same author's *L'omniscienza di Dio*, Turin, 1955, pp. 501ff.

powers, and man is obliged to reckon with them. Varuna "knows the tracks of the birds flying through the air . . . he knows the directions of the winds . . . and he, who knows everything, spies out all secrets, all actions and all intentions . . ." (*Rig Veda*, I, 35, 7ff.) "He has numbered even the blinking of men's eyes . . ." (*Atharva Veda*, IV, 16, 2–7). Varuna is indeed a powerful god, a Great Magician,[1] and men tremble before him. Ahura Mazda (the "Lord Wisdom") is omniscient: the texts describe him as "he who knows", "he who is not deceived", "he who knows how"; "he is infallible, endowed with an infallible, omniscient intelligence".[2]

DESTINY OF THE SUPREME BEING

One can see from these few examples that neither the religions called "primitive" nor those classed as polytheistic are ignorant of the idea of a God who is the Creator, omniscient and all-powerful. Yet we have only to look at things a little more closely to realise that such supreme deities enjoy hardly any actual religious worship. We must except Ahura Mazda, who owed his extraordinary religious vitality to the reforms of Zoroaster: we can also leave aside Varuna, whose case is rather complex. Let us, for the moment, keep to the supreme gods of the "primitives". These are not objects of worship: they are regarded as deities so remote as to be inactive, indifferent—*dii otiosi*, in fact. The "primitives" are well enough informed about the primordial power of these Supreme Beings: they know, for instance, that it was they who created the world, and life, and man. But soon afterwards— according to their myths—these Supreme Beings and Creators forsook the earth and withdrew into the highest heaven.[3] In their

---

[1] The "origin" of his power is of course a rather complex matter: Varuna is at once a god of heaven, a divine Sovereign and Magician: see our *Patterns in Comparative Religion*, pp. 68ff.; and *Images et Symboles*, Paris, 1952, Chap. III; the "god who binds" and the symbolism of knots.

[2] See the texts cited in our *Patterns in Comparative Religion*, pp. 72ff.

[3] R. Pettazzoni explains the remoteness and inactivity of the Creator Gods by the simple fact of their having finished the work of creation and having therefore lost actual importance: see *Mythes des origines et mythes de la création*, p. 75. That is part of the truth,

stead they have left with us their sons or their messengers or some other divinity who is subordinate to them, and who continues to be occupied with the creation in some sort, with its perfection or maintenance.

Thus, Ndyambi, the supreme god of the Hereros, has withdrawn into heaven and abandoned mankind to the inferior divinities. "Why should we sacrifice to him?" explained one of the natives. "We have nothing to fear from him; for, unlike our dead (*okakurus*), he does us no harm." The Supreme Being of the Tumbukas is too great "to be interested in the ordinary affairs of men". The remoteness and indifference of the Supreme Being are admirably expressed in a chant of the Fang of Equatorial Africa:

> God (Nzame) is up on high, man down below.
> God is God, man is man;
> Each in his place, each in his house.[1]

There is no need to multiply examples. Everywhere, in these "primitive" religions, the highest heavenly Being has declined in practical religious importance; he has withdrawn from human beings. He is remembered, however, and prayed to as a last resort, when all the petitions put up to other gods and goddesses, demons and ancestors, have been ineffectual. Dzingbe (the All-Father), Supreme Being of the Ewe, is invoked only against drought: "O Heaven to whom we owe thanksgiving, great is the drought! Make it to rain, that the earth may be refreshed and the fields prosper!" The Selk'nam of Tierra del Fuego call their Supreme Being "Dweller in Heaven" or "He who is in Heaven": there is no image of him, nor any priest; but offerings are made to him during crises in the weather, and prayers in cases of illness: "O thou on high, do not take my child; he is still too little!" During a tempest, the Semang pygmies scratch the calves of their legs with bamboo knives and throw the little drops of blood around

but one must not forget that the Creation, the cosmology, continues to serve as the exemplary model for every act of human "creation" (*e.g.*, for the building of a temple, an altar, a palace or a house, etc.) and even for a certain number of *actions* (such as healing and curative work): *cf. The Myth of the Eternal Return*, pp. 17ff.

[1]See our *Patterns of Comparative Religion*, pp. 73 ff.

on every side, crying out: "Ta Pedn! I am not hardened, I pay
for my fault. Accept my debt—I am paying it!" When the help of
other gods and goddesses has proved disappointing, the Oraon
turn to their Supreme Being, Dharmesh: " We have tried everything, but we still have thee for our helper!" and they sacrifice
a white cock to him, crying: "O God, thou art our creator, take
pity upon us!"[1]

Let us note especially these facts; that the Supreme Beings
progressively lose their religious importance, and that they are
replaced by other divine figures nearer to man, more "concrete",
and more "dynamic"—solar gods, Great Goddesses, mythic
Ancestors, etc. These divine figures may end by usurping nearly
the whole of the religious life of the tribe. Yet in case of extreme
distress, when one has tried everything else in vain, above all in
any disaster that comes from heaven—drought, storm or plague—
one turns back to the Supreme Being and prays to him. This
attitude is not peculiar to "primitive" peoples alone. We remember what came to pass among the ancient Hebrews: whenever they were living in a period of economic peace and economic
prosperity, the Hebrews turned away from God towards the
Ba'als and Astartes of their neighbours. Historical catastrophes
alone brought them back into the strait way and compelled them
once again to look to the true God. "And they cried unto the
Lord and said, We have sinned, because we have forsaken the
Lord and served Baalim and Ashtaroth; but now deliver us out of
the hand of our enemies and we will serve thee" (*I Samuel*, 12, 10).

The Hebrews turned again to Jahveh after historic calamities[2]
or in imminent danger of annihilation from historic forces (the
great military empires); and the "primitives" remember their
Supreme Beings in times of cosmic catastrophe. But the meaning
of this return to the Supreme Being is the same in both cases: in
an extremely critical situation, a "limiting case" when the very
existence of the collectivity is at stake, one abandons the divinities
that promote and enhance Life in normal times to return to the
Supreme Being. This appears to be a great paradox; the divinities,

---

[1]See *Patterns in Comparative Religion*, pp. 45ff., 131, etc.
[2]See *The Myth of the Eternal Return*, pp. 102ff.

who among "primitives" are substituted for the Supreme Beings,
are—just like the Ba'als and Astartes of the Hebrews—divinities
of fecundity, riches and the fullness of life; in short, the deities who
exalt and amplify life, the life of the cosmos—its vegetation,
agriculture, herds and flocks—no less than the life of man. To all
appearance these divinities were strong, *powerful*. Their religious
importance was due precisely to their strength, their illimitable
reserves of vitality, their fecundity. And yet their worshippers
—"primitives" as well as Hebrews—had the feeling that all these
Great Goddesses, these solar or agrarian Gods, and all these
Ancestors and Demons, were unable to *save* them, that is, to ensure
their existence in supremely critical moments. For these gods and
goddesses could only *reproduce* life and *augment* it; and what is
more, they could fulfil this function only during a "normal"
epoch; in brief, they were deities who regulated the cosmic
rhythms to admiration, but who proved incapable of saving the
Cosmos or human society in a capital crisis (a "historic" crisis in
the Hebrew case). *If Hebrews really thought this, it would be entirely impossible to explain their total rejection at the*

How do we explain this phenomenon? This we shall see *very*
presently: the different divinities who were substituted for the *beginning of other gods...*
Supreme Being accumulated the most striking and the most *rather,*
tangible powers, the powers of life. But by that very fact they *they would*
were specialised, as it were, in *procreation*, and lost the more *demand the*
subtle, more "noble" and "spiritual" powers of the *creator-Gods*. *existence of*
The whole drama of the so-called "religious degeneracy" of *those same*
humanity resides in this fact, which we shall comment upon later. *gods.*
In discovering the sacredness of life, man allowed himself more
and more to be carried away by his own discovery; he abandoned
himself to the vital hierophanies, to the enjoyments procurable
from the immediate experiences of life, and turned away from the
sanctities which surpass his immediate, everyday needs. The first
"fall" of man—which led to the fall into history that characterises
modern man—was a fall into life: man was intoxicated by the
discovery of the powers and the sacredness of life.

→ Assumes a historical time when man did not know the lower "sacred." It was "discovered" & man turned to it to escape the terror of history. Thus prim. man entered inauthentic existence.

THE "STRONG GODS"

It must always be remembered that it was the *sanctifying* of life, in the first place, of the magico-religious powers of universal fecundity, which displaced the Supreme Beings from worship and from religious primacy. It was not life itself, as we Occidentals of the twentieth century experience it. Now, it is a fact—one that is strange only at first sight—that the more humanity evolves, the more we perfect our means of subsistence and elaborate our civilisation, the more strongly the religious life is solicited by divine forms that reflect in their very epiphanies the mystery of procreation and of universal fertility. The ouranian Supreme Beings, acknowledged everywhere, to some degree, by the "primitives", were almost forgotten in the more highly evolved societies. The discovery of agriculture above all brings about radical changes in the divine hierarchy: it is the Great Goddesses, the Divine Mothers and their spouses the Divine Males, who then thrust their way into the foreground. We will presently quote a few instances of this. But here again, the facts must not be interpreted in a Western—that is, a materialist—perspective. It is not our technical discoveries in themselves, it is the magico-religious acceptation of them which has altered the perspective and the content of the religious life of the traditional societies. Nor must it be supposed that agriculture itself, as a technical innovation, could have had such repercussions upon the spiritual ambience of archaic humanity. Within their horizons there was no separation between the tool—the real, concrete object—and the symbol which gave it value; between a technique and the magico-religious operation which it implied. Let us not forget that the primitive spade symbolised the phallus and the soil the telluric matrix; the agricultural action was assimilated to the generative act: in many Austro-Asiatic languages the spade still has the same name as the phallus.[1] The soil represented Mother Earth, the seeds the *semen virile*, and the rain the *hieros gamos* between Heaven and

[1] See *Patterns in Comparative Religion*, pp. 260, 331ff.; also below, pp. 185ff.

Earth. In brief, all the modifications which, to our eyes, look like changes due to the evolution of technique, are, for traditional societies, so many changes of perspective in a magico-religious universe: certain sanctities are replaced by others, more powerful and more immediately accessible.

This is a universal phenomenon. We have described it in our *Patterns in Comparative Religion*, showing how the ancient gods of Heaven were everywhere supplanted by more dynamic deities— the solar gods, or the gods of the storm or of fecundity. The ancient Indo-Aryan god of heaven, Dyaus, only very rarely appears in the Vedas: already, in that remote epoch, his place had been taken by Varuna, and by Parjanya the storm-god. The latter, in his turn, was effaced by Indra, who became the most popular of the Vedic gods, for he comprises all the *forces* and all the *fertilities*. Indra embodies all the exuberance of life, of the cosmic and the biological energies; he unlooses the waters and opens the clouds, quickens the circulation of the sap and the blood, governs all moistures and ensures all fecundities. The texts name him as the god "of a thousand testicles", the "master of the field", the "bull of the earth", fertiliser of the fields, of animals and of women. All the attributes and powers of Indra are of a piece and all the domains he rules are complementary. Whether we are reading of his thunderbolts that strike Vritra and release the waters, of the storm that precedes the rain, or of the absorption of fabulous quantities of *soma*, of his fertilisation of the fields or of his gigantic sexual potencies, we are being continually presented with an epiphany of the forces of life. His least gesture springs from an excess of fullness, even his boasting and bragging. The myth of Indra is a wonderful expression of the profound unity that underlies all the abounding manifestations of life.

Here is another example—one of the most ancient Mesopotamian gods was Anu, whose name signifies "heaven", and he appears well before the fourth millennium. But in the historical age Anu became a somewhat abstract deity, and his worship hardly survived. His place was taken by his son Enlil (or Bêl), god of the storm and of fertility, and husband of the Great Mother; and she, known also as the Great Cow, was generally invoked by the name of Bêltu or Bêlit, "Mistress". For, in Mesopotamia and the Middle East above all, the substitution of "strong" and "potent" gods is accompanied by another phenomenon of no less importance; the god of fertility becomes the husband of a Great Goddess, of an agrarian *Magna Mater*; he is no longer autonomous and all-powerful like the ancient gods of the sky, he is reduced to the status of partner in a divine marriage. The cosmogony—which was the essential attribute of the old celestial gods—is now replaced by a hierogamy: the fecundating God no longer creates the world; he is content to fertilise it.[1] And, in some cultures, the male, fecundating deity is reduced to rather a modest position; for it is the Great Goddess by herself who ensures the fecundity of the world; in time, her husband gives place to her son, who is at the same time his mother's lover: these are the well-known vegetation gods, of the type of Tammuz, Attis and Adonis, characterised by the fact that they periodically die and come back to life again.

The ousting of the celestial god in favour of the strong god is also well exemplified by the myth of Ouranos. Admittedly, this myth reflects a number of other transformations which took place in the Greek pantheon and cannot be discussed here.[2] But it is important to remember that Ouranos—whose name means "the sky" and who, with his spouse Gaia, had engendered the other gods, the Cyclops and many monstrous beings—was castrated by one of his children, Kronos. The castration of Ouranos is a mythic image of impotence, and therefore of the inefficacy of the celestial god. His place was afterwards occupied by Zeus, who acquired the attributes both of the sovereign god and of the storm-god.

Certain celestial gods succeeded in preserving their religious importance by revealing themselves as Sovereign Gods: in other words, they reinforced their authority by taking on a magico-religious prestige of another order. Indeed, sovereignty constitutes a source of sacred power capable of maintaining the absolute

[1] See *Patterns in Comparative Religion*, pp. 65ff. and 87ff.
[2] See *e.g.*, Georges Dumézil, *Ouranos-Varuna*, Paris, 1934; W. Staudacher, *Die Trennung von Himmel und Erde. Ein vorgriechischer Schöpfungmythus bei Hesiod und den Orphikern*, Tübingen, 1942; see also *Patterns in Comparative Religion*, pp. 76ff.

ruler in a pantheon: such was the case with Zeus, with Jupiter, with the Chinese T'ien and the god of the Mongols. The notion of sovereignty is found again in Ahura Mazda, the beneficiary of Zoroaster's religious revolution, which elevated him above all the other gods. One might also say that Jahveh, too, includes the elements of a Sovereign God: but the personality of Jahveh is much more complex; we shall have to return to this. For the moment, let it suffice to underline the fact that the monotheistic, prophetic and messianic revolution of the Hebrews (as, moreover, that of Mohammed) succeeded in opposition to the Ba'als and the Bêlits, against the gods of the storm and of fecundity, the great Male and Female divinities. On the one hand are the strong and dynamic gods, the "Bulls", the "begetters", the partners of the Great Mother, the orgiastic divinities, revealing themselves to man in their turbulent epiphanies and rejoicing in rich and dramatic mythologies: there are the Ba'als and Astartes, worshipped with opulent and bloody rites (multiple sacrifices, orgies, etc.). And on the other hand is Jahveh, all alone, who includes all the attributes of the Supreme Being of the "primitives" (being the Creator, omniscient and all-powerful), but who, in addition to this, possesses a power and a religious actuality of an entirely different order. Unlike the Ba'als and the Bêlits, Jahveh is surrounded by no multiple and varied myths; his worship is neither complicated nor orgiastic; he rejects blood sacrifices and the multiplication of rites. He demands from the believer a religious behaviour very different from what is instilled by the worship of the Ba'als and Astartes. Listen to the words of Jahveh as they were written by Isaiah:

To what purpose is the multitude of your sacrifices unto me? saith the Lord: I am full of the burnt offerings of rams, and the fat of fed beasts; and I delight not in the blood of bullocks, or of lambs, or of he-goats.

When ye come to appear before me, who hath required this at your hand, to tread my courts?

Bring no more vain oblations; incense is an abomination unto me; the new moons and sabbaths, the calling of assem-

blies, I cannot away with; it is iniquity, even the solemn
meeting.

Your new moons and your appointed feasts my soul hateth:
they are a trouble unto me; I am weary to bear them . . .
Your hands are full of blood. Wash you, make you clean.
Cease to do evil;

Learn to do well; seek justice, relieve the oppressed, judge
the fatherless, plead for the widow.

Isaiah, I, 11–17

To us, who are heirs and beneficiaries of the great Judæo-
Christian religious revolution, the injunctions of Jahveh seem to
be those of evident good sense, and we may wonder how the
Hebrews of Isaiah's days could possibly have preferred the cult of
the Male God of Procreation to the infinitely purer and simpler
worship of Jahveh. But it must not be forgotten that those
elemental epiphanies of life, by which the Hebrews never ceased
to be allured, imparted undeniable religious experiences. The
paganism to which the Hebrews reverted again and again belonged
to the religious history of all Eastern antiquity; it was a very great
and very ancient religion, dominated by the cosmic hierophanies
and which, therefore, exalted the *sacredness of life*. This religion,
whose roots extended deep and far into the proto-history of the
Orient, reflected the discovery of the sacredness of life, the becoming aware of the unity in which the Cosmos is one with Man and
Man with God. The many and bloody sacrifices that Jahveh
abhorred and his prophets never ceased to denounce, ensured the
circulation of the sacred energy between the different regions of
the Cosmos; it was thanks to this circulation that the whole of
Life was able to subsist. Even the hateful sacrifice of children
offered to Moloch had a profoundly religious meaning. By that
sacrifice, one gave back to the divinity what belonged to him;
for the first child was often regarded as the child of the god;
indeed, throughout the archaic Orient it was customary for young
women to spend a night in the temple in order to conceive by the
god (that is, by his representative the priest or his envoy "the
stranger"). The blood of the child thus augmented the spent

energy of the god, for the so-called fertility divinities expended their own substance in the efforts required to sustain the world and ensure its wealth: they were in need themselves, therefore, of being regenerated from time to time.[1]

The worship of Jahveh rejected all these sanguinary rites supposed to ensure the continuation of life and the fecundity of the Cosmos. Jahveh's power was of a wholly different order; it was in no need of periodical reinforcement. It is a remarkable fact that the simplicity of worship which is characteristic of monotheism and of Jewish propheticism corresponds to the original simplicity of the worship of the Supreme Beings among the "primitives". As we have already observed, this worship has almost disappeared, but we know in what it consisted: its offerings, first-fruits and its prayers addressed to the Supreme Beings. The Jewish monotheism reverted to this simplicity of cultural means. Moreover, the Mosaic dispensation laid the emphasis upon *faith*, upon a religious experience which implied an interiorisation of worship, and this was its greatest novelty. One might say that the discovery of faith as a religious category was the one novelty introduced into the history of religion since neolithic times. Let us note that Jahveh continues to be a "strong" God, all-powerful and omniscient; but, although able to manifest this power and wisdom in the great cosmic events, he prefers to address himself directly to human beings, and takes an interest in their spiritual life. The religious forces set in motion by Jahveh are *spiritual forces*. This modification of perspective is highly important, and we shall have to return to it.

INDIAN RELIGIONS OF POWER

For the present, let us again consider a religion in which the myths, cults and philosophies of sacred power attained to proportions hitherto unknown: we refer to India, and that great religious movement which embraced Shaktism, Tantrism and the various cults of the Great Goddess. It is extremely difficult to

[1] See *The Myth of the Eternal Return*, pp. 110ff.

present a conspectus of this religious complex; but let us recall a few essential facts. The Tantra may be regarded as the religious experience most appropriate to the present condition of man—that of life in *kali-yuga*, the age of darkness. Since the spirit is, in our times, excessively conditioned by the flesh, the Tantra places adequate means at the disposal of whosoever may be seeking deliverance. It would be useless now, in *kali-yuga*, to seek liberation by the methods employed in the ancient days of the Vedas and Upanishads. Humanity is fallen; it is now a case of swimming against the stream, starting from the actual "occultation" of the spirit in the flesh. For this reason the Tantra renounces asceticism and pure contemplation and appeals to other techniques for mastering the world and eventually obtaining deliverance. The tantrika does not renounce the world, as the sage of the Upanishad, the yogi or the Buddha does; instead, he tries to overcome it, while enjoying perfect freedom.

Now, what is the theoretical basis of all the Tantric schools? That the world is created and ruled by two polar principles, Shiva and Shakti. But because Shiva represents absolute passivity, the immobility of the Spirit, all movement, and therefore all Creation and Life upon every cosmic level, are due to the manifestation of Shakti. Deliverance can be attained only by the union of these two principles in the very body of the tantrika. In his *body*—and not only in his psycho-mental experience. We will not go into the details. Suffice it to say that, in Tantrism, the important part is played by the Shakti manifesting in the multiple forms of the Great Goddess, but also active in Woman. It is the Shakti, the universal Force, which continually creates the world. And since we are part and parcel of the world and are its prisoners it is in vain to seek deliverance without having recourse to Her who engenders, nourishes and sustains the world, Shakti. The texts constantly insist upon this point: "Shakti is the root of all that exists," says the *Tantra-tattva*; "it is out of Her that the Universes are manifested, it is She who sustains them and, at the end of time, it is in Her that the worlds will be re-absorbed."[1] Another

---

[1]The *Tantratattva* of Siva-candra Vidyārnava Bhattacārya, trans. by A. Avalon, London–Madras, 1914, Vol. II, p. xvii.

text has this in her praise: "It is thanks to thy power alone that Brahma creates, Vishnu preserves, and that Shiva, at the end of time, will destroy, the Universe. Without thee they are powerless to fulfil their missions: therefore it is thou who, truth to tell, art the creator, preserver and destroyer of the world."[1] "Thou, O Devi," says Shiva to the Goddess in the *Mahânirvâna Tantra*, "thou verily art my real self!"

The conception of this cosmic Force personified in a Great Goddess was not invented by Tantrism. Pre-Aryan India, and the popular India in which it survives, have known the worship of the Great Mother since neolithic times, whatever its forms, names and myths may have been.[2] The Indian cults of the Great Mother were much like all those other fertility cults which were prevalent in the Middle East of antiquity. The Tantra not only assimilated a great deal of the mythology and ritual of the *Magna Mater*; it re-interpreted and systematised them and, above all, it transformed this immemorial heritage into a mystical technique of deliverance. Tantrism strove to re-discover in the body and the psyche themselves the cosmic power personified in the Great Goddess. The Tantric procedure consists primarily in the awakening of this force, known as the *kundalini*, and in making it ascend from the base of the torso where it is slumbering right up into the brain, to re-unite it with Shiva. The "awakening" of the *kundalini* is manifested by a sensation of very lively warmth, a fact that merits our special attention. For one of the most popular myths of India tells how the Great Goddess came to birth—from the fiery energy of all the gods. When a monstrous demon, Mahisha, was endangering the Universe and the very existence of the gods, Brahma and the entire pantheon had sought the assistance of Vishnu and Shiva. Bursting with anger, all the gods together sent forth their energies in the form of a fire flaming from their mouths. These fires, combining together, gave birth to a fiery cloud, which finally took the form of a Goddess with eighteen arms: and it was this Goddess, Shakti, who succeeded in crushing the monster Mahisha and thereby saved the world. As

---

[1] *Devi-Bhâgavata*, quoted by A. Avalon, *Hymns to the Goddess*, London, 1913.
[2] See *Yoga, Immortality and Freedom*, pp. 342ff.

Heinrich Zimmer remarks: the gods "had given back their
energies to Shakti, the Only Power, the source from which all
things issued at the beginning. The result was a great renewal of
the primitive state of the universal power."[1]

THE "MAGICAL HEAT"

However, not enough emphasis has been laid on the fact that the
"powers" of the gods, increased by anger, manifested in the shape
of flames. Heat and fire, on the plane of mystical physiology,
indicate the awakening of a magico-religious power. In yoga and
Tantrism, these phenomena are of rather frequent occurrence.
As we were saying above, he who awakens the *kundalini* feels an
intense warmth; the progression of the *kundalini* through the
body reveals itself by the fact that the lower parts become inert
and ice-cold like a corpse, while the part of the body traversed by
the *kundalini* is burning hot.[2] Other Tantric texts specify that this
"magical heat" is obtained by the "transmutation" of the sexual
energy.[3] These techniques are not a Tantric innovation. The
Majjhima-nikâya (I, 244, etc.) refers to the "heat" obtained by
control of the respiration; and other Buddhist texts, the *Dhammapada* (387) for example, aver that the Buddha is "burning". The
Buddha "burns" with heat because he is practising asceticism
(*tapas*). The original meaning of that term, incidentally, was
"extreme heat"; but *tapas* has come to denote the ascetic striving
in general. *Tapas* is already enjoined in the *Rig Veda*, and its
powers are creative both upon the spiritual and upon the cosmic
planes; through *tapas* the ascetic becomes clairvoyant and may
incorporate the gods. On their side too, the cosmic god Prajapati
creates the world by "heating" himself up to an extreme degree

[1]Heinrich Zimmer, *Myths and Symbols in Indian Art and Civilisation*, New York, 1946,
p. 191.
[2]*Cf.* A. Avalon, *The Serpent Power*, (2nd edn.), Madras, 1924, p. 242.
[3]Lama Kasi Dawa Samdup, and W. Y. Evans-Wentz, *Le Yoga Tibétain et les doctrines
secrètes* (Fr. trans.), Paris, 1938, pp. 315ff., 322ff. See also H. Maspero, "Les procédés de
'nourrir le principe vital' dans la religion taoiste ancienne", in the *Journal Asiatique*,
April-June, July-September, 1937, pp. 177–252, 353–430, and p. 205.

by asceticism: he creates it, indeed, by a magical perspiration, just as do certain gods in the cosmogonies of North American tribes.[1]

Here we touch upon an extremely important problem concerning not only Indian religion but the history of religions in general: the excess of *power*, the magico-religious *force*, is experienced as a very vivid warmth. This is no longer a question of the *myths* and *symbols* of power, but of an experience which modifies the very physiology of the ascetic. There is every reason to believe that this experience was known by the mystics and magicians of the most ancient times. A great many "primitive" tribes conceive the magico-religious power as "burning" and express it by terms that signify "heat", "burn", "very hot", etc. That is why "primitive" sorcerers and magicians drink salted or peppered water or eat exceedingly hot-flavoured herbs; they think this heightens their inner "heat". In modern India the Mohammedans think that by communicating with God a man becomes "burning", and one who works miracles is said to be "boiling". By extension of the same idea, all kinds of persons, possessing any kind of magico-religious "power" whatever, are supposed to be "burning". It must be remembered, too, that all over the world shamans and sorcerers are reputedly "masters of fire", and swallow burning embers, handle red-hot iron and walk over fire. On the other hand they exhibit great resistance to cold. The shamans of the Arctic regions, as well as the ascetics of the Himalayas, thanks to their "magical heat", perform feats of a resistance to cold that passes imagination.[2]

As we mentioned on an earlier occasion (p. 95), the meaning of all these techniques of "mastering fire" lies deeper: they indicate the attainment of a certain ecstatic state, a non-conditioned state of spiritual freedom. But a *sacred power* experienced as an intense warmth is obtained by other means besides shamanic and mystical techniques. It may come from the forces aroused during military initiations. Several terms in the Indo-European "heroic" vocabulary—*furor, ferg, wut, menos*—express just that "extreme warmth" and "choler" which in other spheres of the sacred accompany the

[1] Concerning *tapas* and its shamanic valencies, see our book, *Le Chamanisme et les techniques archaïques de l'extase*, pp. 370ff.

[2] *Cf.* our *Le Chamanisme*, pp. 412ff.; see also above pp. 92ff.

incarnation of the "power".[1] Just like a yogi or a young shaman, the young hero grows "hot" during his initiatory combat. The Irish hero Cuchulain emerges from his first exploit (which, as Georges Dumézil has shown, is equivalent to an initiation of the warrior type) so "hot" that three tubs of water are brought to cool him. "They put him in the first tub, and he gave the water such a heat that it burst the staves and hoops of the tub as one would crack a nutshell. In the second tub the water boiled up in bubbles as big as your fist. In the third tub the heat was such as some men can bear but others cannot. Then the fury (*ferg*) of the little boy diminished, and they put him into his clothes."[2]

This "fury" which is manifested as an intense warmth is a magico-religious experience; there is nothing "ordinary" or "natural" about it, it belongs to the syndrome of possession by something sacred. Being a *sacred energy*, it can be transformed, differentiated, subtilised by a further process of integration or "sublimation". The Indian word *kratu*, which once used to mean "the energy typical of an ardent warrior, especially of Indra", came to signify "victorious strength, heroic strength and ardour, bravery and love of combat" and then, by extension, "power" and "majesty" in general, and finally was used to denote "the power of the pious man, which makes him able to follow the injunctions of the *rita* and attain to happiness."[3]

As one would expect, however, the "fury" and the "heat" aroused by a violent and excessive access of *power* strike fear into the majority of mortals: power of that kind, in its crude state, is chiefly of interest to magicians and warriors: those who are looking to religion for confidence and equilibrium would rather

---

[1] See the fine books of Georges Dumézil, *Mythes et dieux des Germains*, Paris, 1939, and *Horaces et les Curiaces*, Paris, 1942.

[2] *Táin bô Cuâlnge*, summarised and translated in Dumézil, *Horaces et les Curiaces*, pp. 35ff. The same "mystical heat" (of the "warrior" type) distinguishes the heroes of the Nartes, Batradz; *cf.* G. Dumézil, *Légendes sur les Nartes*, pp. 50ff., 179ff.; and his *Horaces et les Curiaces*, pp. 55ff.

[3] Kasten Rönnow, "Ved. *kratu*, eine wortgeschichtliche Untersuchung" in *Le Monde Oriental*, Vol. 26, 1932, pp. 1–90; Georges Dumézil, *Naissance d'archanges*, Paris, 1945, p. 145ff. In the Gatha, "the meaning of *khratu* is the religious striving of the man of piety, or what might be called the pious bravery of the man in this combat with evil which occupies the whole life of the believer" (Dumézil, *op. cit.*, p. 145).

protect themselves against magical "warmth" and "fire". The term *shânti*, which in Sanskrit means tranquillity and peace of soul, absence of passion and suffering relieved, is derived from the root *Sham*, which originally included such meanings as the extinguishing of "fire", and the cooling-down of anger or, indeed, of the "heat" aroused by demonic *powers*.[1] The Indian of Vedic times felt the danger of magic; he resisted temptations to acquire more power.[2] Let us recall, by the way, that the true yogi, also, has to overcome the temptation of "magical powers" (*siddhi*)— the temptations of acquiring the power to fly, or to become invisible, etc.—if he is to reach the perfectly non-conditioned state of *samâdhi*. We must not however draw the conclusion that experience of this "heat" and the obtaining of "the powers" belong exclusively to the sphere of magic: "heat", "burning", "interior fire" and luminous epiphanies, like every other kind of "power", are attested everywhere in the history of religions and in the most highly-evolved mysticisms. A saint, a shaman, a yogi or a "hero" are all apt to feel the supernatural warmth to the degree that, *each upon his appointed plane of being*, they surpass the profane human condition and become embodiments of the sacred.

"POWERS" AND "HISTORY"

We must try not to lose the thread. We have seen, among the Jews, the conflict between the *true* religion of Jahveh and their experience of the cosmic sanctity divinised in the Ba'als and Astartes. Conflict between religious *powers* of entirely different orders: on the one side, the ancient cosmic hierophanies, on the other, the sacred as revealed in the form of a Person, Jahveh manifesting himself not only in the Cosmos, but above all in History. We left off our analysis of the faith in Jahveh at this point

[1] *Cf.* D. J. Hoens, *Sânti. A contribution to ancient Indian religious terminology*, 's-Gravenhage, 1951, esp. pp. 177ff.

[2] One can discern, in this attitude, the ambivalent reaction to the sacred: on the one hand, there is an attraction to magico-religious *power*, and on the other hand, a feeling of repulsion. Upon the meaning of this ambivalence, see our *Patterns in Comparative Religion*, pp. 16ff., 46off.

and turned to India; for it is there that the *religion of power* appeared to have reached its highest peak, in the worship of Shakti and in the Tantra. In the fallen world of *kali yuga* one can obtain deliverance only by awakening the cosmic energy that is asleep in one's own body, by forcing it to rise up into the *sahasraracakra* and unite itself with the pure consciousness symbolised by Shiva. Already one can see how different this is from the popular religions of Oriental proto-history exemplified by the cults of the Ba'als and the Great Goddesses. Tantrism represents an audacious act of interiorisation: the pantheon, the iconography and the ritual of Tantrism have value only in so far as they are interiorised, assimilated, "realised" in a complex experience which engages the body no less than the psyche and the consciousness. In appearance, the part played by Shakti is considerable; but we must not forget that deliverance is obtained through the *union* of Shakti with Shiva. In Tantrism, Shiva the pure Consciousness is passive; his "impotence" is analogous to the state of the *deus otiosus* in "primitive" religions, when the Supreme Beings have become passive, indifferent, "absent", and their places have been taken by *strong, powerful* divine figures. We are reminded of the myth of the birth of Shakti; of how the Gods, with the Supreme Being at their head, exerted all their "powers" in unison to create that Goddess; that it was she, thenceforth, who was the dispenser of strength and of life. But the tantrika strives to *repeat this process the reverse way.* The pure Spirit, Shiva, having become "impotent" and passive, it is necessary, in order to "dynamise" it, to unite it with its own Shakti, now detached from it (by the act of creation) and dispersed throughout the Cosmos. The fulfilment of that paradoxical aim—the unification of the two contrary principles—manifests itself physically by a very vivid warmth. This, as we saw, is a phenomenon universal among the magicians and mystics, and we understand its meaning: the supernatural heat signalises *the realisation of a paradox by which the human condition is surpassed.* If we wish to represent this process in terms of the primitive religions, we may say that the tantrika is trying to "re-dynamise" the Supreme Being by unifying him with the "powers" that have taken his place. Shiva being the symbol of pure Spirit, of absolute consciousness, the effort to "activate" him by union with his Shakti denotes, among other things, the respect and veneration in which the Supreme Being is still held even when he has become "impotent".

In truth, this Supreme Being never entirely disappears from what we might call the religious subconscious of humanity. Even when he has become inoperative and therefore unworshipped, his essential attributes—his transcendence, omniscience and cosmogonic powers—survive in rituals and symbolisms which apparently have nothing to do with the Supreme Being. Everywhere in the world celestial symbolism expresses the *sacredness of the transcendent*: that which is "on high", which is "uplifted", is pre-eminently representative of the sacred. Fading from the mythology and supplanted in the cult, the Celestial retains an important place in the symbolism: and this symbolism of the Celestial reveals itself in numerous rites (of ascension, of scaling heights, of initiation, royalty, etc.), in myths (the Cosmic Tree, the Cosmic Mountain, the chain of arrows, etc.), in legends (the magic flight, etc.). The symbolism of the "Centre", which plays a considerable part in every religion is integral with the symbolism of Heaven: it is at the "Centre of the World" that the break through the plane may take place, making it possible to enter into Heaven.[1]

Furthermore, the cosmogony—which, as we saw, is the achievement of the Supreme Beings—continues to hold its privileged place in the religious consciousness of archaic societies. The creation of the world becomes the archetype of all "creation", all construction, of all real and effectual action. So we see this strange phenomenon; that, while *the Creator* no longer receives direct religious attention, his *creation* becomes the pattern for all kinds of actions. When one is building an altar for sacrifices, or a house, or a canoe; or taking action for the cure of a sick person or the enthronement of a king; when one is celebrating the conjugal rite or trying to cure barrenness in a woman; or when one is setting out for war or seeking poetic inspiration—on these and many other occasions of importance for the collectivity or the

[1] See *Patterns in Comparative Religion*, pp. 38ff., 109ff.; and *Images et Symboles*, pp. 33ff.

individual, one recites the cosmogonic myth: ritually or symbolically one imitates the creation of the world.

More can be said of this: every year a symbolic destruction of the world (and thereby of human society) is celebrated—in order to create it anew; every year the cosmogony is repeated, in ritual imitation of the archetypal gesture of the Creation.[1] All these things show that the symbolisms derived from the nature and the acts of the supreme Heavenly Beings have continued to dominate the religious life of archaic humanity, even when those beings are no longer worshipped: the symbolism has perpetuated, in an occult and allusive way, the memory of the divine Person who had withdrawn from the world.

Symbolism does not mean rationalism, rather the reverse: yet, seen from the point of view of religious experience of a personalist type, symbolism becomes tinged with rationalism: it grows "abstract", it takes no account of the divine Person, of that "Living God" with his *tremenda majestas* and *mysterium fascinans*, whom Rudolf Otto describes. True faith therefore rejects the divinising of life itself, as exemplified by the Ba'al and Astarte cults, no less than the "abstract" religiosity founded only upon symbols and ideas. Jahveh is the divine Person who reveals himself in *history*; therein lies his great novelty. Elsewhere, God had been revealed as a Person; we remember the terrible epiphany of Krishna in the *Bhagavad Gîtâ* (XI, 5 *et seq.*): but this revelation of the Supreme Being under the form of Krishna occurs in a mythical locality, Kurukshetra, and in a mythical time—that of the great battle between the Kauravas and the Pândavas. In contrast to this, the fall of Samaria actually did occur in history, and it was an event willed and provoked by Jahveh: that was theophany of a new type, hitherto unknown—the *intervention of Jahveh in history*. It was therefore something irreversible and unrepeatable. The fall of Jerusalem does not repeat the fall of Samaria: the ruin of Jerusalem presents a new historic theophany, another "wrath" of Jahveh. Such deeds of "wrath" reveal the *tremenda majestas* attaching to a *Person*, Jahveh; it is no longer that of a religious,

[1] *The Myth of the Eternal Return*, pp. 17ff., 51ff.; *Patterns in Comparative Religion*, pp. 410; see also above p. 80.

transpersonal *power*. Because he is a Person—that is, a Being who enjoys perfect freedom—Jahveh stands out from the world of abstractions, of symbols and generalities; he acts in history and enters into relations with actual historical beings. And when God the Father "shows" himself in a radical and complete manner by becoming incarnate in Jesus Christ, then all history becomes a theophany. The conceptions of mythical time and of the eternal return are definitely superseded.[1]

This was a very great religious revolution—too great, indeed, to have been assimilated even after two thousand years of Christian life. Let us explain why. When the sacred made itself known only in the Cosmos it was easily recognisable: for a pre-Christian religious man it was, on the whole, easy to distinguish a sign that was charged with power—a spiral, a circle or a swastika, etc.—from all those that were not; easy, even, to separate liturgical time from profane time. At a certain moment profane time ceased to flow, and—by the simple fact that the ritual had commenced—liturgical, sacred time began. But in Judæism, and above all in Christianity, divinity had manifested itself in History. The Christ and his contemporaries were part of History. Not of History only, of course; but the Son of God, by his incarnation, had accepted existence in History—even as the sacredness revealed in this or that object in the Cosmos paradoxically accepted the innumerable conditions of that object's existence. To the Christian, consequently, there was a radical, additional difference between different historical events: certain events were theophanies (above all, the presence of Christ in history) while others were merely secular events. But the Christ, in his Mystical Body the Church, continued to be present in History. And this, for the true Christian, creates an exceedingly difficult situation: he can no longer repudiate History, but neither can he accept it all. He has continually to *choose*, to try to distinguish, in the tangle of historical events, the event which, *for him*, may be charged with a saving significance.

We know how difficult it is, this choice: in History, the separateness of the sacred from the profane—so clear-cut in pre-

[1] See *The Myth of the Eternal Return*, pp. 141ff.; and *Images et Symboles*, pp. 225ff.

Christian times—is no longer obvious. All the more is this the case, since for two centuries past the fall of man into history has been precipitous. By the "fall into history" we mean the modern man's having become aware of the multiple "conditioning" by history of which he is the victim. How a modern Christian might envy the good luck of the Hindu! For in the Indian conception the man of *kali yuga* is *ipso facto* fallen—that is, conditioned by the carnal life till the occultation of the spirit is almost total—and one must go out of the flesh to recover spiritual freedom. But the modern Christian feels that he is fallen not only because of his carnal condition, but also because of his historical condition. It is no longer the Cosmos and the Flesh—Life—which is creating obstacles for him upon the path of salvation: it is History, the terror of History.

The modern Christian may perhaps succeed in defending himself against the temptations of life, but it is impossible for him, as a Christian, to resist History when once he has become involved in its workings. For we live in an epoch when one can no longer disengage oneself from the wheels of History, unless by some audacious act of evasion. But evasion is forbidden to the Christian. And for him there is no other issue; since the Incarnation took place in History, since the Advent of Christ marks the last and the highest manifestation of the sacred in the world—the Christian can save himself only within the concrete, historical life, the life that was chosen and lived by Christ. We know what he must expect: the "fear and anguish", the "sweat like great drops of blood", the "agony" and the "sadness unto death" (*Luke* 22, 44; *Mark*, 14, 34).

VII

Mother Earth and
the Cosmic Hierogamies

TERRA GENETRIX

AN AMERICAN-Indian prophet, Smohalla, of the tribe of Umatilla, refused to till the soil. "It is a sin," he said, "to wound or cut, to tear or scratch our common mother by working at agriculture." And he added: "You ask me to dig in the earth? Am I to take a knife and plunge it into the breast of my mother? But then, when I die, she will not gather me again into her bosom. You tell me to dig up and take away the stones. Must I mutilate her flesh so as to get at her bones? Then I can never again enter into her body and be born again. You ask me to cut the grass and the corn and sell them, to get rich like the white men. But how dare I crop the hair of my mother?"[1]

Those words were spoken not much more than half a century ago. But they come to us from very distant ages. The emotion that we feel when we hear them is our response to what they evoke with their wonderful freshness and spontaneity—the primordial image of the Earth-Mother. It is an image that we find everywhere in the world, in countless forms and varieties which it would be a fascinating task to classify, showing how they have developed, how they have been passed on from one civilisation to another. But such a work would take up a whole volume: and to do it properly one would have to enter into technical details of interest mainly, or only, to specialists—in this case, to the ethnologists and the historians of religion. Which means that it cannot be attempted here. For our purpose another and pleasanter way

[1] James Mooney, "The Ghost-Dance Religion, and the Sioux outbreak of 1890" in the *Annual Report of the Bureau of American Ethnology*, XIV, 2, Washington, 1896 (pp. 641–1136), p. 721.

presents itself: to review in succession certain images of the Earth-Mother, trying to understand what they reveal to us, to decipher their message. Every primordial image is the bearer of a message of direct relevance to the condition of humanity, for the image unveils aspects of ultimate reality that are otherwise inaccessible.

What is revealed to us by the words of the American-Indian prophet we have just quoted? He denounces and refuses labour on the land, because he will not wound the body of his Mother the Earth. Stones he regards as the bones of this Mother, the soil as her flesh, and the vegetation as her hair. As we shall see later, the correspondence between bodily organs and cosmic substances or regions, and the image of a divine anthropocosmic being, are to be found in other forms also; sometimes in that of a primordial androgyne Giant, or even—though far more rarely—a great cosmic male. We shall see how these variations of sex may be interpreted. For the moment, let us look more attentively at this image of the Earth as Woman, as the Mother. This is the *Terra Mater* or *Tellus Mater*, well known in the Mediterranean religions, who gives birth to all beings. The prophet Smohalla does not tell us in what way men were born of this telluric Mother. But the American myths do reveal to us how things came to pass in the beginning, *in illo tempore*: the first men lived for a certain time in the body of their Mother; that is, deep in the Earth, in its bowels. There, in the telluric profundities, they lived a life only half human; they were, so to speak, embryos as yet imperfectly formed. So, at least, say the Lenni Lenape, or Delaware Indians, who formerly dwelt in Pennsylvania. According to their myths, the Creator who had already prepared for men, on the surface of the Earth, all the things that they now enjoy, nevertheless decided that they should remain for some time longer in the womb of their telluric Mother where they could best develop and mature. Some say that the ancestors who lived underground were already of human form; but according to others they were more like animals.[1]

[1]The Rev. John Heckenwelder (1819), quoted by J. G. Frazer, *The Worship of Nature*, London, 1926, p. 427.

This is not an isolated myth. The Iroquois recall an epoch when they lived under the earth: down there it was always night, for the rays of the sun never penetrated to them. But one fine day one of them found an opening, and climbed up on to the surface of the Earth. While he was walking in the strange and beautiful landscape he came across a deer, which he killed, and took back with him underground. The meat of the deer was good; and all that he had to tell of the other world, the world of light, greatly interested his companions. They unanimously decided to climb up to the surface.[1] Other Indian myths speak of a remote age in which the Earth-Mother produced human beings in the same manner as she now produces bushes or reeds.[2] This notion of men being born in the same way as plants will engage our attention later.

THE MYTHS OF EMERGENCE

But, for the present, let us look into a few more myths about gestation and parturition. In the Navajo language the Earth is called Naëstsán, literally, the "horizontal" or "recumbent" Woman. According to the Navajo there are four subterranean worlds, one below the other; and the Zuni call these four worlds the four wombs of the Earth. It was right down in the deepest womb of the Earth that men lived in the beginning. They came out on to the surface through a lake or a spring, or, according to other traditions, by climbing up a vine (the Mandau opinion) or a reed (as the Navajo think). A Zuni myth recounts that, in the beginning of time, *in illo tempore*, the "Twins of War" came down through a lake into the underground world. There they met with a "vapourish and unstable" people who took no solid nourishment but lived solely upon the "steams and smells" of food. These men were horrified to see the Twins feeding upon solid substances, for in the underground world such food was

[1]The Rev. C. Pyraeus (1743), quoted in Frazer, *op. cit.*, p. 428.
[2]Myths of the Salivas, a tribe of the Orinoco: J. Gumilla (1758), quoted by Frazer, *op. cit.*, p. 432. A good many myths of origin can be found in the recent volume by Raffaele Pettazzoni, *Miti e Legende, III: America Settentrionale*, Turin, 1953.

thrown away. After numerous adventures, the Twins returned to the surface, bringing back with them a certain number of these subterranean men, and it is from these that our present humanity is descended. And that, continues the myth, is the reason why the newly-born feed exclusively upon "wind" until the moment when the "invisible cord" is cut: only then can they begin to absorb milk and very light nourishment, and even that with very great difficulty.[1]

We can see how this myth connects the ontogenetic with the phylogenetic: the condition of the new-born babe is homologised with a mythical pre-existence of the human race in the bowels of the Earth: every infant, in its pre-natal state, is re-living the life of that primordial humanity. The assimilation of the human mother to the Great telluric Mother is complete. We shall better understand this symmetry between individual birth and anthropogeny—or, to use the scientific terms, between ontogenesis and phylogenesis—when we have considered the Zuni myth of the creation of the world and man. Here is the gist of it:

In the beginning, there was only Awonawílono the Creator—the Maker and Container of all. He was quite alone in the universal void. He transformed himself into the Sun and, out of his own substance, he produced two seeds with which he impregnated the Great Waters: under the extreme warmth of his light, the waters of the sea turned green and a foam appeared, which grew continually until finally it took the form of the Earth-Mother and of the Father-Heaven (Awitelin Tsíta, the "Four-fold Containing Mother-Earth" and Apoyan Tächu the "All-covering Father Sky"). From the union between these two cosmic twins, the Heaven and the Earth, life was engendered in the forms of myriads of creatures. But the Earth-Mother kept all these beings within her body, in what the myth calls "the four wombs of the World". In the deepest of all these cavernous wombs the seeds of men and of the other creatures germinate little by little and finally hatch

[1]F. H. Cushing, *Zuni Folk-tales*, New York, 1901, p. 409; Washington Matthews, "Myths of Gestation and Parturition" in the *American Anthropologist*, N.S. IV, 1902, pp. 737–742, p. 740. For the Navajo myths, see A. M. Stephen, "Navajo Origin Legend" in the *Journal of American Folk-lore*, Vol. 43, 1930, pp. 88–104; and R. Pettazzoni, *op. cit.*, pp. 233ff.

out; they do so, indeed, like a chick coming out of the egg. But these are still imperfect beings: heaped and crowded together in the darkness, they crawl over one another like reptiles, grumbling, lamenting, spitting, and using indecent and insulting language. A few among them try to escape, however, and this effort is followed by some increase in the wisdom of mankind. One above all, distinguished from all the others as the most intelligent, is the master Póshaiyank'ya, who somehow participates in the divine condition; for the myth tells us that he made his appearance *under* the primordial Waters in the same manner as the Sun manifested itself above the Waters. This great sage— who probably symbolises the nocturnal Sun—emerges all alone into the light after having traversed all the four telluric "cavern-wombs" one after another. He arrives on the surface of the Earth, which has the appearance of a vast island, humid and unstable; and he makes his way towards the Father-Sun to implore him to deliver subterranean humanity.

The Sun then repeats the process of the Creation, but this time it is creation of another order: the Sun wishes to produce intelligent, free and powerful beings. He again impregnates the foam of the Earth-Mother, and from this foam twins are born. The Sun endows them with every kind of magical power and ordains them to be Ancestors and Lords of men. The Twins then lift up the sky and, with their knives—which are "thunderstones" —they break open the mountains and go down into the darkness underground. There, in the depths of the Earth, are all sorts of herbs and climbing plants: the Twins breathe upon one of these, causing it to grow till it reaches up to the light. They then fashion it into a ladder by which men and the other creatures can climb up as far as the second cavern. A number of them fall by the way, and those will remain for ever in the depths: they become monsters who provoke earthquakes and other cataclysms. In the second Cavern-womb it was still dark, but there was a little more room, for, as the myth tells us, this cavern was "nearer to the Earth's navel". (Note, by the way, this allusion to the symbolism of the Centre: the Zuni, like so many other peoples, think that the Creation of man took place at the Centre of the World.) This second Cavern-womb bears the name of "the Umbilical Matrix or Place of Gestation".

Again the Twins cause the ladder to grow, and then carefully lead the underground people by groups, one after another— groups which, later on, are to become the ancestors of the six human races. They reach the third Cavern-womb, larger and lighter: this is the "vaginal-womb, or Place of generation or gestation"—a cavern still larger and better-lit, like a valley under the stars. The human beings remain here for some time, and multiply, before the Twins guide them up to the fourth and last cavern, which is called the "last discoverable (cavern), or the Womb of Parturition". Here, the light is like that of dawn; and men begin to perceive the world and develop intellectually, each one in conformity with his own nature. The Twins, looking after them as if they were little children, also complete their education: they teach them above all things to look to the Sun-Father, for it is he who will reveal wisdom to them.

But this cave in its turn becomes too small, for humanity never ceases to multiply; so the Twins send them up to the surface of the Earth, which is named the "World of disseminated light, or of Knowledge, or of Sight". When they had emerged completely to the surface, these beings were still of a sub-human appearance; they were dark, cold and damp; they had membranous ears like bats and toes joined together like the palmipeds: they also had tails. They were as yet unable to walk upright, but leaped like frogs or crawled like lizards. The weather, too, had a different rhythm: eight years lasted four days and four nights—for the world was new and fresh.[1]

We need not comment upon the gynæcological and obstetric symbolism of this fine myth of the origin of man. The image of the Earth perfectly corresponds to that of the Mother: the anthropogeny is described in terms of ontogeny. The formation

[1] F. H. Cushing, *Outlines of Zuni Creation Myths*, in the *Annual Report* of the Bureau of American Ethnology, Washington, 1896 (pp. 325–462), pp. 379–384. Another variant of the Zuni myth, one that contains hardly any gynæcological symbolism, has been published by Elsie C. Parsons, *Pueblo Indian religion*, Chicago, 1939, pp. 218–236, and reproduced by R. Pettazzoni, *op. cit.*, pp. 520–532. F. H. Cushing has also published a Hopi myth; cf. *Origin Myth from Oraibi* in the *Journal of American Folk-lore*, Vol. 36, 1923, pp. 163–170 (Trans. by Pettazzoni, *op. cit.*, pp. 510–515). The myth of emergence is also found elsewhere, *e.g.*, among the Pima; cf. Pettazzoni, pp. 569–571.

of the embryo and the birth repeat the cosmic act of the birth of mankind, conceived as an emergence from the profoundest Cavern-womb in the chthonic depths. Yet, as we have seen, this emergence occurs under the sign of the Spirit; it is the Sun who, through the intermediation of the Twins, leads and helps mankind to reach the surface of the Earth. Life—although it was the creation of the first hierogamy between Earth and Heaven—would, if left to itself, have remained forever at the level of fœtal existence. So the Zuni myth tells us, perfectly clearly: in the deepest of the Cavern-wombs the human beings lived like larvæ; they were a grumbling throng, moaning and reviling each other in the dark. Their progression to the light is homologous with the emergence of mind. The solar Twins lead embryonic humanity up to the threshold of consciousness.

Like all myths, this one is also exemplary—that is, it serves as the pattern and model to a great many human activities. Indeed, it must not be imagined that cosmogonic and anthropogenic myths are narrated only to answer such questions as "who are we?" and "whence do we come?" Such myths also constitute examples to be followed whenever it is a case of *creating* something, or of restoring or regenerating a human being. For, to the "primitive" mind all regeneration implies a return to the origins, a repetition of the cosmogony. We can realise the value of such myths by observing, for instance, what happens among the Navajo: it is generally during certain ceremonies performed for the cure of an illness or the initiation of a shaman-apprentice that they recount the myth of the emergence of men from the bosom of the Earth and the laborious journey to the surface of the soil and into the light.[1] This means that the myths of the origin of the human race still exert an important influence on the religious life of the tribe; they are not just recited no matter when or no matter how, but only to accompany and justify a ritual designed to *re-make* something (health, the vital integrity of the sick person), or to *make*, to create a new spiritual factor (the shaman) or situation. To restore the health of a patient they re-enact, in his

---

[1] *Cf.* Mary C. Wheelwright, *Navajo Creation Myth, the Story of the Emergence*, Museum of Navajo Ceremonial Art, Santa Fé, New Mexico, 1942, p. 19 *et passim*.

presence, the coming into being of the world; they re-actualise the emergence of the first human beings from the bosom of the Earth. It is because this anthropogeny is rendered present and active (preceded, moreover, by a recitation of the cosmogony), that the patient recovers: he feels in his intimate being the primordial process of emergence. In other terms, he becomes again contemporary with the cosmogony and the anthropogeny. This return to origins—in the present case to the Earth-Mother— this repetition of the cosmogony and the anthropogeny in order to bring about a cure, constitutes an important type of archaic therapeutics.

MEMORIES AND NOSTALGIAS

These myths of emergence from the depths of the Earth may be compared with the memories of pre-natal existence which certain North American shamans claim to have rather clearly preserved. The memories in question relate to the insertion of the shaman's soul into the maternal womb, its sojourn in the amniotic darkness and its final passing out into the light. Such memories of pre-natal existence may not seem, at first sight, to have much to do with myths of the emergence of ancestors from the bosom of the Earth. But the image is the same: the personal recollections of the shamans illustrate the myth of a subterranean life followed by an arrival upon the face of the Earth, with, of course, differences due to the fact that these memories are those of an individual obstetrical birth. Here are a few examples: a shaman tells us that his soul had decided to become incarnate among the Iowa; the soul entered into a hut at the door of which there was a bear-skin fur and stayed there for some time; afterwards it came out of the hut —and the shaman had been born.[1] Winnebago, a shaman, recounted the vicissitudes of one of his reincarnations: he had entered, not into a woman but into a room. "Down there, I remained conscious all the time. One day I heard the sounds of

[1] Alanson Skinner, "Traditions of the Iowa Indians", in the *Journal of American Folklore*, 1925, Vol. 38, p. 479, quoted by Ake Hultkrantz, *Conceptions of the Soul among North American Indians*, Stockholm, 1953, p. 421.

little children outside, and other sounds too, and I decided to go out. Then it seemed to me that I went through a door, but in reality I was just newly born from a woman. As soon as I had come out, the cool air chilled me and I began to cry."[1]

The nostalgia for a return to the Earth-Mother sometimes becomes a collective phenomenon; and then it is a sign that the society has given up the struggle and is nearing complete disappearance. That is the case with the Yaruros of South America, a people as primitive as the Fuegians, for they are ignorant of agriculture and have no domestic animal except the dog. The Great Mother of the Yaruros lives in the East, in a distant region called the Land of Kuma. The dead go away thither, into the land of the Mother; there they are re-born and rejoice in a paradisiac existence—the life which the Yaruros declare that they knew before the coming of the white men. During their trance, the shamans travel to the Land of Kuma, and recount what they see there. The whole tribe suffers from a nostalgia for this lost Paradise; the Yaruros are impatient to die and re-enter the land of the Mother. Perhaps by now they have done so; for twenty years ago, when Petrullo visited them, only a few hundred remained...[2]

MOTHER EARTH

That human beings were born from the Earth is a belief of universal distribution: one need only look at the few books written on this subject, such as the *Mutter Erde* of Dieterich, or Nyberg's *Kind und Erde*.[3] In many languages man is named "the Earth-born".[4] The belief is that babies "come" from the depths

---

[1]Paul Radin, *The Road of Life and Death*, New York, 1945, p. 8. But the shamans' memories of pre-natal existence are much more varied and more complex; see Hultkrantz, *op. cit.*, pp. 418–426.

[2]Vicenco Petrullo, *The Yaruros of the Capanaparo River, Venezuela*, Smithsonian Institution, Bureau of American Ethnology, Bulletin 123, Anthropological Papers No. 11, Washington, 1939, (pp. 167–289), pp. 226ff., 244, 249, 250.

[3]A. Dieterich, *Mutter Erde, ein Versuch über Volksreligion*, Leipzig–Berlin, 1905, 3rd edn., 1925, augmented and completed by E. Fehrle; Bertel Nyberg, *Kind und Erde. Ethnologische Studien zur Urgeschichte der Elternschaft und des Kinderschutzes*, Helsinki, 1931; see also our *Patterns in Comparative Religion*, Paris, 1949, pp. 239-264, with supplementary bibliography.

[4]In Russian songs, myths of the Lapps and Esthonians, etc., Dieterich, *op. cit.*, p. 14.

of the Earth, from caves, grottoes, fissures, but also from swamps and streams. In the form of legends, superstitions or simply of metaphors, similar beliefs still survive in Europe. Every region, and almost every town and village, knows a rock or a spring which "brings" children, by some such name as *Kinderbrunnen, Kinderteiche* or *Bubenquellen*.[1]

We should be wary of supposing that these superstitions or metaphors are no more than explanations for the children: the reality is not so simple. Even among Europeans of today there lingers an obscure feeling of mystical unity with the native Earth; and this is not just a secular sentiment of love for one's country or province, nor admiration for the familiar landscape or veneration for the ancestors buried for generations around the village churches. There is also something quite different; the mystical experience of autochthony, the profound feeling of having come from the soil, of having been born of the Earth in the same way that the Earth, with her inexhaustible fecundity, gives birth to the rocks, rivers, trees and flowers. It is in this sense that autochthony should be understood: men feel that they are *people of the place*, and this is a feeling of cosmic relatedness deeper than that of familial and ancestral solidarity. We know that in many cultures the father played a subordinate part; he only legitimised the child, and gave it recognition. *Mater semper certa, pater incertus*. And this principle was long maintained: as they used to say in monarchic France: "The King is the child of the Queen." But this itself was not the original position, which was that the mother did no more than *receive* the child. According to innumerable beliefs, women became pregnant whenever they approached certain places; rocks, caves, trees or rivers. The souls of the children then entered their bodies and the women conceived. Whatever was the condition of these child-souls—whether they were or were not the souls of ancestors—one thing was certain: in order to become incarnate, they had been waiting hidden somewhere, in crevasses or hollows, in pools or woods. Already, then, they were leading some sort of embryonic life in the womb of their real Mother, the Earth. That was where children came from. And thence it was, according

---

[1] Dieterich, *op. cit.*, p. 19ff., 126ff.

to other beliefs still surviving among Europeans of the nineteenth century, that they were brought by certain aquatic animals—fish, or frogs, and especially by storks.

Now, this obscure belief in a pre-existence within the bosom of the Earth has had considerable consequences: it has created in man a sense of cosmic relatedness with his local environment; one might even say that, in those times, man had not so much a consciousness of belonging to the human race as a sense of cosmo-biological participation in the life around him. He knew, of course, that he had an "immediate" mother, her whom he saw still near him, but he also knew that he came from farther away, that he had been brought to her by the storks or the frogs, that he had lived in the caves or in the rivers. And all this has left its traces in language: the Romans called a bastard *terrae filius*; the Rumanians even today call him the "child of flowers".

This kind of cosmo-biological experience rooted man in a mystical solidarity with *the place* which was intense enough to have survived till now in folk-lore and popular traditions. The mother did no more than bring to completion the creation of the Earth-Mother: and, at death, the great desire was to return to the Earth-Mother, to be interred in the native soil—that "native soil" of which we can now see the profound meaning. Hence the fear of having one's remains buried anywhere else; hence, above all, the satisfaction of having them re-integrated with the "mother land"—a satisfaction often expressed in Roman sepulchral inscriptions: *hic natus hic situs est*, "here he was born, here he is laid"; *hic situs est patriæ; hic quo natus fuerat, optans erat illo reverti*— "hither, where he was born, he desired to return".[1] Perfect autochthony comprises the whole cycle from birth to death; one has to go back to the Mother. "Creep back to the earth thy mother!" says the *Rig Veda* (X, 18, 10). "Thou, who art earth, I put thee into the Earth!" is written in the *Atharva Veda* (XVIII, 4, 48). "Let the flesh and the bones return once more to the Earth!" as they say during the Chinese funeral ceremonies.[2]

[1] A. Brelich, *Aspetti della morte nelle iscrizioni sepolcrali dell' Impero Romano*, Budapest, 1937, pp. 36ff.
[2] *Li Ki*, trans. by Couvreur, I, p. 246.

HUMI POSITIO: THE PLACING OF
THE INFANT ON THE SOIL

This fundamental conception—that a mother is only the representative of the telluric Great Mother—lies at the origin of customs without number. Let us recall, for example, that of giving birth upon the soil (the *humi positio*), a ritual found here and there all over the world from Australia to China, from Africa to South America. Among the Greeks and Romans this custom had disappeared by historic times, but there is no doubt it had existed in a more distant past: certain statues of the goddesses of birth (Eileithia, Damia, Auxeia) represent them kneeling exactly in the position of a woman giving birth upon the ground. In Egyptian demotic texts, the expression "to be seated on the earth" signified "giving birth" or "child-bed".[1]

We can easily grasp the religious meaning of this custom: giving birth and parturition are the microcosmic version of an exemplary action accomplished by the Earth; every human mother is but imitating and repeating that primordial act by which Life appeared in the womb of the Earth. Therefore every mother ought to find herself in direct contact with the Great Genetrix, and let herself be guided by her in the accomplishment of the mystery of the birth of a new life, so as to share in her benefic energies and her maternal protection.

Still more widely practised is the custom of depositing the new-born child upon the earth. This is still done even now among the Abruzzi, who place the infant, as soon as it is washed and dressed, upon the soil itself. This ritual is found among the Scandinavians, the Germans and the Parsees; in Japan and in other places. The child is then picked up by the father (*de terra tollere*) to express his gratitude.[2] Marcel Granet has studied this placing

---

[1] Ernst Samter, *Geburt, Hochzeit und Tod. Beiträge zur vergleichenden Volkskunde*, Leipzig–Berlin, 1911, pp. 5ff.; Nyberg, *Kind und Erde*, pp. 131ff.; Uberto Pestalozza, *Religione Mediterranea*, Milan, 1951, p. 254.

[2] Dieterich, *Mutter Erde*, pp. 7ff.; Nyberg, *Kind und Erde*, pp. 31, 158ff.; Robert Briffault, *The Mothers; a study of the origin of sentiments and institutions*, London, 1927, Vol. III, p. 58.

of the infant on the earth in ancient China, and has very well interpreted the meaning of the rite.[1] "*The dying person, like the new-born babe,*" writes Granet, "*is deposited on the soil.* When they have collected the last breath upon wadding, when they have tried in vain to call back the soul's breath, which is the first to go, they all weep around the body as it lies on the earth (just as the infant whimpers upon the soil for three days) . . . To be born or to die, to enter into the living family or into the ancestral family (or to go out of either of them), there is the same threshold, the natal Earth. That is not only the place where life and the after-life begin, it is also the great witness of the initiation into the new kind of existence: it is the sovereign power that adjudges success in the Ordalia that that initiation implies . . . When the new-born child or the dying person is laid upon the Earth, it is for Her to say whether the birth or the death is valid, whether they are to be taken as regular and accomplished facts . . . The rite of depositing them on the soil implies the idea that there is a substantial identity between the Race and the Soil. This idea is expressed, indeed, in the sentiment of autochthony which is the most vivid of all those that we discern in the beginnings of Chinese history: the idea of a close alliance between a country and its inhabitants is so profoundly believed in, that it has remained at the heart of the religious institutions and of public rights."[2]

Thanks to Granet's analysis, here we can seize upon the living process of the formation of the image of the Earth-Mother. At first she appears "under the neutral aspect of the Holy Place as the principle of all solidarity". A little later on, "in the totality of images and conceptions determined by a family organisation based upon maternal affiliation, the domestic Earth was conceived with the characteristics of a maternal and nourishing power" (Granet, p. 201). It is very probable that in ancient times the dead were buried within the domestic enclosure (*ibid.* p. 199) where the seeds were kept. Now, the woman retained, for a long time, the keeping of the seeds. "In the times of the Tcheu, the grains

---

[1] Marcel Granet, "Le dépôt de l'enfant sur le sol: Rites anciens et ordalies mythiques", in the *Revue Archéologique*, 1922, republished in *Etudes Sociologiques sur la Chine*, Paris, 1953, pp. 159-202

[2] Marcel Granet, *Etudes sociologiques*, pp. 192-193, 197-198.

to be sown in the royal field were not kept in the chamber of the Son of Heaven, but preserved in the apartments of the Queen" (*ibid*, p. 200). "If, in a noble house, the father of the family puts his bed where the seeds are, and where the souls haunt, he has usurped the place of the mother of the family. There was a time when the family was uterine and when the husband, in the conjugal house, was only the son-in-law." (*Ibid*, p. 201.) It was only later, with the rise of the agnatic family and the seigneurial power, that the Soil became a God.[1]

Let us note this fact: that before being represented as a Mother, the Earth was felt as a pure cosmic creative power—a-sexual or, if one prefers it, supra-sexual. The conception is the same as that we have just described, of mystical autochthony; the infants are thought of as "coming" from the Soil itself. Obviously the Soil which produces children as it produces rocks, springs and plants is always a Mother, even though the feminine attributes of this maternity may not always be in evidence. One might, in this case, speak of it as an *Ur-Mutter*, a Primordial Mother. It represents perhaps an obscure memory of the androgyny of the Tellus Mater, or of its capacities of autogenesis or parthenogenesis; but that is an important problem to which we shall return.

[1] Marcel Granet, we think, happily corrects the interpretation proposed by Edouard Chavannes in his fine study *Le T'ai Chan. Essai de monographie d'un culte chinois*, Paris, 1910, Annales du Musée Guimet, Bibliothèque d'Etudes (especially pp. 520–525). According to Chavannes, the personification of the Soil as a great Earth-Goddess was a rather late phenomenon, which seemed to have taken place about the beginning of the Han dynasty in the second century B.C.; before that date there had been only local cults that developed around certain *gods* of the soil (Chavannes, *op. cit.*, p. 437). But Granet has shown that these gods were substituted for very ancient feminine or "neuter" divinities which had preceded them. The researches of Carl Hentze into the pre-history and proto-history of the Chinese religions have confirmed these views: the lunar and aquatic myths elucidated by Hentze are integral with a religion of the Earth-Mother. See his *Mythes et Symboles lunaires*, Antwerp, 1932; *Objets rituels, croyances et dieux de la Chine antique et de l'Amérique*, Antwerp, 1936; *Frühchinesische Bronzen*, Antwerp, 1938. As early as 1912, B. Laufer wrote that: "Primarily, Earth was neither a distinctly female nor a distinctly male deity, but rather sexless; nevertheless, it falls under the category *yin*, the negative, dark, female principle, as already indicated in the Book of mutations (*I Ching*), where the notion of *yin* is defined as the action of the Earth (*yin ti tao*). It is certainly doubtful whether the word *yin* conveyed in the beginning a clear sex notion, which may be regarded as a philosophical abstraction of later times; but there is no doubt that the combination *yin yang* signified the combined action of Heaven and Earth in the production and transformation of beings, or the creative powers of these two great forces. In the sacrifices to the deity Earth, all the paraphernalia are derived from the sphere *yin* . . ." (B. Laufer, *Jade; a study of Chinese archæology and religion*, Field Museum, Chicago, 1912, pp. 144ff.) Against these views, *cf.* Bernhard Karlgren, "Some fecundity Symbols in ancient China" in the *Bulletin of the Museum of Far Eastern Antiquities*, No. 2, Stockholm, 1930 (pp. 1–54) pp. 14ff.

THE SUBTERRANEAN WOMB
THE EMBRYOS

For the moment, let us note that the conception of the Earth as universal Genetrix is verified even upon what might be called the geological plane of existence. If the Earth is a living and fecund Mother, all that she brings forth is at the same time organic and animated, not only men and trees but also stones and minerals. A great many myths mention stones as the bones of the Earth-Mother. Deucalion threw "the bones of his mother" over his shoulder in order to re-populate the world. Those "bones" were stones; but in the oldest traditions of the hunting peoples—traditions which go back to the paleolithic—the bone represented the very source of life: it was in the bones that the ultimate essence of life was concentrated; and from them that animals as well as men were re-born. By scattering stones, Deucalion was really sowing the seeds of a new humanity.

If the Earth is likened to a Mother, all the things that she carries in her bowels are homologous with embryos, or living beings in course of "gestation"—that is, of growth and development. This conception is very clearly expressed in the mineralogical terminology of the various traditions. For example, the Indian treatises on mineralogy describe the emerald in its "matrix" in the rock as an embryo. The Sanskrit name for emerald is *aҫmagarbhaja*, the "rock-born". Another text distinguishes the diamond from the crystal as though it were a difference of age, expressing this in biological terms: the diamond is *pakka*—that is, "ripe"—while the crystal is *kaccha*, "unripe", "green", insufficiently developed.

Such conceptions are extremely ancient. Mines, just like the mouths of rivers, were likened to the womb of the Earth-Mother. In Babylonian, the term *pû* signifies both "source of a river" and "vagina"; in Egyptian the word *bi* means both "vagina" and "gallery of a mine"; the Sumerian *buru* also means "vagina" and "river". It is probable that the ores extracted from a mine were likened to embryos. The Babylonian word *an-kubu* is by certain authors translated "embryo" and by others "abortion". There is, at all events, a hidden symmetry between metallurgy and obstetrics; the sacrifice that was sometimes performed before the smelting furnace resembled the obstetrical sacrifice; the furnace was likened to a womb, it was there that the "embryonic ores" had to complete their growth, and do so in a considerably shorter time than this would have required had they remained hidden underground. The metallurgical operation, much like agricultural labour—and equally implying the fertility of the Earth-Mother —at last created in man a feeling of confidence, and even of pride: man felt that he was capable of co-operating in the work of Nature, able to promote the processes of growth that were taking place in the bosom of the Earth. Man hustles and quickens the rhythm of these slow chthonic maturations; in a sense, he is *taking the place of Time.*

Alchemy was pursued within this same spiritual horizon. The alchemist takes up and completes the work of Nature, working at the same time to "perfect" himself.[1] Gold is the noblest metal because it is perfectly "mature"; if left in their chthonic womb, the other ores would turn into gold—but only after hundreds of thousands of centuries. Like the metallurgist, who transforms "embryos" into metals by accelerating the growth begun within the Earth-Mother, so the alchemist dreams of intensifying that acceleration until the crowning and final transmutation of all the baser metals—"base" because still immature—into the "noble" and perfectly "ripe" metal, which is gold. This is what Ben Jonson is telling us in Act II, Scene 1, of his play *The Alchemist.*

Subtle: The same we say of lead and other metals,
           Which would be gold, if they had time.
Mammon: And that our art doth further.

[1]See our book, *Forgerons et Alchimistes*, 1956.

LABYRINTHS

But let us go back to the image of the Earth depicted as a giant Mother. Clearly, if the galleries of mines and the mouths of rivers were likened to the *vagina* of the Earth-Mother, the same symbolism applied *a fortiori* to grottoes and caverns. And we know that caverns had a religious significance in the paleolithic period. In prehistoric times the cavern, often resembling, or ritually transformed into, a labyrinth, was at once a theatre of initiation and a place where the dead were buried. The labyrinth, in its turn, was homologised with the body of the Earth-Mother.[1] To penetrate into a labyrinth or a cavern was the equivalent of a mystical return to the Mother—an end pursued in the rites of initiation as well as in funeral obsequies. The researches of Jackson Knight have shown us how slow it is to disappear, this symbolism of the labyrinth regarded as the body of a telluric Goddess.[2] Troy was felt to be like the Earth, that is, like a Goddess: the inviolability of the ancient cities was homologised with the virginity of the protective divinity. All these symbols, overlapping and complementing one another, attest the perennial sway of the primordial image of the Earth-Woman.

But it was not only initiations and funerals that were conducted in caverns; it was there too that certain mythological marriages were celebrated. The marriages, for example, of Peleus and Thetis, of Jason and Medea, and, in the *Aeneid* of Virgil, the marriage of Aeneas and Dido (IV, 165–166). At the consummation of their union, Virgil tells us, a storm broke out: while the nymphs were crying on the heights of the mountain, the thunder boomed and the lightning flashed—a sign that the God of Heaven was approaching his spouse, the Earth-Mother. The marriage of Aeneas and Dido is but an imitation of the exemplary union—the cosmic hierogamy. But Dido did not conceive; no offspring came

[1] We must note, however, that the symbolism of the labyrinth is rather complex, and is not to be reduced to a single "motif".

[2] W. F. Jackson Knight, *Cumæan Gates. A reference of the sixth Aeneid to Initiation Pattern*, Oxford, 1936, pp. 122ff., and *passim*.

to sanctify the union; and it was for this that she was abandoned by Aeneas; she had not worthily represented the Earth-Mother. Their union remained sterile, and after Aeneas's departure Dido mounted the funeral pyre. For, after all, her marriage had not been a happy hierogamy. When Heaven meets Earth, life bursts forth in forms innumerable, at every level of existence. The hierogamy is an act of Creation, it is at once cosmogony and biogony, both the Creation of the Universe and the creation of Life.

COSMIC HIEROGAMIES

The cosmic hierogamy, the marriage between Heaven and Earth, is a cosmogonic myth of the widest distribution. It is found above all in Oceania, from Indonesia to Micronesia; but also in Asia, Africa and the two Americas.[1] This myth is more or less similar to that of which Hesiod tells us in his *Theogony* (126, etc.). Ouranos, Heaven, unites with Gaia, the Earth, and the divine pair engender the gods, the Cyclops and other monstrous beings. "The holy Heaven is intoxicated (with desire) to penetrate the body of the Earth," says Aeschylus in his *Danaïds* (Nauck, fragm. 44). All that exists—the Cosmos, the Gods and Life—takes birth from this marriage.

Although so widely distributed, the myth of the cosmic hierogamy is not, however, universal: thus, it is not recorded from among the Australians, the Arctic peoples, the Fuegians or the hunting and herding peoples of Northern or Central Asia, etc. Some of these peoples—the Australian and the Fuegian, for instance—are reckoned among the most ancient; their culture is, indeed, still at the paleolithic stage. According to their traditional mythology, the Universe was created by a celestial Supreme Being; sometimes, we are even told that this God is a creator *ex nihilo*.[2] When he has a consort and children, it is still he himself who created them. One may presume that, at the paleo-

[1] *Cf.* our *Patterns in Comparative Religion*, pp. 240ff.
[2] *Ibid.*, pp. 41ff.

lithic stage of culture and religion, the myth of the cosmic hierogamy was unknown. This does not necessarily mean that nothing was known about a great Goddess of the Earth and of universal fertility. On the contrary, paleolithic deposits in Asia and Europe have yielded a great many bone statuettes representing a nude Goddess,[1] very probably the prototype of the innumerable goddesses of fecundity, of which some occur everywhere from all times since the neolithic. We know, on the other hand, that Mother-Goddesses are not an appanage of the agricultural societies; they only attained to their privileged position after the invention of agriculture. Great Goddesses were also known to the hunting peoples: there is, for instance, the Great Mother of the Animals, Mother of the Wild Beasts, whom we find in the Far North of Asia and in the Arctic regions.

Nevertheless the absence of the hierogamic myth from the earliest strata of the "primitive" religions is of significance from our point of view. Two hypotheses could be advanced to explain it. The first is as follows: at the archaic stage of culture—which, be it remembered, corresponds with the paleolithic period—hierogamy was inconceivable, because the supreme Being, a god of celestial character, was believed to have created the world, life and men, all by himself. It follows that the figurines of bone found in paleolithic sites are easy to explain—assuming that they do indeed represent goddesses—in the light of the Australian, Fuegian or Arctic religions and mythologies: such Mother-Goddesses had themselves been created by the supreme Being, as is the case, for instance, among the Australians and in the Zuni myth we have described above. In any case, we cannot deduce from the *presence* of the paleolithic female statuettes, the *non-existence* of the worship of a divine masculine Being. In still more ancient paleolithic sites—namely, the caves of Wildkirchli, Wildemannlisloch and Drachenloch, in the Swiss Alps, and in that of Petershöhle in Mittelfranken—remains of sacrifices have been found, which it is allowable to identify as offerings to the

---

[1] Of the 80 statuettes known, 35 are reproduced in the recent study by Herbert Kühn, *Das Problem des Urmonotheismus* (Akademie der Wissenschaften und der Literatur, Abh. d. Geistesund Sozial—wissenschaftlichen Klasse, 1950, No. 22, Wiesbaden, 1951, pp. 1639-1672, fig. 12 *et seq.*, pp. 1660ff).

heavenly Gods.[1] There is, indeed, an astonishing resemblance between these remains—skulls of cave-bears set up on stones built into the form of an altar—and the sacrifice of the heads of animals which the hunting peoples of the Arctic regions, even today, are still offering up to the heavenly Gods.[2]

This hypothesis would appear to have a very good chance of proving correct. The trouble is that it applies only to the paleolithic, and can tell us nothing about the situation before the stone ages. Men had been living for about half a million years before they left us any traces—either of their culture or of their religion. About that pre-lithic humanity we have no exact knowledge.

ANDROGYNY AND WHOLENESS

We could advance another hypothesis to explain the absence of hierogamy in the archaic religions: that their supreme Beings were androgyne, at once male and female, both Heavenly and Earthly. That being so, hierogamy would have been unnecessary for creation; for the very being of the primordial divinity would have constituted a hierogamy in itself. This hypothesis is not to be rejected *a priori*. We do know, in fact, that a certain number of the Supreme Beings of the archaic peoples were androgyne.[3] But the phenomenon of divine androgyny is very complex: it signifies more than the co-existence—or rather coalescence—of the sexes in the divine being. Androgyny is an archaic and universal formula for the expression of *wholeness*, the co-existence of the contraries, or *coincidentia oppositorum*. More than a state of sexual completeness and autarchy, androgyny symbolises the perfection

[1]Emil Baechler, *Das Alpine Paläolithikum der Schweiz*, Basle, 1940; Konrad Hoermann, *Die Petershöhle bei Velden in Mittelfranken*, Abhandlugen der Naturhistorischen Gesellschaft zu Nürnberg, 1923; Oswald Menghin, "Der Nachweis des Opfers im Altpaläolithikum", in the *Wiener Prähistorische Zeitschrift*, XIII, 1926, pp. 14–19; *cf.* also H. Kühn, *op. cit.*, pp. 1643ff.

[2]A. Gahs, "Kopf-, Schädel- und Langknochenopfer bei Rentiervölkern", in the *Festschrift für Wilhelm Schmidt*, Vienna, 1928, pp. 231–268. But see also Karl Meuli, "Griechische Opferbräuche", in *Phyllobolia für Pieter von der Mühll*, Basle, 1946 (pp. 185–288), pp. 237ff. *Cf.* W. Schmidt, "Die Primizialopfer in den Urkulturen" in *Corona Amicorum, Festschrift für E. Bächler*, St Gallen, 1948, pp. 81–92.

[3]*Cf.* A. Bertholet, *Das Geschlecht der Gottheit*, Tübingen, 1934; see our *Patterns in Comparative Religion*, pp. 420ff. Then see Hermann Baumann, *Das Doppelte Geschlecht*, Berlin, 1955.

of a primordial, non-conditioned state. It is for this reason that androgyny is not attributed to supreme Beings only. Cosmic Giants, or mythical Ancestors of humanity are also androgynous. Adam, for example, was regarded as an androgyne. The *Bereshit Rabbâ* (I, 4, fol. 6, col. 2) affirmed that he was "man on the right side and woman on the left side, but God has cloven him into two halves".[1] A mythical Ancestor symbolises the *commencement* of a new mode of existence; and every beginning is made in the *wholeness* of the being.

Also androgyne are the great divinities of vegetation and of fertility in general. We find traces of androgyny among the gods —such as Attis, Adonis and Dionysus—as well as in goddesses like Cybele.[2] And this is understandable enough, since life springs from an over-fullness, from a wholeness. To men of the traditional cultures, one must hasten to add, all life was a hierophany, a manifestation of the sacred. Creation—at every cosmic level— presupposed the intervention of a holy power. Accordingly, the divinities of life and of fertility represented sources of holiness and of power, and of this their androgyny was confirmatory. But *androgyny extends even to divinities who are pre-eminently masculine, or feminine.* This means that androgyny has become a general formula signifying *autonomy, strength, wholeness;* to say of a divinity that it is androgyne is as much as to say that it is the ultimate being, the ultimate reality. We can see, then, that the androgyny of a Supreme Being can no longer be regarded as a specific characteristic; for, on the one hand, this androgyny is an archetype of universal distribution; and, on the other hand, it becomes, after all, an attribute of divinity which tells us nothing about the actual nature of that divinity. A pre-eminently male God may also be androgyne, and so may a Mother-Goddess. So, if we say that the Supreme Beings of the primitives are—or were —androgyne, this in no way excludes their "masculinity" or their "femininity"; and, in the end, this second hypothesis brings us no nearer the solution of our problem.

[1] A. H. Krappe, "The Birth of Eve" in the *Gaster Anniversary Volume*, London, 1936, pp. 312–322.
[2] *Cf. Patterns in Comparative Religion*, pp. 420ff., 265ff.

A HISTORICO-CULTURAL HYPOTHESIS

It has been attempted to interpret these facts—the absence or presence of hierogamies, the preponderance of Heavenly Beings or of telluric Goddesses—in a historical perspective. According to the historico-cultural school,[1] the earliest phase of human civilisation, the *Urkultur*, was that of an economy of food-gathering (*Sammelwirtschaft*) and hunting of small animals: the social structure was one of monogamy and equal rights between husband and wife; while the dominant religion must have been a kind of primitive monotheism (*Urmonotheismus*). Corresponding more or less to this stage today are the cultures and religions of the oldest Australians, the Pygmies, the Fuegians and some other primitive peoples. When the means of existence changed, that is, when men had learnt how to hunt big game, and women had found out how to cultivate plants, the *Urkultur* gave birth to two more complex and clearly distinct forms of society, the *Primärkulturen*: on the one hand, the totemic society, in which man was predominant, and on the other hand the matrilocal and matriarchal society, where women were dominant. It was in the latter that the worship of the Earth-Mother originated and reached its highest development.

It is probable that this schema corresponds, in a great measure, to the realities. But it is impossible to prove that evolution proceeded in this order from the beginnings of humanity: at the most, this schema renders an account of human evolution since the paleolithic era. Even limited to that lapse of time, the schema put forward by the historico-cultural school needs correction and modification. We should speak of *tendencies* rather than *historical realities*. We can no longer doubt the existence of a supreme Being, of what has been called the *Urmonotheismus*; but this, we must not fail to add, is a primordial monotheism, conceived within the mental horizon of archaic man, and not that of

[1] See, for instance, Wilhelm Schmidt, *Rassen und Völker in Vorgeschichte und Geschichte des Abendlandes*, Lucerne, 1946, I, pp. 245ff.

eighteenth-century theism. And this means that, for symbolical thinking—the only kind that is vital and creative at this archaic stage of humanity—the Supreme Being may very well manifest himself in the shape of an Animal without thereby losing anything of his celestial divinity. And concurrently with belief in such a Supreme Being other religious beliefs were held also. This is to say that, so far as we can judge from the available data, there was then no "pure religion", but only the tendency for a certain form of religion to become predominant.

These observations apply to the primordial phase of civilisation, the *Urkultur*. With regard to the cultures that succeeded this, the *Primärkulturen*, things are more complicated. We do not know whether the matriarchate ever existed as an independent cycle of culture[1]—in other words, whether a certain stage in the history of mankind was ever characterised by the absolute ascendancy of woman and by an exclusively feminine religion. It is more prudent to say that matriarchal *tendencies* or *predispositions* are manifest in certain religious and social customs. It is true that certain social structures—for example, uterine descent, matrilocalism, the avunculate and gynæcocracy—show the social, juridical and religious importance of woman. But *importance* does not mean absolute *predominance*.

Whatever one may think about the existence or non-existence of the matriarchate, ethnologists are in agreement upon one specific point—that matriarchy cannot have been a primordial phenomenon. It cannot have come about until *after* the discovery of the cultivation of plants, and of property in cultivable land. And such innovations as these could not have taken place until after the first phase of civilisation, the *Urkultur* characterised, as we saw, by food-gathering and the hunting of small game.

Hitherto, we have done no more than summarise the conclu-

[1]Against the existence of a matriarchal cycle of culture, see the arguments of Ad. E. Jensen, "Gab es eine mutterrechtliche Kultur?" in *Studium Generale*, Jg. 3, Heft 8, Berlin–Heidelberg, 1950, pp. 418–433. See also Josef Haekel, "Zum Problem des Mutterrechtes", in *Paideuma*, Vol. V, H.6, June 1953, pp. 298–322. Difficulties arise above all when it is a question of applying the general theory of a matriarchal culture-cycle to a clearly-defined cultural zone: see, for instance, the state of things in Africa as described in the excellent monograph of Ephraim Andersson, *Contribution à l'Ethnographie des Kuta*, I, Upsala, 1953, pp. 308ff. See also Wilhelm Schmidt, *Das Mutterrecht*, Vienna–Mödling, 1955.

sions of ethnology and paleontology. These conclusions are important; but we must not therefore forget that our problem— that of the Earth-Mother—belongs to the history of religions. And the history of religions is concerned not only with the *historical becoming* of a religious form, but also with its *structure*. For religious forms are non-temporal; they are not necessarily bound to time. We have no proof that religious structures are created by certain types of civilisation or by certain historic moments. All one can say is that the predominance of this or that religious structure is occasioned or favoured by a certain kind of civilisation or by a certain historic moment. When we consider religious structures historically, it is their statistical frequency which matters. But religious reality is more complex: it transcends the plane of history. Judaic monotheism was not the creation of a certain type of civilisation: on the contrary, arising from the religious experience of an élite, the Judaic, like every other form of monotheism, had to struggle against contemporaneous forms of religion. Civilisations, societies and historical moments furnish *opportunities* for the manifestation or the predominance of these non-temporal structures. Yet, being non-temporal, the religious structures never triumph in a definitive manner. One cannot say, for example, that the modern world is monotheist because it calls itself Israelite or Christian: other religious forms co-exist with Judæo-Christian monotheism—magic, for instance, polytheism or fetishism. On the other hand, the monotheistic experience is attested in cultures which, in the formal sense, are still at a polytheistic or totemistic stage.

THE "PRIMORDIAL SITUATION"

Therefore, turning once more to our problem—the absence of the hierogamic myth in the most ancient of the primitive cultures —here is the conclusion that one might propose: the Earth-Mother is a very old divinity, known since paleolithic times. But we cannot say that she was ever the *sole* primordial divinity, and this for the simple reason that "femininity" does not seem to have been thought of as a primordial mode of being. "Femininity", like "masculinity" also, is already a particular mode of being, and, for mythical thinking, this particular mode is necessarily preceded by a *whole* mode of being. When we have to do with Creators, with *Urheber*, it seems that the emphasis falls on their *capacity* to *create*, and this capacity is felt as an undifferentiated plenitude, otherwise unspecified. One might call this primordial state a *neuter and creative wholeness*. This aspect of the matter is very happily prominent in the Chinese instances we have mentioned above: we saw how the celestial God and the patriarchal ideology took the place of an Earth-Goddess and a matriarchal ideology; but this matriarchal ideology in its turn had been preceded by a religious situation which was neither matriarchal nor patriarchal; Granet calls it "the neuter aspect of the holy Place". This "holy place" was perceived as an undifferentiated religious power, as a primordial *Grund* which preceded and supported all subsequent manifestation.

One might say that such "primordial situations" explain the absence of hierogamy in the oldest religions. In these religions too, the cosmogony plays an important part—but it is the act itself of creation upon which all the interest is centred. And we now know that all creation implies a wholeness that precedes it, an *Urgrund*. Hierogamy is only one of the forms of explanation of Creation from a primordial *Urgrund*; there are other cosmogonic myths besides the hierogamic; but they all presuppose the prior existence of an undifferentiated unity.

IZANAGI AND IZANAMI

We shall better understand all these aspects after a closer examination of certain cosmic myths which deal with the Heaven-Earth hierogamy as well as with the creation effected solely by the Earth-Mother. Here, for example, is what the Japanese cosmogonic myth reveals to us: in the beginning, Heaven and Earth, Izanagi and Izanami, were not separate; together they constituted a Chaos, which was like an egg in the midst of which was a germ.

When Heaven and Earth were thus intermingled, the two principles, male and female, did not yet exist. One may therefore say
that this Chaos represented the perfect totality and, consequently,
it was also androgyne. The separation of Heaven from Earth
marked the first pre-eminently cosmogonic act, and the rupture
of the primordial unity.[1]

The first phase of the Creation presents itself in the following
way: a little island, unstable and amorphous, is surrounded by the
sea, and in the midst of this island there is a Reed. From this
Reed the gods are to be born, and their births symbolise the
different stages in the organisation of the world. The "reed" is
the germ that could be distinguished in the middle of the cosmic
egg. It is like a vegetative *Grund*; and it is the first form taken by
the Earth-Mother. As soon as they separate from one another,
Heaven and Earth also manifest themselves in the human forms
of a man and a woman.

And now a strange fact presents itself: the *Nihongi* tells us
that "the three celestial divinities" command Heaven and Earth
to complete the Creation; that is, to create the land of Japan.
According to the other Japanese text describing the cosmogony,
the *Kojiki*, it cannot be decided whether the three celestial divinities existed *before*, or only appeared in Heaven *after* the separation
of Heaven from Earth. We are therefore dealing with two distinct and contradictory traditions: according to the former, the
cosmos developed spontaneously from a primordial egg in which
the two polar principles co-existed; while according to the latter
the celestial gods had always dwelt in the sky and it was they who
decreed the Creation. It is very probable that this second tradition
—which implies the pre-existence of a primordial and all-
powerful heavenly god—is chronologically the more ancient, for
in Japanese cosmology this tradition is already on the way to disappearance. The phenomenon of a gradual fading-out of the
heavenly gods is well known elsewhere. Celestial gods lose their

[1]The different variants of the Japanese cosmogonic myth, as they have been preserved
in *Kojiki* and *Nihonji*, betray Taoist influences; *yin* and *yang* correspond to Izanagi and
Izanami; *cf.* Franz Kiichi Numazawa, *Die Weltfange in der Japanischen Mythologie*, Paris–
Lucerne 1946, pp. 41ff. But it is likely that the Japanese knew the cosmogonic myth before
having come under Chinese influence. In China itself, the Taoist mythology is not autochthonous; it seems to have been of a southern origin (*cf.* Numazawa, *op. cit.*, p. 428).

religious importance, withdraw themselves from the Earth and human beings and grow indifferent—*dii otiosi*.

That is what is happening in the Japanese cosmology. Whatever may be the truth about those three celestial gods, their function is limited to ordering Izanami and Izanagi to continue and complete the Creation. They do not intervene in that tremendous work. Their function is of a spiritual order; they make regulations and see to it that a certain norm is respected. For example, when Heaven and Earth are wedded, and it is Earth who first pronounces the formula of marriage, the three gods annul the rite, for it ought to have proceeded in just the opposite way: it is for Heaven—that is, the husband—to speak first; the woman has to do no more than repeat the formula. We can discern in this the conflict between the two ideologies, the matriarchal and the patriarchal, and the victory of the latter. Indeed, their first child, born of the matriarchal type of union, who is called the "bloodsucker", is abandoned as too weak.[1] After having repeated the marriage formula in the patriarchal form, Heaven and Earth unite again, and give birth to all the Japanese archipelago and to all the gods. The last-born is the god of Fire. But this child-birth is fatal to Izanami; the fire burns her in the womb and she dies. During her agony, Izanami gives birth from her own body—that is, without hierogamy—to other gods, especially to aquatic and agricultural divinities; and this is a very important mythological motif, to which we shall have to return.

After death, Izanami descends beneath the earth. The husband Izanagi goes in search of her, just like Orpheus descending into the Shades to recover Eurydice. Under the earth it is very dark; but Izanagi finally meets his wife and offers to bring her back with him. Izanami begs him to wait at the door of the subterranean palace, and not to show a light. But the husband loses patience; he lights a tooth of his comb and enters the palace where, by the flame of this torch, he perceives Izanami in process of decomposition; and, seized with panic, he takes to flight. His dead wife pursues him, but Izanagi manages to escape by the same way that

[1]This is, in reality, a case of the myth of the abandonment of the solar hero; *cf.*, Numazawa, *op. cit.*, pp. 197ff. *Cf.* also L. Frobenius, *Das Zeitalter des Sonnengottes*, Berlin 1904, pp. 225ff.

he had gone down under the earth, and casts a great rock down over the aperture. Husband and wife talk together for the last time, separated from each other by this rock. Izanagi pronounces the sacramental formula for separation between them, and then goes up to heaven; while Izanami goes down for ever into the subterranean regions. She becomes the Goddess of the dead, and this corresponds to what is generally the case with chthonic and agricultural Goddesses, who are divinities of fecundity and, at the same time, of death, of birth, and of re-entry into the maternal bosom.

SEXUALITY, DEATH, CREATION

This Japanese myth is important in several respects: (1) it shows us the primordial situation, the *whole* which presented itself as a *coincidentia oppositorum*, and therefore also as androgynous; (2) this wholeness was antecedent to the hierogamy, the marriage of Heaven and Earth, but nevertheless it already bore within itself a "germ", an *Urgrund* which could be regarded as the progeny of the divine androgyny; (3) the cosmogony begins with the separation of Heaven from Earth; the primordial "germ" transforms itself into a Reed out of which spring a number of gods; (4) it is after the separation that we have what can be called a hierogamy —that the union of the two cosmic principles produces the creation of the world and at the same time of the other gods; and lastly (5) it should be emphasised that the Earth-Mother dies in giving birth to Fire (a homologue for the Sun) and that the divinities of telluric and vegetative fecundity are born from her body. It is this last motif which interests us above all. For it tells us of the creation of the edible plants out of the actual body of the Goddess, not as the result of the hierogamy: it is a creation coincident with the death of Izanami—that is, with her sacrifice.

For this is a case of sacrifice, of an immolation. That emerges very clearly from the story of another divinity, Ukemochi, daughter of Izanami. According to the *Nihongi*, Ukemochi was murdered by the god of the Sun, Tsukiyomi, and from her dead body all sorts of animal and vegetable species were born: the bull and the horse came out of the top of her head, millet from her forehead, the silk-worms from her eyebrows; different varieties of beans from her vagina.[1] Let us specially note that the creation is completed and perfected either by a hierogamy or else by a violent death; which means that the creation depends both upon sexuality and upon sacrifice, voluntary sacrifice above all. Indeed, the myth of the origin of the edible plants—a myth very widely distributed—always has to do with the spontaneous sacrifice of a divine being; who may be a mother, or a young woman, a child or a man. In Indonesia, for instance, it is almost always a mother or a girl who immolates herself in order to produce from her own body various kinds of edible plants;[2] in New Guinea, in Melanesia and Polynesia, it is generally a masculine divine being.[3]

CREATION AND SACRIFICE

Let us linger a moment over this mythic motif, for the matter is becoming complicated. It would seem that we are now dealing with a myth of extremely wide distribution, and one which appears in a considerable number of forms and variants. But this is the essential theme: that Creation cannot take place except from *a living being who is immolated*—a primordial androgynous giant, or a cosmic Male, or a Mother Goddess or a mythic Young Woman. We note, too, that this "Creation" applies on all the levels of existence: it may refer to the Creation of the Cosmos, or of humanity, or of only one particular human race, or of certain vegetable species or certain animals. The mythic pattern remains the same: nothing can be created without immolation, without sacrifice. It is thus that certain myths tell us about the creation of the world out of the actual body of a primordial Giant: Ymir, P'an-Ku, Purusha. Other myths reveal to us how human races or different social classes came to birth, always from a primordial

[1] F. K. Numazawa, *op. cit.*, pp. 244–245. See also his pp. 246ff., the myth recounted by *Kojiki*: the goddess Oho-ge-tsu-hime put to death by Susanowo.

[2] *Cf.* Ad. E. Jensen, *Hainuwele*, Frankfurt a-M, 1939, pp. 59ff.; also the same author's *Das religiöse Weltbild einer frühen Kultur*, Stuttgart, 1948.

[3] *Cf.* Gudmund Hatt, "The Corn-Mother in America and Indonesia" in *Anthropos*, XLVI, 1951, (pp. 853–914), p. 892.

Giant or an Ancestor who is sacrificed and dismembered.[1] Finally, as we have just seen, the edible plants have a similar origin; they sprang from the body of an immolated divine being.[2]

This myth of creation by a violent death transcends, therefore, the mythology of the Earth-Mother. The fundamental idea is that Life can only take birth from another life which is sacrificed. The violent death is creative—in this sense, that the life which is sacrificed manifests itself in a more brilliant form upon another plane of existence. The sacrifice brings about a tremendous transference: the life concentrated in one person overflows that person and manifests itself on the cosmic or collective scale. A single being transforms itself into a Cosmos, or takes multiple re-birth in a whole vegetable species or race of mankind. A living "whole" bursts into fragments and disperses itself in myriads of animated forms. In other terms, here again we find the well-known cosmogonic pattern of the primordial "wholeness" broken into fragments by the act of Creation.

From this we can understand why the myth of the creation of the useful plants and animals out of the body of a sacrificed divine being was incorporated into the mythology of the Earth-Mother. The Earth is the universal Genetrix and Nurse above all others: she creates by hierogamy with Heaven, but also by parthenogenesis or by self-immolation. Traces of the parthenogenesis of the Earth-Mother survive even in highly evolved mythologies like the Greek: Hera, for instance, conceived by herself to give birth to Typhon, to Haephestos and to Ares.[3] The Earth-Mother embodies the archetype of fecundity, of inexhaustible creativity. That is why she has a tendency to assimilate the attributes and the myths of the divinities of fertility, whether they are human, aquatic or agricultural. But the converse of this is also true: these divinities appropriate the attributes of the Earth-Mother, and sometimes even replace her in the cult. And we can see why: the Waters, like the Mother, are rich with the germs of life, and the

[1] See A. W. Macdonald, "A propos de Prajâpati" in the *Journal Asiatique*, Vol. CCXL, 1052, pp. 323-338.

[2] *Cf.* also Mircea Eliade, "Le mandragore et les mythes de la naissance miraculeuse", *Zalmoxis*, III, Bucharest, 1942, pp. 3-48, for the survival of this mythic motif in folk-lore.

[3] Upon parthenogenesis and the autonomy of the Greek and Mediterranean goddesses, see Uberto Pestalozza, *Religione mediterranea*, pp. 191ff., and *passim*.

Moon, too, symbolises the universal becoming, the periodical creation and destruction. As for the goddesses of vegetation and agriculture, it is sometimes difficult to distinguish these from telluric goddesses; their myths reveal to us the same mystery of birth, of creation, and of dramatic death followed by resurrection. Reciprocal borrowings and mutual entanglements occur between the mythologies of all these divinities. One might say that the Earth-Mother constitutes a form that is "open" to, or susceptible of, indefinite enrichment, and that is why it takes in all the myths dealing with Life and Death, with Creation and generation, with sexuality and voluntary sacrifice.

RITES OF THE EARTH-MOTHER

This point stands out clearly in the rituals of the telluric goddesses. For their rites are repetitions of what happened *in illo tempore*, in mythical time; they re-actualise the primordial events recounted in the myths. Thus, in the rituals of the *Terra Mater*, we meet with the same mystery, a revelation of how Life was born from a seed hidden in an undifferentiated "whole", or how it was produced in consequence of the hierogamy between Heaven and Earth or, again, how it sprang from a violent death, in most cases voluntary.

We shall recall only a few of the examples, for they are well enough known. We know that in rituals that relate to the *Terra Mater* and the goddesses of telluric fecundity (who, as we saw, are also goddesses of vegetation and of agriculture) the women play important parts. We need not re-emphasise the symbolic assimilation of woman with the land and of the sexual act with agricultural labour. That symbolism is found everywhere to some degree in agrarian cultures, and has even survived in highly evolved civilisations. "Your women are unto you as fields," says the Korân. "The woman is the field and the male is the bestower of the seed," writes an Indian author.[1] It is because of this mystical

---

[1] Narada, commenting on this passage from Manu (IX, 33), writes: "The woman may be regarded as a field, the male as the seed." Upon the homologising of the woman with the furrow, and the double symbolism, sexual and agricultural, see our *Patterns in Comparative Religion*, pp. 257ff., 354ff.

identification of the woman with the land that the presence of women in agricultural operations is so much appreciated. But the religious function of the woman is attested especially by the ceremonial union in the fields, or by the orgies which mark certain dates in the agricultural calendar. For example, among the Oraons of Central India, the hierogamy which precedes and assures the harvest is ritually repeated every year; the marriage between Heaven and Earth is mimed by the priest and his wife; and until this ritual has been celebrated no work is done in the fields, for the earth is thought to be still virgin. The imitation of the divine marriage sometimes gives rise to veritable orgies.[1] But the meaning of the orgy is not difficult to understand; the orgy is a symbolic re-entry into chaos, into the primordial and un-differentiated state. It re-enacts the "confusion", the "totality" before the Creation, the cosmic Night, the cosmogonic egg. And one can guess why a whole community should re-actualise this regression into the undifferentiated.[2] It is to recover the original wholeness out of which sprang differentiated Life, and from which the Cosmos emerged. It is by such a symbolical and lurid reinte-gration into the pre-cosmological state that they hope to ensure an abundant harvest. For the harvest represents the Creation, the triumphal manifestation of a young, rich and perfect Form. "Perfection" is produced in the beginnings, *ab origine*. They hope, therefore, to recover the vital reserves and the germinal riches which were made manifest for the first time in the majestic act of the Creation.

But all this, let us repeat it, has religious significance. It must not be assumed that the cults of the Earth-Mother encourage immorality in the profane sense of the term. Sexual union and the orgy are rites celebrated in order to re-actualise primordial events. The rest of the time—that is, apart from the decisive moments of the agricultural calendar—the Earth-Mother is the guardian of the norms: among the Yahengo of the French Sudan she is the champion of morality and justice; among the Kulango of the

---

[1]*Cf.* Sir James Frazer, *The Magic Art and the Evolution of Kings*, Vol. I, pp. 76ff.; *Adonis, Attis, Osiris*, I, pp. 47ff.; *The Worship of Nature*, pp. 379ff.

[2]Upon the symbolism and ritual function of the orgy, see our *Patterns in Comparative Religion*, pp. 356ff.

Ivory Coast, the goddess hates criminals, thieves, magicians and malefactors. In Africa in general, the sins most abhorred by the Earth-Mother are crime, adultery, incest and all kinds of sexual misdemeanour[1]: in ancient Greece, both bloodshed and incest rendered the Earth barren.[2]

HUMAN SACRIFICES

We have just seen in what sense the myths of creation, either starting from a primordial wholeness, or by way of hierogamy, are re-enacted in the rituals of the Earth-Mother—rituals which include either ceremonial union (replica of the hierogamy) or the orgy (regression into the primordial chaos). It remains for us now to recapitulate a few rites in relation with that other myth of the Creation, which reveals the mystery of the Creation of the food-bearing plants through the sacrifice of a chthonic goddess. Now, there is evidence of human sacrifice almost everywhere in the agrarian religions, although such sacrifice had generally become only symbolical.[3] We possess, however, documentary proofs of real sacrifices: the best known being those of the *meriah* of the Khonds of India, and the sacrifices of women among the Aztecs.

Here, in a few words, is what these sacrifices consisted of. The *meriah* was a voluntary victim, bought by the community: he was allowed to live for years, he could marry and have children. A few days before the sacrifice, the *meriah* was consecrated, that is, he was identified with the divinity to be sacrificed; the people danced around, and worshipped him. After this, they prayed to the Earth: "O Goddess, we offer thee this sacrifice; give us good harvests, good seasons and good health!" And they added, turning to the victim: "We have bought thee and have not seized thee by force: now we sacrifice thee, and may no sin be accounted to us!" The ceremony also included an orgy lasting several days. Finally the *meriah* was drugged with opium, and,

[1]*Cf.* Frazer, *The Worship of Nature*, pp. 403, 405, 409, 420ff.
[2]*Cf.* our *Patterns in Comparative Religion*, pp. 255ff.
[3]See Frazer, *Spirits of the Corn*, I, pp. 149ff.; *The Golden Bough* (abridged edn.), pp. 406ff.; and our *Patterns in Comparative Religion*, pp. 341ff.

after they had strangled him, they cut him into pieces. Each of the villages received a fragment of his body which they buried in the fields. The remainder of the body was burnt, and the ashes strewn over the land.[1]

This bloody rite evidently corresponds to the myth of the dismemberment of a primordial divinity. The orgy which accompanies it enables us to glimpse another meaning as well: the fragments of the victim's body were assimilated to the seed that fecundates the Earth-Mother.[2]

Among the Aztecs, a very young woman, Xilonen, who symbolised the young maize, was beheaded; and three months later another woman, incarnating the goddess Toci, "Our Mother" (who represented the maize already harvested and ready for use), was also beheaded and flayed.[3] This was the ritual repetition of the birth of the plants by the self-sacrifice of the Goddess. Elsewhere, for example among the Pawnees, the body of the young woman was cut up and the pieces buried in the fields.[4]

Here we must stop, though we are far from having dealt with all the attributes or all the significant myths of the Earth-Mother. We have had to select, and inevitably some aspects of the subject have been left aside. We have said little of the nocturnal and funerary aspect of the Earth-Mother as the Goddess of Death, and nothing of her aggressive, terrifying and agonising characteristics. But even in respect of these negative aspects, one thing that must never be lost sight of, is that when the Earth becomes a goddess of Death, it is simply because she is felt to be the universal womb, the inexhaustible source of all creation. Death is not, in itself, a definitive end, not an absolute annihilation, as it is sometimes thought to be in the modern world. Death is likened to the seed

---

[1] *Cf.* Frazer, *Spirits of the Corn*, I, pp. 245ff.; *The Worship of Nature*, pp. 386ff.; and our *Patterns in Comparative Religion*, pp. 343ff.

[2] *Cf.* A. W.Macdonald, *A propos de Prajâpati*, pp. 332ff. Needless to say, the ritual of the dismemberment of a victim assimilated to any divinity whatever has a far more complex history; in the final analysis, the rites and myths of dismemberment come under the lunar symbolism, and consequently also imply the ideas of becoming, of death and resurrection, initiation, etc. (Upon the lunar symbolism, see our *Patterns in Comparative Religion*, pp. 154ff.)

[3] The classic description is still that of B. de Sahagun, *Histoire générale des choses de la Nouvelle-Espagne* (translated and annotated by D. Jourdanet and R. Simeon, Paris, 1880), pp. 94ff.; see Frazer's summary in *The Worship of Nature*, pp. 434ff. *Cf.* G. Hatt, "The Corn-Mother in America and Indonesia" in *Anthropos*, XLVI, 1951, pp. 870–871.

[4] Frazer, *Spirits of the Corn*, I, pp. 175ff.

which is sown in the bosom of the Earth-Mother to give birth to a new plant. Thus, one might speak of an optimistic view of death, since death is regarded as a return to the Mother, a temporary re-entry into the maternal bosom. That is why bodies buried in neolithic times are found lying in the embryonic position; the dead were laid in the earth in the attitude of the embryo in the womb, as though they were expected to come back to life again and again. The Earth-Mother, as the Japanese myth told us, was the first to die; but this death of Izanami was at the same time a sacrifice made in order to augment and extend the Creation. It followed that men, too, in their dying and being buried, were sacrifices to the Earth. It is thanks to that sacrifice, after all, that life can continue, and that the dead hope to be able to come back to life. The frightening aspect of the Earth-Mother, as the Goddess of Death, is explained by the cosmic necessity of sacrifice, which alone makes possible the passage from one mode of being to another and also ensures the uninterrupted circulation of Life.

However, one must not lose sight of this important point—that religious life has rarely been monopolised by one single "principle"; rarely has it given itself up to the veneration of a single god or a single goddess. As we have observed before, nowhere do we find a "pure and simple" religion, reducible to one form or one structure. The predominance of cults either celestial or telluric does not in the least exclude the co-existence of other cults and other symbolisms. In the study of a certain religious form, one is always in danger of giving it an exaggerated importance and passing too lightly over other religious practices which are really complementary, though sometimes they may appear incompatible. In studying the symbolism and worship of the Earth-Mother, one always has to take into account a whole mass of beliefs co-existent with this, which are often liable to pass unnoticed. "I am the son of the Earth and of the starry Heaven" is inscribed upon an Orphic tablet—and that declaration holds good for a very great number of religions.

VIII

Mysteries and Spiritual Regeneration

AUSTRALIAN COSMOGONY AND MYTHOLOGY

To THE Karadjeri, the mysteries—that is, their secret ceremonies of initiation—are connected with the cosmogony. More precisely, their entire ritual life depends upon the cosmogony. In *burari* times (the "times of the dream"), when the world was created and human societies were founded in the form that they still have today, the rites were also inaugurated—and ever since then they have been repeated with the greatest care, and without modification. As with the other archaic societies, so in the eyes of the Karadjeri, history is limited to a few events that took place in mythical times, *in illo tempore*; the acts of divine beings and of civilising Heroes. The Karadjeri do not regard themselves as having any right to intervene in history—to make, for their own part, a history that would be exclusive and proper to themselves, an "original" history; on the whole they do not recognise any originality: they repeat the exemplary actions performed in the dawn of time. But since these exemplary deeds were done by gods and divine beings, their periodic and obligatory repetition expresses, for archaic men, the desire to keep themselves in the sacred atmosphere of the cosmogony. The rejection of originality amounts, in fact, to a rejection of the profane world, a lack of interest in human history. The existence of archaic man consists, in the final reckoning, of a perpetual repetition of the exemplary models revealed at the beginning of Time. As we shall see presently, the mysteries are perpetuated by periodical re-presentations of these primordial revelations.

Here, then, is the knowledge of the Karadjeri.[1] In the times

---

[1] *Cf.* Ralph Piddington, "Karadjeri Initiation", in *Oceania*, III, 1932–33, pp. 46-8 7; and *An Introduction to Social Anthropology*, Edinburgh–London, 1950, pp. 91–105.

of the dream, two brothers named Bagadjimbiri came up out of the earth in the form of dingos; they afterwards turned into two human giants, so tall that their heads touched the sky. Before the appearance of the Bagadjimbiri nothing existed—neither trees, nor animals nor human beings. They came out of the earth just before dawn on the "first day". A few moments later they heard the cry of a little bird (*duru*) which always sings at break of day; and they knew that it was dawn. Until then, the Bagadjimbiri had known nothing. The two brothers afterwards saw the animals and the plants, and gave them names; and it was from that moment, because they had names, that plants and animals began *really* to exist. One of the Bagadjimbiri stopped to urinate; from curiosity, his brother stopped too, and imitated him. That is the reason why the Australian Karadjeri stop and take up a special position in order to urinate: they are imitating the primordial gesture.

The Bagadjimbiri afterwards turn towards the North. They see a star and the moon, and they give these the names of "star" and "moon". They meet with men and women: their family relationships, their divisions into clans, were defective, and the Bagadjimbiri organised them on the system which remains in force until this day. These human beings were, moreover, imperfect: they were without genital organs—and the two Bagadjimbiri took two species of mushrooms and thus provided them with the organs that they have now. The brothers stopped and ate a certain grain raw; but they immediately burst into laughter, because they knew that one ought not to eat it so; it had to be cooked—and since then men imitate them whenever they have this grain cooked. The Bagadjimbiri threw a *pirmal* (a kind of large baton) at an animal and killed it—and that is how men have done it ever since. A great many myths describe the manner in which the brothers Bagadjimbiri founded all the customs of the Karadjeri, and even their behaviour. Finally, they instituted the initiation ceremonies, and for the first time used the instruments of the mystery, which became sacred—the flint knife, the *rhombe* (bull-roarer) and the *pimbal*. But one man, Ngariman, killed the two brothers with a lance. Their mother, Dilga (for some myths say that they had a mother, although their gestation had been extra-uterine), who was far away, detected the odour of corpses upon the wind. At once milk began to flow from her breasts, fell upon the earth and, as a subterranean current, this flood of milk flowed to the place where the two heroes lay dead; and there it gushed like a torrent, revived the two brothers and drowned the murderer. Later on, the two Bagadjimbiri transformed themselves into water-snakes; and their spirits rose up into the sky, there to become what Europeans call the Cloud of Magellan.

THE KARADJERI INITIATION

These traditions make up the mythological foundation of Karadjeri life. The initiation mystery re-enacts the ceremonies instituted by the brothers Bagadjimbiri, although the meaning of some of the rituals is not altogether clear. It should be noted that initiation includes a good many ceremonies, spaced out over several years. Thus it is not a question of one rite of passage from adolescence to maturity: rather, it is a matter of one initiation, properly so-called, which is progressive, divided into degrees; and by means of which the boy is not only instructed in the myths, the traditions and social customs of the clan, but is trained, in the true sense of the term. He not only becomes physiologically adult, but is made capable of coping with the human condition, such as it was declared to be by the two mythical Bagadjimbiri beings.

The rites are somewhat complicated and difficult to summarise; we shall also have to restrict our account to the most important of them. The first, *milya*, marks the break with childhood: about the age of twelve, the boy is taken into the bush, and there he is anointed from head to foot with human blood. Some few months later his nose is pierced and a quill is introduced into the wound; the boy then receives a special name. The second and most important rite, that of circumcision, takes place two or three years later. It constitutes a mystery properly so-called. The boy is mourned by his family and the whole clan, as though he had died. In a sense he is already dead, for he is carried, at night, into the forest, where he hears the sacred songs for the first time. And the forest is a symbol for the beyond: we shall meet with it again in many of the initiatory rites and mysteries of primitive peoples. But other signs also indicate that the boy is in process of dying, that he is undergoing a radical change of being. On the next day, each of the men opens a vein in his arm and lets the blood flow into a receptacle. The boy, completely nude, with eyes bandaged and ears plugged so that he can neither see nor hear, and seated near a fire amid the smoke, has to drink a large quantity of blood. He is convinced that the blood will kill him, but happily, a little later, he sees that those of his relatives who are conducting his initiation are also drinking it. The boy still remains on the ground, with a shield over his knees; and the men come to him one by one, and let the blood flowing from their opened veins drip down upon his head. One of the relatives then girds him with a girdle made of human hair; and the whole group returns to the camp where the women and his relatives mourn for him once again. After the ritual meal the neophyte is given a torch ready lit for fire-lighting, and is told that this will enable him to light a fire in which his genital organs will be burnt up. On the following day a journey is begun, and this continues for twenty-four days, marked by a great many ceremonies which we cannot stop to describe. The boy is accompanied by some of his male relatives. During the ritual journey he must not speak; he may, at most, only give out a special sound to attract attention, and then intimate by gestures whatever he may be in need of. Moreover, during the whole time of his noviciate (that is, so long as he is a *malulu*, a boy in process of being initiated) he may not move without being led by the hand; he keeps his head lowered all the time and—from what observers have reported—his face is completely devoid of expression. "If it were not for the spontaneity with which he responds to the instructions," writes Piddington, " he might give one the impression of a mental defective."[1]

Upon his return to the camp, the neophyte receives visits from groups of all the clans that he has met with on his journey. When

---

[1] R. Piddington, *Karadjeri Initiation*, pp. 68–69.

these are approaching the camp, the women welcome them by throwing vegetables at their heads, and the visitors return the compliment with their boomerangs. This is a mock battle of a ritual character, but it may happen that a boomerang touches one of the women, and then a real brawl ensues. The neophyte, whose return to the camp has given rise to renewed lamentations and voluntary self-mutilations by his relatives, does not join in the festival, which follows at nightfall and consists of songs and dances representing various mythical events. Before dawn, the neophyte is led into the bush to be circumcised. He remains seated, with bandaged eyes and plugged ears, while several operators work in turn, using flint knives. This circumcision, it must be said, is rather complicated and terribly painful: the operators make an incision at the base of the genital organ and remove the whole of the epidermis of the member. All this while the relations are weeping in the camp.

When all is done, the operators—and they, too, are all weeping—file before the initiate, who remains seated with bent head and closed eyes. The operators throw boomerangs by way of presents, and tell him their real names. A group of young men, recently initiated, swing the bull-roarers which they show to the neophyte; the latter now sees these terrifying instruments for the first time; just like the women and all the non-initiated, he had always believed that the din made by the bull-roarer was the voice of a divine being.

When the blood on his wound is dry, the operators show him the flint instruments. And with that ceremony the initiation as such comes to an end; but the boy stays several nights longer in the bush. On the day of his return to the camp, his body is anointed all over with blood, and he arrives heralded by the noise of the bull-roarers, ceaselessly sounded by the young men. In the camp, the women and children hide themselves under branches and do not dare to come out until the men have finished burying the bull-roarers. The women receive the initiate with lamentations, and offer him food.

For two or three years, the circumcised young man remains at this stage of initiation and is called *miangu*. He then undergoes another operation, the sub-incision, a rite of less importance which only occupies a single day, and to which few neighbours are convened. Some time later a further ceremony is held, called *laribuga*: in the forest, while the men are singing a sacred song, the initiate climbs a tree. Piddington tells us that the subject of the song is connected with a myth about the tree, but that the Karadjeri have forgotten what it signifies. We can guess, however, the meaning of this ritual: the tree symbolises the axis of the cosmos, the Tree of the World: and by climbing it the initiate enters into Heaven. It is a case of the symbolic ascension to Heaven which is attested elsewhere by a great many Australian myths and rituals.[1] But fully initiated status is not yet attained. At certain intervals other ceremonies take place which cannot be described here. Let us merely observe that at the end of several years the *midedi* ceremony is held: the initiate, led by an old man, is shown the places where the *pirmal* (which are a sort of ritual poles) are buried. This is a long journey, almost an expedition, and the revelation is made by means of songs and, above all, of dances symbolising the journeys of the Bagadjimbiri. Finally, they explain to him how the Bagadjimbiri invented the ceremony of the *pirmal*.

MYSTERY AND INITIATION

We have dwelt upon the initiation of the Karadjeri because it is always instructive to know in detail at least one rite of the kind being studied. We are consequently obliged to deal briefly with the other initiations, but the example of the Karadjeri has shown us that things are not so simple as one might be led to believe by an over-concise presentation. We shall better understand the profound meaning of the Karadjeri initiation when we have reviewed some similar ceremonies among other peoples; but we are already able to point out certain specific features. As we said, more is involved than a mere rite of passage out of one age group into another. The initiation goes on for years, and the revelations

[1] *Cf.* M. Eliade, *Le chamanisme et les techniques de l'extase*, pp. 55ff., 125ff., etc.

are of several orders. There is, to begin with, the first and most terrible revelation, that of the sacred as the *tremendum*. The adolescent begins by being terrorised by a supernatural reality of which he experiences, for the first time, the power, the autonomy, the incommensurability; and, following upon this encounter with the divine terror, the neophyte dies: he dies to childhood—that is, to ignorance and irresponsibility. That is why his family lament and weep for him: when he comes back from the forest he will be another; he will no longer be the child he was. As we have just seen, he will have undergone a series of initiatory ordeals which compel him to confront fear, suffering and torture, but which compel him above all to assume a new mode of being, that which is proper to an adult—namely, that which is conditioned by the almost simultaneous revelation of the sacred, of death and of sexuality.

It must not be imagined that the Australians are conscious of all this, or that they invented the mystery of initiation consciously and voluntarily, as we invent a modern system of pedagogy. Their behaviour, like all the behaviour of archaic humanity, is existential: the Australians have reacted in this manner because they felt, in the depths of their being, their peculiar situation in the Universe—that is, when they realised the mystery of human existence. This mystery, we have just said, belongs to the experience of the sacred, to the revelation of sexuality and the consciousness of death. The child knows nothing of all these experiences; the adult man assumes them, one after another, and incorporates them into his new personality, that which he obtains after his ritual death and resurrection. These motifs—the *tremendum*, death and sexuality—recur endlessly, as we shall find in the course of our exposition. Let us say, at once, that the neophyte, when he dies to his infantile, profane and unregenerate life to be re-born into a new, sanctified existence, is also re-born to a mode of being which makes knowledge, consciousness and *wisdom* possible. The initiate is not only new-born; he is a man who is *informed*, who knows the mysteries, who has had revelations of a metaphysical order. During his training, he learns the holy secrets, the myths about the gods and the origin of the world, the true names of the gods, the realities behind the bull-roarers, the ritual knives, etc. Initiation is equivalent to becoming spiritually mature; and this, throughout the entire religious history of mankind, is an ever-recurrent theme—the initiate, he who has known the mysteries, is the man who is *informed*. But, as we saw, the initiation of the Karadjeri is only a faithful reproduction of the exemplary actions of the Bagadjimbiri. Still, these actions constitute a cosmogony, for it was the Bagadjimbiri who founded the world even as it is today. By repeating the acts of the two mythical brothers, the Karadjeri periodically recommence the creation of the world, they repeat the cosmogony. In short, at the initiation of each adolescent, one is present at a new cosmogony. The genesis of the world serves as the model for the "formation" of a man.

Everywhere one meets with mysteries of initiation, and everywhere, even in the most archaic societies, they include the symbolism of a death and a new birth. We cannot here undertake a historical analysis of initiation—such as might enable us to elucidate the relations between this and that cultural structure and the types of initiation—but let us retain at least certain characteristic features that are common to the majority of these secret ceremonies.[1]

(1) Everywhere the mystery begins with the separation of the neophyte from his family, and a "retreat" into the forest. In this there is already a symbolisation of death; the forest, the jungle and the darkness symbolise "the beyond", the Shades. In certain places it is believed that a tiger comes and carries the candidates into the jungle on its back; the wild animal incarnates the mythical Ancestor, the Master of the initiation who conducts the adolescents to the Shades. In other places the neophyte is supposed to be swallowed by a monster—an initiatory motif that will claim our attention later on: for the moment we are concerned with the

[1]*Cf.* Heinrich Schurtz, *Altersklassen und Männerbünde*, Berlin, 1902; H. Webster, *Primitive Secret Societies*, New York, 1908; J. G. Frazer, *Totemism and Exogamy*, 1910, III, pp. 457–550; E. M. Loeb, *Tribal Initiation and Secret Societies*, University of California Publications in American Archæology and Ethnology, Berkeley, 1929, Vol. 25, 3, pp. 249–288; Ad. E. Jensen, *Beschneidung und Reifezeremonien bei Naturvölkern*, Stuttgart, 1932. See also *Semaine d'Ethnologie Religieuse*; *compte rendu analytique de la IIIième session*, Enghien-Moedling, 1923, especially pp. 329–456. *Cf.* Richard Thurnwald, "Primitive Initiations-und Wiedergeburtsriten" in *Eranos Jahrbuch*, 1939, VII, Zürich, 1940, pp. 321–398; and M. Eliade, *Birth and Rebirth*, New York, 1958.

symbolism of darkness. In the belly of the monster it is cosmic Night; this is the embryonic mode of existence, both upon the plane of the cosmos and on the plane of human life.

(2) In many regions, there is a hut for initiations in the bush. It is there that young candidates undergo a part of their ordeals and are instructed in the secret traditions of the tribe. And the initiation-cabin symbolises the maternal womb.[1] The death of the neophyte signifies a regression to the embryonic state, but this must not be understood only in terms of human physiology but also, and chiefly, in cosmological terms; the fœtal condition is equivalent to a temporary regression into the *virtual*, or precosmic mode of being before "the dawn of the first day" as the Karadjeri say. We shall have an opportunity to return to this multivalent symbol of a new birth expressed in terms of gestation. For the present, let us add this: the candidate's regression to the pre-natal stage is meant to render him contemporary with the creation of the world. He now lives no longer in the maternal womb as he did before his biological birth, but in the cosmic Night and in expectation of the "dawn"—that is, of the Creation. To become a new man, he has to re-live the cosmology.

(3) Other rituals throw light upon the symbolism of the initiatory death. Among certain peoples, the candidates are buried or laid out in newly dug graves. They are either covered with branches, and remain motionless like the dead; or they are rubbed with a white powder to make them look like ghosts. The neophytes also imitate the behaviour of ghosts: they do not use their fingers in eating, but pick up the food directly with the teeth as the souls of the dead are believed to do. Finally, the tortures that they undergo, and which of course have a multitude of meanings, have this one among others: the tortured and mutilated neophyte is supposed to be tortured, dismembered, boiled or grilled by the demon-masters of initiation—that is by the mythic Ancestors. His physical sufferings correspond to the situation of the man who is "eaten" by the demonic wild animal, is cut to pieces between the jaws of that initiatory monster and is digested in his belly.

[1] R. Thurnwald, "Primitive Initiations- und Wiedergeburtsriten", p. 393. See also Frazer, *Spirits of the Corn*, I, pp. 225ff.

The initiates' mutilations, too, are charged with a symbolism of death. The majority of those mutilations come under the lunar deities. Now, the Moon disappears—that is, dies—periodically, to be born again three nights later; and this lunar symbolism stresses the idea that death is the first condition of all mystical regeneration.

(4) Besides specific operations—such as circumcision and sub-incision—and apart from initiatory mutilations (extractions of teeth, amputations of fingers, etc.), there are other external marks of death and resurrection, such as tattooings and scarifications. As for the symbolism of the mystical rebirth, it presents itself in many forms. The candidates are given new names which for the future are to be their real names. In certain tribes, the young initiates are deemed to have forgotten all their previous lives; immediately after initiation they are fed like little children, led by the hand and taught how to behave in every way, as though they were babies. In the bush, they generally learn a new language, or at least a secret vocabulary known only to the initiates. Thus, we see, at an initiation everything begins anew. *Incipit vita nova.* Sometimes the symbolism of the "second birth" is expressed in concrete gestures. Among some Bantu peoples the boy who is to be circumcised is the object of a ceremony known explicitly as "being born anew".[1] The father sacrifices a ram; and three days later he envelops the child in the animal's stomach-membrane and in its skin. Before being thus attired, the child has to climb into the bed beside his mother and cry like a new-born infant. He remains in the ram's skin for three days and, on the fourth, the father cohabits with his wife. Among these same people, the dead are buried in rams' skins and in the embryonic position. We will say no more here about the symbolism of the mystical rebirth for which one is ritually dressed in the skin of an animal—a symbolism that is attested both in ancient Egypt and in India.[2]

(5) Finally, we must say a few words about another motif which appears in a great many initiations, and not always in the

[1] M. Canney, "The Skin of Rebirth", in *Man*, July, 1939, No. 91, pp. 104-105; *cf.* C. W. Hobley, *Bantu Beliefs and Magic*, London, 1922, pp. 78ff. and 98ff.

[2] *Cf.* E. A. Wallis Budge, *From Fetish to God in Ancient Egypt*, Oxford, 1934, p. 494; S. Stevenson, *The Rites of the Twice-born*, London, 1920, pp. 33, 40, etc.

most primitive societies. It concerns the injunction to kill a man. Here, for instance, is what happens among the Papuan Koko.[1] The candidate has first to undergo ordeals analogous to those of any other initiation—prolonged fasting, solitude, tortures, the revelation of the bull-roarer and traditional instruction. But in the end they say to him: "Now you have seen the Spirit, and you are a real man. In order to prove that in your own eyes, you must slay a man." Head-hunting, and certain forms of cannibalism, are parts of the same initiatory schema. Before pronouncing a moral judgment upon these customs, one should remember this—that to kill a man, and eat him or preserve his head as a trophy, is to imitate the behaviour of the Spirits, or of the gods. Thus, replaced in its own context, the act is a religious one, a ritual. The neophyte must kill a man because the god did so before him; furthermore he, the neophyte, has just been killed by the god during initiation; he has known death. He has to repeat what has been revealed to him: the mystery instituted by the gods in mythic times.

We have alluded to this type of ritual because it has played a very great part in military initiations, above all in proto-historical Europe. The warrior hero is not only a killer of dragons and other monsters; he is also a killer of men. The heroic duel is a sacrifice: war is a decadent ritual in which a holocaust of in-numerable victims is offered up to the gods of victory.

Let us come back once more to the primitive mysteries of initiation. Everywhere we have found the symbolism of death as the ground of all spiritual birth—that is, of regeneration. In all these contexts death signifies the surpassing of the profane, non-sanctified condition, the condition of the "natural man", ignorant of religion and blind to the spiritual. The mystery of initiation discloses to the neophyte, little by little, the true dimensions of existence; by introducing him to the sacred, the mystery obliges him to assume the responsibilities of a man. Let us remember this fact, for it is important—that access to the spiritual is expressed, in archaic societies, by a symbolism of Death.

[1] E. W. P. Chinnery and W. N. Beaver, "Notes on the Initiation Ceremony of the Koko; Papua" in *Journal of the Royal Anthropological Institute*, No. 45, 1915, (pp. 69–78), especially pp. 76ff.

"MEN'S SOCIETIES" AND SECRET SOCIETIES

Besides these ceremonies held at the attainment of puberty, there are other mysteries reserved to the adult: these are the "men's societies", the *Männerbünde*, or the secret societies, of which no one can gain knowledge or become a member until he has endured another series of initiatory ordeals. The morphology of these *Männerbünde* is considerable, and we cannot depict their structure or history here.[1] As for the history of the men's secret societies, the most commonly admitted hypothesis is the one suggested by Frobenius and adopted by the historico-cultural school[2]: according to this hypothesis, the masculine secret societies were a creation of the matriarchal cycle; their object was to terrify the women, chiefly by leading them to believe that the masquerades were those of demons and spirits of the dead, and this in order to shake off the feminine domination produced by the matriarchate. For reasons we cannot develop here, this hypothesis does not seem to us well founded. It is possible that the societies of maskers played a part in the struggle for male supremacy, but there is no proof that the secret societies, as a general phenomenon, were a consequence of the matriarchate. We find, on the contrary, a perfect continuity between the rites of puberty which we have just analysed, and the ordeals of initiation into membership of the men's secret societies. Throughout Oceania, for example, both the initiations of the boys and those required for membership of the men's secret societies included the same symbolic ritual of death, through being swallowed by a monster, and of a subsequent resurrection: which proves that these forms derive from the same source.[3] Hence the alternative conclusion, which seems to us irresistible, is that the men's secret societies, the *Männerbünde*, derive from the mysteries of the tribal initiation.

[1] See the works quoted above in footnote on p. 197 of the present chapter. *Cf.* also C. H. Wedgwood, "The Nature and Function of Secret Societies" in *Oceania* I, 2, 1930, pp. 129-151; Will-Erich Peuckert, *Geheimkulte*, Heidelberg, 1951.

[2] *Cf. e.g.*, *Semaine d'Ethnologie Religieuse* III, pp. 335ff.; and W. Schmidt, *Das Mutterrecht*, Vienna, 1955, pp. 170ff.

[3] *Cf.* E. M. Loeb, *Tribal Initiation and Secret Societies*, p. 262.

It remains for us now to explain the origin and aim of these new secret associations. First of all, we must remark that there are both exclusively masculine and exclusively feminine societies of the mysteries, although the latter are fewer in number. One is tempted to ascribe the emergence of feminine secret societies to a desire to copy the associations of the men; and it is quite possible that such a process of imitation might be verified in certain regions. But, as we shall see later, the secret societies of women, the *Weiberbünde*, derive some feminine rites from the pubertal initiation connected with the first menstruation. Nothing therefore obliges us to assume that the men organised themselves into secret societies in reaction against the matriarchate, nor that the women in their turn imitated the men by organising *Weiberbünde* to forearm themselves against terrorism by the men. It is not denied —let us repeat—that such a phenomenon of reaction and counter-reaction may often be observed in the religious history of humanity, but this is not something innate and originative. The original phenomenon is the initiation mystery which is enacted by both the young men and the girls at the age of puberty. All other kinds of mysteries derive from this primordial revelation that everyone has to receive in order to become a *man* or a *woman*. And the only plausible explanation for the appearance of secret societies devoted to the mysteries is to be sought in the desire to live, as intensely as possible, the sacraments specific to each of the two sexes.

It is for this reason that initiation into the secret societies so closely resembles the rites of initiation at puberty; we find here the same ordeals, the same symbols of death and resurrection, the same revelation of a traditional and secret doctrine—and we meet with these because the initiation-scenario constitutes the condition *sine qua non* of a new and more complete experience of the sacred. A difference of degree has, however, been observed: in the *Männerbünde*, secrecy plays a greater part than it does in tribal initiations. Rites of puberty do exist which are not absolutely secret (this is the case with the Fuegians, for instance)—but there is no mystery-society without its oath of secrecy, or, to be more exact, there were none so long as the indigenous peoples preserved their ancestral traditions intact. For this there are two reasons: first, that membership of a secret society already implies selection; not all of those who have undergone the tribal initiation will take part in the secret society, even if all would like to. The second reason for the reinforcement of secrecy is more of a historic order: the world changes, even for primitive peoples, and certain ancestral traditions are in danger of decay. To prevent their deterioration, the teachings are transmitted more and more under the veil of secrecy. This is the well-known phenomenon of the "occultation" of a doctrine when the society which has preserved it is in course of radical transformation. The same thing came to pass in Europe, after the urban societies had been Christianised; the pre-Christian religious traditions were conserved, camouflaged or superficially Christianised, in the countryside; but above all they were hidden in the closed circles of the sorcerers. It would be an illusion, then, to suppose that we know the actual traditions transmitted by the secret mystery societies. As a rule, observers have been able to record no more than some secondary rituals and a few songs. Nevertheless, their symbolism is clear—and that is how we are enabled to discover the meaning of their ceremonies.

Here, for example, is the rite of initiation into the secret cult of Ngoye (Ndsasa) among the Kuta—a brotherhood "so exclusive that only the chiefs of the clan can belong to it".[1] The adepts are whipped with a thong of panther hide; and, after that, are bound to a horizontal pole placed about a yard from the ground—and "it is in the course of this rite", we are told, "that many neophytes are seized with dread, and make desperate efforts to escape."[2] Yet from the description given, it is difficult to see the cause of their terror, and this leads us to suspect that some more formidable rite is involved which the ethnologists have not been able to observe. The neophytes are then rubbed with "stinging leaves" and their bodies and their hair are coated with a plant which causes frightful itching. We may observe, by the way, that to be whipped or rubbed with nettles is a ritual that symbolises the neophyte's being cut to pieces and put to death by demons. We find the

[1] E. Andersson, *Contribution à l'Ethnographie des Kuta*, I, Upsala, 1953, p. 211.
[2] E. Andersson, *op. cit.*, pp. 213–219.

same symbolism and the same rites again in shamanic initiations.[1] Lastly, another ordeal "consists in making the adept climb a tree five or six metres high, where he has to drink a medicament preserved in a *mukungu*. On re-entering the village, the neophyte is welcomed by the women in tears: they weep . . . as though the neophyte were about to die." Among some other Kuta tribes, the neophyte is beaten with extreme violence, and they say that they are "killing" his old name, so as to be able to give him another. We need not comment at length on these rites. As in the case of the initiations at puberty, they are concerned with a symbolical death and resurrection followed by an ascension into heaven.

Among the Mandja and the Banda, there is a society known by the name of Ngakola. "According to the myth that is recounted to the neophytes when they are being initiated, Ngakola once used to live on earth. His body was very dark and covered with long hair. No one knew whence he came, but he lived in the bush near to a swampy stream of water . . . He had the power to kill a man and afterwards breathe a new life into him; he could even make a better man of him." So he proclaimed to mankind: "Send me some people, and I will eat them and then vomit them forth renovated!" They took his advice, but when Ngakola gave back only half as many as he had swallowed, men decided to avenge themselves: they gave him "to eat great quantities of cassava, with stones mingled in it—so much, that they managed to weaken the monster until they could kill it with knives and assegais". This myth forms the basis and the justification for the secret society's ritual. A sacred flat stone plays a great part in the initiation ceremonies: according to tradition, this sacred stone was taken out of the body of Ngakola. The neophyte is shut up in a little hut which symbolises the body of the monster: it is there that he hears the lugubrious voice of Ngakola; it is there that he is whipped and undergoes tortures; for, as they tell him, "he has now entered into the body of Ngakola" and is in process of being digested. The other initiates chant in chorus, "Ngakola, take our bowels from all of us! Ngakola, take the livers from us all!" After further ordeals, the master initiator finally announces that

[1] *Cf.* M. Eliade, *Le Chamanisme* . . . pp. 47ff., 55ff., 65ff.

Ngakola, having eaten up the neophyte, has just given him back again.[1]

Here we find, again, the symbolism of death in the belly of a monster—which plays so great a part in the initiations of puberty. Observe, once more, that the rites of entry into a secret society correspond at all points to the tribal initiations: seclusion, initiatory tortures and ordeals, death and resurrection, imposition of a new name, the learning of a secret language, etc. This emerges still more clearly from the description given us by a Belgian missionary, Léo Bittremieux, of the secret society of the Bakhimba of Mayumba.[2] Here the initiation-ordeals continue for from two to five years, and the most important consists of a ceremony of death and resurrection. The neophyte has to be "killed", a scene which is acted at night, and the old initiates "sing, to the rhythm of the dance-drums, the dirge of the mothers and relatives over those who are about to die". The candidate is scourged, and drinks, for the first time, a narcotic beverage called "the drink of death", but he also eats some calabash seeds, which symbolise the intelligence—a significant detail, for it indicates that through death one attains to wisdom. When he has drunk the "drink of death" the candidate is seized by the hand, and one of the old men makes him turn round and round until he falls to the ground. Then they cry, "O, so-and-so is dead!" A native informant states that "they roll the dead man to earth while the chorus intone a funeral dirge: 'He is quite dead, ah! he is quite dead! The Khimba —I shall never see him again!'"

And in the same way, in the village, he is also mourned by his mother, his brother and his sister. Afterwards "the dead" are carried away, on their backs, by relatives who are already initiated, into a consecrated enclosure called "the court of resurrection". There they are laid, naked, in a grave dug in the form of a cross, and remain there until the dawn of the day of "commutation" or of "resurrection", which is on the first day of the natives' four-day week. The neophytes then have their heads shaven, are beaten,

[1] E. Andersson, *op. cit.*, pp. 264–266.
[2] Léo Bittremieux, *La Société secrète des Bakhimba au Mayombe*, Brussels, 1936. A very important African secret society is the *poro* of Sierra Leone and Liberia: see, lastly, K. Little, "The Poro Society as an Arbiter of Culture" in *African Studies*, VII, 1948, pp. 1–15.

thrown down to earth and, lastly, are revived by letting a few drops of a very peppery liquid drip into their eyes and nostrils. But before the "resurrection" they have to take the oath of absolute secrecy: "All that I shall see here, I will tell to nobody, neither to a woman nor to a man; to no profane person, nor to any white one; blow me up, kill me if I do!"[1] *All that I shall see here*—the neophyte, then, has not yet *seen* the true mystery. His initiation—that is, his ritual death and resurrection—is only the condition *sine qua non* for his attendance at the sacred mysteries, and about these we have very little information.

It is impossible for us to discuss the other male secret societies —those of Oceania,[2] for instance, especially the *dukduk*, whose mysteries, and the terror it wields over the non-initiated, have so deeply impressed observers; or the masculine fraternities of North America, celebrated for their initiatory tortures. It is known, for example, that among the Mandan—where the rite of tribal initiation was at the same time that of entry into the secret con-fraternity—the torture surpassed all imagination: two men thrust knives into the muscles of the victim's breast and back, put their fingers deep into the wounds, passed a loop under the muscles, attached it to cords and hoisted the neophyte into the air; but before slinging him up, they inserted, through the muscles of the arms and legs, pegs to which they had tied heavy stones and buffalo heads. The way in which the young men endured this terrible torture, says Catlin,[3] verges on the fabulous: not a feature of their faces moved while the torturers were butchering their flesh. Once the victim was suspended in the air, a man began to make him spin like a top, faster and faster, until the wretched man lost consciousness and his body hung as though dislocated.

[1] *Ibid.*, pp. 50–52.

[2] Concerning the *dukduk*, see the classic description of Romilly, *The Western Pacific and New Guinea*, pp. 27–33, reproduced by Webster, *Secret Societies*, pp. 111ff., and by O. E. Briem, *Les Sociétés secrètes de mystères* (trans. from the Swedish), Paris, 1941, pp. 38ff. See also R. Piddington, *Introduction to Social Anthropology*, pp. 208–209. The *arioi* secret societies of the Society Islands represent another type of brotherhood; *cf.* R. W. William-son and R. Piddington, *Essays in Polynesian Mythology*, Cambridge, 1939, pp. 113–153; and then W. E. Mühlmann, *Arioi und Mamaia*, Wiesbaden, 1955.

[3] George Catlin, *O-Kee-Pa*, London, 1867, pp. 13ff., 28ff.; and the same author in the *Annual Report of the Smithsonian Institution for 1885*, Washington, 1886, 2nd Part, pp. 309ff. *Cf.* the summary given by O. E. Briem, *Les Sociétés secrètes de mystères*, pp. 94–95.

THE INITIATORY SIGNIFICANCE
OF SUFFERING

What can be the meaning of such tortures? The first European observers used to speak of the innate cruelty of the natives. However, that is not the explanation: the natives are no more cruel than the civilised. But for every traditional society, suffering has a ritual value, for the torture is believed to be inflicted by superhuman beings and its purpose is the spiritual transmutation of the victim. The torture is, in itself, an expression of initiatory death. To be tortured means that one is cut into pieces by the demon-masters of initiation, that one is put to death by dismemberment. We may recall how St Anthony was tortured by devils; he was lifted into the air, smothered under the earth; the devils gashed his flesh, dislocated his limbs and cut him to pieces. Christian tradition calls these tortures "the temptation of St Anthony"—and that is true to the degree that the temptation is homologised with the initiatory ordeal. In confronting all these ordeals victoriously—that is, in resisting all the "temptations"— the monk Anthony becomes holy. That is to say that he has "killed" the profane man that he was, and has come to life again as another, a regenerated man, a saint. But in a non-Christian perspective, this also means that the demons have succeeded in their aim, which was just that of "killing" the profane man and enabling him to regenerate himself. In identifying the forces of evil with the devils Christianity has deprived them of any positive function in the economy of salvation: but before Christianity the demons were, among others, masters of initiation. They seized the neophytes, tortured them, subjected them to a great number of ordeals, and finally killed them so that they could be born again, regenerated both in body and soul. It is significant that they discharge the same initiatory function in the temptation of St Anthony; for, after all, it was their tortures and "temptations" that provided opportunity for St Anthony to attain to sainthood.

These reflections are not a digression from our subject. What we want to emphasise is this: that the initiatory tortures of the Mandan were not inspired by an innate cruelty in the American-Indian nature; that they were of a ritual significance, namely, that of being cut to pieces by the demons of initiation. This religious evaluation of suffering is confirmed by other facts: certain grave illnesses, psycho-mental maladies above all, are regarded by the primitives as "demonic possession", in the sense that the sufferer has been chosen by divine beings to become a shaman and a mystic: it follows that he is in process of being initiated—that is, tortured, cut to pieces and "killed" by "demons". We have recorded elsewhere a number of examples of such initiatory maladies suffered by future shamans.[1] Our conclusion, therefore, must be as follows: that sufferings, both physical and psychic, are homologous with the tortures that are inseparable from initiation; illness was esteemed among primitives as the sign of a supernatural election; and was therefore regarded as an initiatory ordeal. One had to "die" to something to be able to be re-born; that is, to be cured: one died to what one was before, died to the profane condition; the man who was effecting this cure was another, a newborn man—in this case, a shaman, a mystic.

At different levels and in various contexts we find the same initiatory schema comprising ordeals, tortures, ritual putting-to-death, and symbolic resurrection. We have now identified this scenario of spiritual regeneration both in the initiations effected at puberty, which are obligatory for all members of the clan, and in the secret associations of the men, which create a "closed circle" within the clan. But we observe, furthermore, that individual mythical vocations, as well as the initiatory illnesses of future shamans, comprise the same scenario of sufferings, torture, death and resurrection; and all this compels us to conclude that the mystery of spiritual regeneration consists of an archetypal process which is realised on different planes in many ways; it is effected whenever the need is to surpass one mode of being and to

[1] See *Le Chamanisme . . .* pp. 45ff., and above, pp. 75ff. Upon the alchemical symbolism of the "torture" in its psychological context, see the work of C. G. Jung, *Psychology and Alchemy*, London, 1953, pp. 320ff. *et passim; Von den Wurzeln des Bewusstseins*, Zurich, 1954, pp. 154ff., 211ff., etc.

enter upon another, higher mode; or, more precisely, whenever it is a question of spiritual transmutation.

The perfect solidarity and continuity between the mystery of the pubertal initiations, the rituals of the secret societies and the intimate experiences which determine the mystical vocation seem to us highly significant; we shall, however, come back to this later.

THE "WOMEN'S MYSTERIES"

There has been less study of what may be called the Women's Mysteries, for which reason we are still poorly informed about the content of feminine initiations. Nevertheless, there are striking resemblances between the two classes of mysteries, masculine and feminine. Corresponding to the rites of passage from one age group to the next, there is the segregation of the young women following upon the first menstruation; the societies of men, the *Männerbünde*, are matched by the women's societies, the *Weiberbünde*; and, lastly, the initiatory rites constitutive of the men's confraternities are also found in exclusively feminine mysteries. Admittedly, these are correspondences of a general order; in the initiatory rites and mysteries reserved to women we should not expect to find symbolism, or, more precisely, symbolical expressions, identical with those we have just discovered in the men's initiations and fraternities. There is, however, one common element: it is always a profound religious experience that is the basis of all these rites and mysteries. It is the *access to the sacred*, as it reveals itself upon assuming the condition of woman, that constitutes the aim and object, both of the initiatory rites of puberty and of the feminine secret societies.

Initiation begins at the first menstruation. The physiological symptom ordains a rupture, the uprooting of the girl from her familiar world: she is immediately isolated, separated from the community. We need not concern ourselves here with the myths evoked by the natives to account for both the appearance of the first menstrual blood and its malefic character. We may also ignore the theories elaborated by ethnologists and modern sociologists to account for this strange behaviour. It is enough to mention that isolation is imposed at once, that it takes place in a special hut or cabin in the bush, or in some obscure corner of the habitation, and that the young menstruant has to remain there in a special, rather uncomfortable position, and must avoid being "seen" by the sun, or touched by any person whomsoever. She wears a special dress, or a sign or a colour in some way exclusive to her, and must feed herself with uncooked food.[1]

Certain details strike one at once—segregation and seclusion in shadow, in a dark hut in the bush. This reminds one of the symbolism of the initiatory death of the boys, alone in the forest, shut up in huts. Only there is this difference that, with the girls, seclusion takes place immediately upon the first menstruation and is therefore individual; whereas the boys' initiation is performed in a group. But that difference explains itself by the physiological aspect of the end of childhood, more manifest in the girls. Their being set apart individually as soon as the menstrual signs appear, accounts for the feminine initiatory rites being rather few. Nevertheless they exist even in Australia among the Aranda, and in many regions of Africa.[2] One thing not to be overlooked, is that the period of isolation varies from one culture to another: from three days, as in India, to twenty months in New Ireland, or even several years in Cambodia. This means that the young women finally constitute a group, and then their initiation is completed collectively, under the admonition of old women. As we said just now, very little is known about the initiation of the girls. We do know, however, that they receive a fairly complete education in regard to certain traditions of the tribe[3] (as for instance among the Basuto), as well as in the secrets of sexuality. The period of initia-

[1]*Cf.* H. Ploss and M. Bartels, *Das Weib in der Natur- und Völkerkunde* I, Leipzig, 1908, pp. 454–502; Frazer, *Tabu and the Perils of the Soul*, pp. 204–233; R. Briffault, *The Mothers*, London, 1927, II, pp. 365–412; W. Schmidt and W. Koppers, *Völker und Kulturen*, I, Regensburg, 1924, pp. 273–275 (diffusion of the custom).

[2]B. Spencer and F. G. Gillen, *Native Tribes of Central Australia*, London, 1899, pp. 92ff., 269; and *Northern Tribes of Central Australia*, London, 1904, pp. 133ff.; C. H. Wedgwood, "Girls' Puberty Rites in Manam Island, New Guinea", in *Oceania*, IV, 2, 1933, pp. 132–155; Webster, *op. cit.*, pp. 45ff. (Africa).

[3]*Cf. e.g.*, Hehaka Sapa, *Les rites secrets des Indiens Sioux* (French translation), Paris, 1953, pp. 146ff.

tion comes to an end with a collective dance (a custom already observed among the *Pflanzervölker*[1]); in many regions the girl initiates are put on exhibition and fêted,[2] or they pay visits in procession, to receive gifts.[3] They may also be marked with external signs denoting the completion of initiation; tattooing, for example, or blackening of the teeth.[4]

There is no room here to study in greater detail the rites and customs of the young women's initiations. Let us recall, however, the ritual importance of certain feminine crafts which the neophytes are taught during the period of seclusion; in the first place, spinning and weaving, which play essential parts in the symbolism of numerous cosmologies.[5] It is the Moon that spins the Time, she who "weaves" the lives of humanity: the goddesses of fate are spinners. Creation or re-creation of the World, the spinning of Time and of destiny, on the one hand; and, on the other, nocturnal work, feminine work that must be done far from the light of the sun and in secret, almost in hiding; we can see the occult correspondence between the two orders of mystic reality. In certain places—as in Japan[6]—one can still discern the mythological memory of a lasting tension, and even a conflict, between the secret societies of young women and the societies of men, the *Männerbünde*. The men and their gods, during the night, attack the spinsters, destroy their work, break their shuttles and weaving-tackle. In other regions, it is during the initiatory seclusion that the old women teach, besides the art of spinning, the feminine ritual songs and dances, most of them erotic or even obscene. Their seclusion at an end, the young women continue to meet in the house of an old woman at spinning parties. We must underline the ritual character of this feminine occupation; spinning is very dangerous, and that is why it can only be done in special houses

---

[1] W. E. Peuckert, *Geheimkulte*, p. 258.
[2] Ploss and Bartels, *op. cit.*, I, pp. 464ff.; E. Gasparini, *Nozze, società e abitazione degli antichi Slavi*, Venice, 1954, (lithographed). Appendices 1 and 2, p. 13.
[3] Gasparini, *op. cit.*, p. 14.
[4] *Cf.* the bibliographical references in E. Gasparini, *op. cit.*, pp. 15ff., where one finds also an analysis of similar Slav customs.
[5] Mircea Eliade, *Images et Symboles*; *Essais sur le symbolisme magico-religieux*, pp. 120ff.
[6] *Cf.* Alex Slawik, "Kultische Geheimbünde der Japaner und Germanen" in *Wiener Beiträge zur Kulturgeschichte und Linguistik*, IV, Vienna, 1936, (pp. 675–675) pp. 737ff.; W. E. Peuckert, *Geheimkulte*, p. 253.

and only during certain periods and before certain hours. In some parts of the world they have given up spinning, and they have even forgotten it altogether, because of its magical danger.[1] Similar beliefs still persist in Europe in our own days (*cf.* Percht, Holda, Frau Holle, etc.). In short there is a secret link between the feminine initiations, spinning and sexuality.[2]

The young women enjoy a degree of pre-marital freedom, and the meetings with the boys take place in the house where spinning-meetings are held. The custom was still known in Russia at the beginning of the nineteenth century.[3] It is surprising that in the very cultures where virginity was held in high esteem, one finds that meetings between the young women and the young men were not only tolerated but encouraged by the parents. To Western observers—and in Europe to the clergy above all—such customs seemed to connote a dissolution of morals. Yet that is not the case here; it is not a question of morals, but of something deeper, essential to life. For the secret behind it is the revelation of the sacredness of the feminine; it concerns the sources of life and of fecundity. These pre-marital liberties of the young women are not of an erotic, but of a ritual character: they represent vestiges of a forgotten mystery and not profane enjoyments. We cannot otherwise explain the fact that in societies where modesty and chastity are obligatory, the girls and the women behave on certain sacred occasions—and that of marriage above all—in a manner that has so terribly shocked the observers. Thus—to mention but one example—in the Ukraine the women lift their skirts up to the waist to jump over the fire; they are said to be "burning the hair of the bride".[4] This complete reversal of behaviour—from modesty to exhibitionism—serves a ritual purpose, and is therefore in the interests of the whole community. The orgiastic character of this feminine mystery is explained by the need for a periodic abolition

---

[1] R. Heine-Geldern, *Südostasien*—G. Bushan, *Illustrierte Völkerkunde*, II, Stuttgart, 1923, p. 841; Gasparini, *op. cit.*, pp. 18ff.

[2] Marcel Granet, *La civilisation chinoise*, Paris, 1929, pp. 406ff.; E. Gasparini, *op. cit.*, pp. 20ff.; upon the "devil" of the spinning in popular Slav belief, *cf.* Gasparini, *op. cit.*, p. 40.

[3] D. Zelenin, *Russische (ostslavische) Volkskunde*, Berlin, 1927, pp. 337ff.; but see also Gasparini, *op. cit.*, pp. 22–23.

[4] Th. Volkov, "Rites et usages nuptiaux en Ukraine" in *Anthropologie*, 1891–1892, summarised in Gasparini, *op. cit.*, pp. 42ff.

of the norms that govern profane existence—in other words, the necessity of suspending the law that bears like a dead weight upon the customary, and of re-entering into a state of absolute spontaneity.

In certain regions, the feminine initiation is of several degrees. For example, among the Yao, initiation begins with the first menstruation, is renewed and deepened during the first pregnancy, and completed after the birth of the first child.[1] The mystery of giving birth—that is, the woman's discovery that *she is creative upon the plane of life*—amounts to a religious experience untranslatable in terms of masculine experience. One can understand, then, why childbirth has given rise to secret feminine rituals, sometimes developed into veritable mysteries; and traces of these have been preserved even in Europe. In the north of Schleswig, all the village women used to run almost wild: they all went to the house of the mother dancing and shouting; if they met with any men they snatched their hats off and filled them with dung; if they came across a cart, they broke it in pieces and set the horse at liberty (here one can perceive the feminine reaction against the work of the men). When they were all assembled at the house of the new birth, there was a frantic race through the village; the women ran all together, like Maenads, shouting and crying hurrah! They went into the houses, took all the food and drink they wanted, and if there were any men present, they compelled them to dance.[2] It is very probable that, in ancient times, certain secret rituals were performed in the houses of childbirth. According to an account from the thirteenth century, the following custom was observed in Denmark: the women met together in the house and sang and shouted while they made a manikin of straw which they called the Ox. Two women took this between them and danced with it, making lewd gestures, and finally cried out: "Sing for the Ox." Then another woman began to sing in a deep, coarse voice, using terrible words.[3] This information,

[1] R. P. Heckel, "Miscellanea", in *Anthropos*, XXX, 1935, p. 875, and Gasparini, *op. cit.*, pp. 42ff.
[2] Richard Wolfram, "Weiberbünde" in the *Zeitschrift für Volkskunde*, 42, 1933, pp. 143ff.
[3] R. Wolfram, *op. cit.*, p. 144; W. E. Peuckert, *Geheimkulte*, p. 230.

handed down by a monk, tells us nothing further; however, it is
likely enough that the ritual was more complex, and that the
dialogue with the Ox had a meaning of "mystery".

FEMININE SECRET SOCIETIES

The secret conclaves of women are always concerned with the
mystery of birth and fertility. When the women of the Trobriand
islands are planting their gardens, they have the right to attack
and overthrow any man who comes too near their work. Several
types of secret women's associations have remained in being to
this day; their rites always include fertility symbols. Here, for
example, are some details concerning the secret society of women
among the Mordvins. Men, unmarried girls and children are
rigorously excluded. The mascot of the association is a hobby-
horse, and the women who accompany it are called "horses":
they suspend from their necks a bag full of millet, decorated with
stripes, which represents the horse's belly, and to which they
attach little balls representing testicles. Every year, in the house
of one of the old women, the association holds a ritual feast; and
as the young married women enter, they receive three strokes of
a whip from the old women, who call out: "Lay an egg!" upon
which each young woman produces a cooked egg from her bodice.
The banquet, to which every member of the society has to contri-
bute victuals, drink and money, very soon becomes orgiastic.
At nightfall, half of the members pay a visit to the other half—for
each village is divided between two parties—and this is a carnival
procession, with drunken old women bestriding the hobby-
horses and singing erotic songs. When the two halves of the
society are reunited, the uproar grows indescribable. Men dare
not venture out into the streets. If they do so, they are attacked by
the women, stripped and bullied, and made to pay a ransom before
being set free again.[1]

To obtain a few details about the initiations in feminine secret
societies, let us look more closely at certain African examples.

[1]Uno Harva, *Die religiös n Vo:stell ngen der Mordwinen*, Helsinki, 1952, pp. 386ff.

The specialists are careful to warn us that very little is known of these secret rites; nevertheless, we can discern their general character. Here is what we know of the Lisimbu society among the Kuta of the north (Okondja). A great part of the ceremony takes place near, or even in, a river; and it is important to note henceforward the presence of aquatic symbolism in almost all the secret societies of this part of Africa. In the river itself, they build a hut of branches and leaves: "It has only one entrance, and the summit of the hut is hardly a yard above the surface of the water."[1] The candidates, whose ages vary from twelve to thirty-two years, are brought down to the shore. Each is under the supervision of an initiate, called the "mother". They advance all together, walking in the water, crouching down with only head and shoulders out of the water. Their faces are painted with *pembe*, and each holds a leaf in her mouth (. . .). This procession goes down the river and, on arrival at the hut, they stand up suddenly and dive into the opening. Having entered into the hut they undress completely, and dive out again. Crouching down, they form a semi-circle around the entrance to the hut and proceed to perform the "fishing dance". One of the "mothers" afterwards comes out of the river, tears off her loin-cloth and, thus naked, dances a most salacious dance.[2] After the dance, the candidates have to go into the hut and it is here that their first initiation takes place. The "mothers" take away their clothes, "plunge their heads under water to the verge of suffocation", and rub their bodies with rough leaves. The initiation is continued in the village: the "mother" beats her "daughter", holds the latter's head close to a fire on which they have thrown a handful of pepper and, lastly, taking her by the arm, makes her dance and then pass between her legs. The ceremony includes also a number of dances, one of which symbolises the sexual act. Two months later, another initiation is held, still on the bank of the river. In this case the neophyte undergoes the same ordeals, and, on the bank, her hair is cut all round in the distinctive fashion of the society. Before going back into the village the president breaks an egg over the roof of the

---

[1] E. Andersson, *Les Kuta*, I, p. 216.
[2] E. Andersson, *op. cit.*, p. 217-218.

hut: "This is to ensure that the hunters will catch plenty of game." When they are back in the village, each "mother" rubs the body of her "daughter" on the *kula*, divides a banana in two, gives one piece to the novice, keeps the other, and they both eat the fruit together. Then the "daughter" bows down and passes between the "mother's" legs. After a few more dances, some of which symbolise the sexual act, the candidates are held to be initiated. "They believe that the ceremonies of Lisimbu exert a favourable influence over the whole life of the village; the plantations will give a good return, the hunting and fishing expeditions will be successful, epidemics and quarrels will be averted from the inhabitants."

We will not dwell upon the symbolism of the Lisimbu mystery. Let us only remember this: that the initiation ceremonies take place in the river, and that, as water symbolises chaos, the hut represents the cosmic creation. To penetrate into the waters is to re-enter the pre-cosmic condition, the non-being. Afterwards, the girl is re-born by passing between the legs of the "mother", meaning that she is born to a new spiritual existence. The elements of cosmogony, of sexuality, of the new birth, of fecundity and of luck, all belong together. In other feminine secret societies in the same part of Africa, certain initiatory features in the rituals are still more in evidence. Thus, in the Gaboon, there are the societies called Nyembe or Ndyembe, who also celebrate their secret ceremonies near a stream of water. Among their initiatory ordeals we should note this: a fire must be kept burning continually, and for fuel the novices have to venture alone into the forest, often during the night or in a storm, to gather wood. Another ordeal is that of staring at the burning sun, while a song is being sung. Lastly, each novice has to plunge her hand into a snake-hole and catch a snake; and they bring these into the village coiled around their arms. During the period of an initiation, the women who are already members of the sisterhood perform nude dances, singing obscene songs. But there is also a ritual of death and initiatory resurrection which is performed in the last act of the mystery; this is the leopard dance. It is executed by the leaders, two and two, one representing the leopard, and her partner the mother. Around the latter a dozen of the young girls are assembled and "killed" by the leopard. But when it comes to the mother's turn, she attacks the leopard and kills it. The death of the wild animal is supposed to allow the young women to be liberated from its belly.[1]

Some special points emerge from all that has just been said. We are struck by the initiatory character of these *Weiberbünde* and secret feminine associations. To take part in them, one has to have successfully passed through an ordeal—and not one of a physiological order (like the first menstruation or parturition), but initiatory in the sense that it brings into play the whole being of the young woman or young wife. And this initiation is effected in a cosmic context. We have just seen the ritual importance of the forest, of the water, of the darkness and of the night. The woman receives the revelation of a reality that transcends her although she is a part of it. It is not the natural phenomenon of giving birth that constitutes the mystery; it is the revelation of the feminine sacredness; that is, of the mystic unity between life, woman, nature and the divinity. This revelation is of a transpersonal order; for which reason it is expressed in symbols and actualised in rites. The girl or the initiated woman becomes conscious of a sanctity that emerges from the innermost depths of her being, and this consciousness—obscure though it may be—is experienced in symbols. It is in "realising" and in "living" this sacredness that the woman finds the spiritual meaning of her own existence, she feels that life is both *real* and *sanctified*, that it is not merely an endless series of blind, psycho-physiological automatisms, useless and in the last reckoning absurd. For the women too, initiation is equivalent to a change of level, to the passing out of one mode of being into another; the young woman is brutally separated from the profane world; she undergoes a transformation of a spiritual character which, like all transformation, implies an experience of death. We have just seen how the ordeals of the young women resemble those that are symbolic of the initiatory death. But what is in question is always *a death to something which has to be surpassed*, not a death in the modern and de-sanctified sense of the term. One

[1]Andersson, *op. cit.*, pp. 219–221.

dies to be transformed and attain to a higher level of existence. In the case of the girls, this is death to the indistinct and amorphous state of childhood, in order to be reborn into personality and fecundity.

As with the men's, so also with the women's associations, we have to deal with a number of different forms of progressively greater secrecy and mystery. There are, to begin with, those general initiations through which every girl and every young wife passes, and which lead up to the institution of the women's secret societies (*Weiberbünde*). Then there are the women's associations for the enacting of the mysteries as we find them in Africa or, in antiquity, the closed groups of the Maenads. We know that some sisterhoods of the kind have taken a long time to disappear—such as those of the witches of the Middle Ages in Europe, with their ritual reunions and "orgies". Although the medieval trials for sorcery were in most cases inspired by theological prejudice, and although it is sometimes hard to distinguish the genuine, rural magico-religious traditions, deeply rooted in prehistory, from collective psychoses of a very complex character, it is nevertheless probable that "orgies" of witches did take place, not with the meaning ascribed to them by the ecclesiastical authorities but in the first, authentic sense that they were secret reunions including orgiastic rites—that is, ceremonies related to the mystery of fertility.

The witches, just like the shamans and the mystics of other primitive societies, were only concentrating, intensifying or deepening the religious experience revealed during their initiation. Just like the shamans, the witches were dedicated to a mystical vocation which impelled them to live, more deeply than other women, the revelation of the mysteries.

SWALLOWING BY A MONSTER

Among the women, then, as much as the men, we find a continuity between the primary revelation of the sacred—that which is imparted at pubertal initiation—and the further revelations transmitted through more exclusive circles (*Männerbünde* and *Weiber-bünde*), and even the personal revelations which, for some chosen individuals, constitute the syndrome of their mystic vocation. We have seen (pp. 208ff.) that the same scenario of initiation—comprising tortures, being put to death and resurrecting—was repeated whenever there was a mystery; that is, a process of spiritual regeneration. To gain a better idea of the persistence of such scenarios of initiation and, at the same time, of their capacity for actualisation in many and different situations, we will now examine one of these archetypal themes at greater length. That is, instead of presenting ritual systems classified according to their objects—tribal initiation, rites of entry into *Männer-* or *Weiber-bünde*, etc.—we will now concentrate upon a single symbolic theme and try to see how it enters into all these ritual systems, and to what extent it can enrich their significance.

Several times during our exposition we have met with the initiatory ordeal that consists of being swallowed by a monster. There are innumerable variants of this rite, which can be compared with Jonah's adventure with the whale—and, as we know, the symbolism implied in the story of Jonah has keenly interested the depth-psychologists, especially Professor Jung and Dr Neumann. This initiatory motif has given birth not only to a great number of rites but to myths and legends not always easy of interpretation. The mystery in question is one of symbolic death and rebirth; but let us examine it more closely. In certain regions, the initiatory rites of puberty include the entry into an effigy resembling an aquatic monster (a crocodile, a whale or a great fish). But this ceremony had already fallen into disuse when it was studied by the ethnologists. Thus, among the Papuans of New Guinea,[1] for example, a monstrous creature called a *kaiemunu* is constructed of raffia, and is kept in the men's house. On the occasion of his initiation, the child is put into the belly of the monster. But the initiatory meaning is lost; the novice goes inside the *kaiemunu* while his father is busy completing the contraption.

[1] F. E. Williams, "The Pairama Ceremony in the Purari Delta, Papua", in the *Journal of the Royal Anthropological Institute*, 53, 1923, pp. 363ff. See also Nevermann, *Masken und Geheimbünde Melanesien*, Leipzig, 1933, pp. 51ff.

The significance of the rite having been forgotten, no initiatory terror takes possession of the novice. They continue, however, to put him into the *kaiemunu*, because of the tradition that the ancestors of the tribe did so.

In other regions, they know only that the neophytes are swallowed by a monster,[1] but no longer practise the ritual entry into its belly. Thus, among the natives of Sierra Leone and Liberia, future members of the *Poro*[2] secret society are believed to be swallowed by the monster Namu, who remains pregnant for four years and then gives birth to the initiates after the manner of a woman. Among the Kuta, the Mungala secret society practise the following rite: out of tissues of fibre, painted white, they construct an apparatus four metres long and two metres high which "has vaguely the appearance of an animal". A man enters into this construction and, during the ceremonies, he walks about the forest in it, to terrorise the candidates. Here again, the original meaning is lost. But we have seen how the mythological memory of a monster who swallows and vomits up the candidates was preserved among the Mandja and the Banda (by the Ngakola secret society).[3]

The myths are more eloquent than the rites; they unveil to us the original meaning of this sojourn in the inside of a monster. Let us begin with a famous Polynesian myth, that of Maui. This great Maori hero returns, at the end of a richly adventurous life, to his native country and to the house of his grandmother Hine-nui-te-po, the Great Lady (of the Night). He finds her asleep and, quickly throwing off his clothing, prepares to enter into this giantess's body. But the hero is attended by birds: he takes the precaution of forbidding them to laugh before they see him come out victorious from his adventure. In the end, the birds keep

[1]*Cf.* Hans Schaerer, *Die Gottesidee der Ngadju Dajak in Süd-Borneo*, Leiden, 1946, pp. 102ff.: the disappearance of the man in the crocodile symbolises the initiation. On the same motif, see Carl Hentze, *Bronzegerät, Kultbauten, Religion im ältesten China der Shangzeit*, Antwerp, 1951, pp. 176ff., *et passim*. Upon the *sosom* of the Marind-anim, which swallows up children, see P. Wirz, *Die Marind-anim von Holländisch-Süd-Neu-Guinea*, Hamburg, 1922, pp. 36ff. The map of the distribution of the "Jonah-motif" has been published by L. Frobenius, "Das Archiv für folkloristik", *Paideuma*, I, 1938, p. 9, and reproduced by Peuckert, *op. cit.*, pp. 355ff.

[2]E. Andersson, *Les Kuta*, I, pp. 297ff., and Peuckert, *op. cit.*, pp. 355ff.

[3]See Andersson, *Les Kuta*, I, pp. 263ff.

silence only so long as Maui is passing through the body of his
grandmother; when they see him half-way out again—that is,
when half of the hero's body is still in the giantess's mouth—the
birds burst into laughter, and the Great Lady (of the Night) shuts
her teeth upon him, cutting the hero in two, so that he dies. And
that, say the Maoris, is why man is mortal; if Maui had managed
to emerge unscathed from his grandmother's body, men would
have become immortal.[1]

In this myth we can see another meaning attaching to the
entry into the body of a monster: this is no longer death followed
by a resurrection—the theme common to all initiations—but the
quest for immortality by a heroic descent into the womb of a
giant ancestress. In other words, this time it is a question of
enduring death without dying, of descending into the Kingdom
of Night and of the Dead and yet returning alive—as the shamans
do to this day during their trances. But whereas the shaman enters
the Kingdom of the Dead only *in the spirit*, Maui ventures upon
a descent in the material sense of the word. This is the well-known
difference between the shamanic ecstasy and the heroes' adventures in flesh and blood. We meet with the same difference in the
northern and arctic regions where religious experience is dominated by shamanism. According to some variants of the *Kalevala*
for instance, the sage Väinämöinen sets out on a journey to the
land of the dead, Tuonela. The daughter of Tuoni, the Lord of
the beyond, swallows him up—but, on arrival in the giantess's
stomach, Väinämöinen builds a boat and, as the text puts it,
he rows vigorously "from one end of the intestine to the
other". The giantess is finally obliged to vomit him out into the
sea.[2]

Now, the shamans of Lapland, during their trances, are
supposed to enter into the intestines of a big fish or a whale. One
legend tells us that the son of a shaman awakened his father, who
had been asleep for three years, with these words: "Father! Wake
up and come out of the fish's guts; come out of the third loop of

[1]W. D. Westervelt, *Legends of Ma-ui the Demigod*, Honolulu, 1910, pp. 128ff.; and
J. F. Stimson, *The Legends of Maui and Tahaki*, Honolulu, 1937, pp. 46ff.
[2]Martti Haavio, *Väinämöinen, Eternal Sage*, F F Communications, No. 144, Helsinki,
1952, pp. 117ff.

its intestines!"[1] What is happening in this case is an ecstatic voyage, in the spirit, in the belly of a marine monster. Why the shaman should remain three years in "the third loop of the intestine", we will try to understand presently. For the moment, let us recall some other adventures of the same type. According to a still-surviving tradition in Finland, a blacksmith named Ilmarinen was courting a young woman, and she made it a condition of marriage that he should "walk among the teeth of the old witch Hiisi". Ilmarinen departs on this errand and, on his approaching the sorceress, she swallows him. She then tells him to go out again by the mouth, but Ilmarinen refuses: "I shall make my own door," he answers; and, with blacksmith's tools that he has magically forged, he cuts the old woman's stomach open and makes his way out of her. According to another variant, the condition laid down by the young woman is the capture of a large fish. This fish swallows Ilmarinen; but having entered its stomach he begins to toss and turn, until the fish begs him to go out by the rear. "I'm not going that way," answers the blacksmith. "Just think what people would call me!" The fish then proposes that he should go out by the mouth, but Ilmarinen replies: "I won't do that, for men would call me vomit." So he went on rampaging until at last the fish burst.[2]

The story reappears with many variations. Lucian of Samosata recounts in his *True Stories* the swallowing-up of an entire ship with all hands, by a marine monster. The men lit a great fire, which killed the monster; and to make their way out, they opened its jaws with poles. An analogous story is in circulation in Polynesia: the hero Nganaoa had his boat swallowed by a kind of whale; but the hero took the mast and thrust it into the whale's mouth to prop it open. Then he went down into the monster's stomach, where he found both his parents, still living. Nganaoa lit a fire, killed the monster and came out by its mouth. This motif of folk-lore is widely current in Oceania.[3]

Let us take note of the ambivalent part played by the marine monster. There can be no doubt that the fish that swallows Jonah

---

[1] M. Haavio, *Väinämöinen*, p. 124. [2] *Ibid.* pp. 114ff.
[3] *Cf.* L. Rademacher, "Walfischmythen" in the *Archiv für Religionswissenschaft*, IX, 1906, pp. 246ff.; F. Graebner, *Das Weltbild der Primitiven*, Munich, 1924, pp. 62ff.

and the other mythical heroes symbolises death; its belly represents Hell. In medieval visions, Hell is frequently imagined in the form of an enormous marine monster, which perhaps had its prototype in the biblical Leviathan. To be swallowed by it is therefore equivalent to dying, to the descent into Hell—the experience which all the primitive rites of initiation we have been discussing clearly leave one to infer. But on the other hand, descent into the belly of a monster also signifies the re-entry into a pre-formal, embryonic state of being. As we have already said, the darkness that reigns in the interior of the monster corresponds to the cosmic Night, to the Chaos before the creation. In other words, we are dealing here with a double symbolism: that of death, namely the conclusion of a temporal existence, and consequently of the end of time, and the symbolism of return to the germinal mode of being, which precedes all forms and every temporal existence. Upon the cosmological plane, this double symbolism refers to the *Urzeit* and the *Endzeit*.

SYMBOLISM OF THE INITIATORY DEATH

We can understand, then, why being swallowed by a monster has played so important a part in the initiation rituals,[1] as well as in heroic myths and the mythologies of Death. The mystery in question is one that involves the most terrible of initiatory ordeals, that of death, but which also constitutes the only possible way of abolishing temporal duration—in other words, of annulling historic existence—and of re-entering into the primordial situation. Evidently, this re-entry into the germinal state of "the beginnings" is itself equivalent to death: in effect, one "kills" one's own profane historic existence, now outworn, to re-enter into an immaculate, open existence, untainted by Time.

It follows from this that, in all these initiatory contexts, death has not the meaning that one is generally inclined to give it; what it means above all is that one liquidates the past, one

---

[1]For a psychological interpretation of this symbolism, see also Charles Baudouin, *Le mythe du héros*, Paris, 1952.

puts an end to one existence, which like all profane existence is a failure, to begin again, regenerated, in another. Initiatory death is thus a recommencement, never an end. In no rite or myth do we find the initiatory death as something *final*, but always as the condition *sine qua non* of a transition to another mode of being, a trial indispensable to regeneration; that is, to the beginning of a new life. Let us emphasise, too, the fact that the symbolism of a return to the womb always has cosmological valency. It is the whole world which, symbolically, returns with the neophyte into cosmic Night, in order to be created anew; that is, to become capable of regeneration. And, as we have said elsewhere,[1] a great many archaic therapeutic methods consist of ritual recitations of the cosmogonic myth: in other terms, in order to cure the patient, *he has to be born again*—and the archetypal pattern of this birth is the cosmogony. It is necessary to abolish the work of Time, and to re-enter the auroral instant prior to the Creation: on the human plane, this amounts to saying that one must return to the "blank page" of existence, the absolute commencement when nothing had yet been defiled, nothing as yet spoiled.

To enter into the belly of the monster is equivalent to a regression into the primal indistinctness, into the cosmic Night—and to come out of the monster is equivalent to a cosmogony: it is to pass from Chaos to Creation. The initiatory death repeats this exemplary return to Chaos in order to make possible a renewal of the cosmogony; that is, to prepare for the new birth. The regression into Chaos is sometimes realised literally—as for instance in the initiatory illnesses of the future shamans, which in many cases were regarded as actual madness. We find, in fact, a total crisis, occasionally leading to the disintegration of the personality.[2]

From a certain point of view, one could compare this initiatory "madness" of the shamans to the dissolution of the old personality which follows upon the descent into Hell or the entry into the belly of a monster. Every initiatory adventure of this type ends in the *creation* of something, in the founding of a new world or a new mode of being. We remember how the hero

[1]See above, pp. 48ff.   [2]See above, pp. 79ff.

Maui, entering into the body of his grandmother, was seeking immortality, which amounts to saying that he thought he would be able, through his initiatory exploit, to establish a new human condition, like that of the gods. We also recall the legend of the Lapp shaman who—in the spirit—spent three years in the bowels of an enormous fish. Why did he undertake such an adventure? The answer is perhaps supplied by an ancient Finnish myth concerning Väinämöinen, which says that Väinämöinen built a boat of magic—that is, by singing—but was unable to complete the work, for there were three words he did not know. To learn them, he sought out a famous sorcerer, Antero, a giant who had remained motionless for long years, like an entranced shaman, until a tree grew out of his shoulder and birds nested in his beard. Väinämöinen falls into the mouth of the giant and is quickly swallowed. But once he is in Antero's stomach, he forges himself a suit of iron, and warns the sorcerer that he will stay where he is until he obtains the three magic words for finishing his boat.[1]

What we have here is an initiatory adventure undertaken to gain an item of secret knowledge. One goes down into the belly of a giant or a monster in order to learn *science* or *wisdom*. That is why the Lapp shaman remains in the fish's entrails for three years —to learn the secrets of Nature, to resolve the enigma of life and see into the future. But, if entering into the belly of a monster is equivalent to a descent into Hell, into darkness among the dead —that is, if it symbolises a regression to cosmic Night as well as into the darkness of "madness" where all personality is dissolved —and if we take account of all these homologies and correspondences between Death, Cosmic Night, Chaos, madness as regression to the embryonic condition, etc., then we can see why Death also symbolises Wisdom, why the dead are omniscient and know the future, and why the visionaries and the poets seek inspiration among the tombs. Upon another plane of reference, we can also understand why the future shaman, before becoming a wise man, must first know "madness" and go down into darkness; and why creativity is always found in relation to some "madness" or "orgy" involved with the symbolism of death and darkness.

[1] M. Haavio, *Väinämöinen*, pp. 106ff.

C. G. Jung explains all this as contact with, and reactivation of the collective unconscious. But, to keep within our own domain, we are able to see, above all, why initiation among the primitives always takes place in relation with the revelation of the sacred knowledge, of wisdom. It is during the period of seclusion—that is, when they are supposed to be swallowed up in the belly of a monster or finding themselves in Hell—that the neophytes are instructed in the secret traditions of the tribe. The true knowledge, that which is conveyed by the myths and symbols, is accessible only in the course of, or following upon, the process of spiritual regeneration realised by initiatory death and resurrection.

We are now in a position to understand why the same initiatory schema—consisting of suffering, death and resurrection —reappears in all the mysteries, both in the rites of puberty and in those of entry into a secret society; and why the same scenario can be traced in the shattering personal experiences which precede the mystic vocation. Above all we understand this—that the man of the archaic societies strove to conquer death by according it such an importance that, in the final reckoning, death ceased to present itself as a *cessation* and became a *rite of passage*. In other words, to the primitive one is for ever dying to something that was not essential; one is dying to the profane life. In short, death comes to be regarded as the supreme initiation, namely, as the beginning of a new spiritual existence. Furthermore, generation, death and regeneration were understood as three moments of this same mystery, and all the spiritual energy of archaic man was exerted to show that between these moments there ought to be no division. One cannot *stop* in any one of these three moments, one cannot *instal* oneself anywhere, either in death, for instance, or in generation. The movement—the regeneration—always continues: the cosmogony is tirelessly repeated to make sure that what one is doing is well done—whether it be the production of a child, or a house or entry into a spiritual vocation. That is why we have always found that the rites of initiation have a cosmogonic valency.

Wisdom itself and, by extension, all sacred and creative knowledge are conceived as the fruit of an initiation; that is, as the result both of a cosmogony and of spiritual obstetrics. Socrates was not wrong in comparing himself to a midwife; for he helped men to be born into self-consciousness. Still more clearly did St Paul, in his *Epistle to Titus*, speak of "spiritual sons"—sons whom he had procreated by the faith. And the same symbolism occurs again in the Buddhist tradition: the monk gives up his family name and becomes a "son of Buddha" (*sakya-putto*), because he is "born among the saints" (*ariya*). As Kassapa said, speaking of himself, "Natural son of the Blessed One, born of his mouth, born of the *dhamma*, formed by the *dhamma*", etc. (*Samyutta Nikâya*, II, 221). But this initiatory birth implied death to profane existence. The schema was preserved in Hinduism as well as in Buddhism; the yogi "dies to this life" to be re-born into another mode of being, that which is represented by "liberation". The Buddha taught the way and the means of dying to the profane human condition—that is, to bondage and to ignorance— and of being reborn to freedom, bliss, and the unconditioned state of *nirvâna*. The Indian terminology of initiatory re-birth some- times recalls the archaic symbolism of the "new body" obtained by the neophyte. The Buddha himself proclaims this: "I have shown my disciples the means whereby they may create, on departure from this body (created by the four elements), another body of an intellectual substance (*rûpim manomayam*) complete with its members and endowed with transcendental faculties (*abhinindriyam*)."[1]

All this proves, we think, that the archaic evaluation of death as the supreme means to spiritual regeneration founded an initiatory scenario which survives even in the great world re- ligions and is re-valorised also in Christianity. It is the funda- mental mystery, renewed, relieved, and re-valorised by every new religious experience. But let us look more closely into the ultimate consequence of this mystery: if one knows death already *here below*, if one is continually dying countless deaths in order to be reborn to *something else*—to something that does not belong to the Earth but participates in the sacred—then one is living, we may say, a *beginning of immortality*, or growing more and more

[1]*Majjhima-Nikâya*, II, 17; *cf.* M. Eliade, *Yoga, Immortality and Freedom*, pp. 165ff.

into immortality. It would follow that immortality should not be conceived as a survival *post mortem*, but rather as a situation one is constantly creating for oneself, for which one is preparing, in which one is even participating *from now onward* and from this present world. The deathless, the immortal, ought then to be conceived as a limiting situation, an ideal situation towards which man is straining with his whole being, and that he strives to attain by dying and resurrecting continually.

THE ENCOUNTER:
A TEST-CASE

Religious Symbolism and the Modern Man's Anxiety

WE PROPOSE now to consider the anxiety of the modern man as it appears in the light of the history of religions. To more readers than one, this project may seem singular, if not merely unnecessary. For some of us regard the anxiety of the modern world as a product of historical tensions, belonging specifically to our times, explicable by the fundamental crises of our civilisation, and by nothing else. To what purpose, then, should we compare this historic moment in which we live with the symbolisms and religious ideologies of other epochs and other civilisations long since past? This objection is but half justified. There is no perfectly autonomous civilisation, wholly unrelated to the others that preceded it. The Greek mythology had lost its reality some 2,000 years before it was found that some of the fundamental behaviour of the modern European could be explained by the myth of Oedipus. Psychoanalysis and depth-psychology have accustomed us to such comparisons—at first sight unverifiable—between historical situations apparently unrelated to one another. Some have compared, for example, the ideology of the Christian to that of the totemist; they have tried to explain the notion of the Father God by that of the totem. We will not now enquire how well-founded such comparisons are, or upon what documentary basis. Enough to point out that certain psychological schools make use of comparisons between the most varied types of civilisation to gain a better understanding of the structure of the psyche. The directive principle of this method is that, since the human psyche has a history and, in consequence, cannot be wholly explained by the study of its present situation, all its history, and even its pre-history, should still be discernible in what we call its actual disposition.

This brief allusion to the methods employed by the depth-psychologists will suffice, for we have no intention of proceeding in the same way. In saying that one can study the anxiety of modern times in the perspective of the history of religions, we were thinking of quite another comparative method, which we will now indicate in a few words. We propose to reverse the terms of comparison, to place ourselves outside our civilisation and our own moment of history, and to consider these from the standpoint of other cultures and other religions. We do not think of re-discovering among ourselves, Europeans of the twentieth century, certain attitudes already known to the ancient mythologies—as, for example, Freud did with the Oedipus complex: our aim will be to see ourselves just as an intelligent and sympathetic observer, from the standpoint of an extra-European civilisation, might see and judge us. For greater precision, we will imagine an observer who belongs to another civilisation and judges us according to his own scale of values, not some abstract observer from the planet of Sirius.

Such an approach is, moreover, imposed upon us by our own historic moment. For some time now, Europe has not been the only maker of history: the Asiatic world is actively re-entering the stream of history, soon to be followed by other exotic societies. Upon the plane of culture and of spirituality in general this historic phenomenon will have considerable consequences. European values will lose their privileged status as universally recognised norms: they will be back at the status of local spiritual creations; that is, of cultural tributaries of a certain historic amplitude, conditioned by clearly circumscribed traditions. If Western culture is not to become provincialised, it will be obliged to carry on conversation with the other, non-European cultures, and take care not to be too often mistaken about the meaning of their terms. It is urgent for us to understand how our culture is placed and judged, from their extra-European point of view. It must not be forgotten that all these cultures have a religious structure; that is, they have all grown up, and are constituted, as religious valuations of the world and of human existence. To know how we are regarded and judged by the representatives of other cultures we must learn how to compare ourselves with them, which will be possible only if we can manage to view ourselves in the perspective of their religious traditions: in no other perspective will this comparison be valid and helpful. For it is less instructive for us to know how a cultured Indian, or Chinese, or Indonesian, who has been educated in our Western tradition, may judge us. He will reproach us for defects and contradictions of which we ourselves are well aware: he may tell us we are not sufficiently Christian, not intelligent enough, or too intolerant—which we know already from our own critics and moralists, our own reformers.

We need, then, not only to have good knowledge of the religious values of other cultures but above all to strive to see ourselves as they see us. And this feat is possible, thanks to the history of religions and religious ethnology. That is the explanation and justification of our present enterprise; in trying to understand the symbolism of anxiety in the non-Christian religions, we have a good chance of learning what would be thought of our present crisis in Oriental and archaic societies. Evidently, such an enquiry will not *only* show us the point of view of the "others", the non-Europeans: for any confrontation with another person leads to enlightenment about one's own situation.

It is sometimes surprising to see how certain cultural habits, which have grown so familiar to us that we regard them as the natural behaviour of every civilised man, disclose unexpected meanings as soon as they are viewed in the perspective of another culture. We need only instance one of the most specific features of our own civilisation—namely, the modern man's passionate, almost abnormal interest in History. This interest is manifested in two distinct ways, which are however related: first, in what may be called a passion for historiography, the desire for an ever more complete and more exact knowledge of the past of humanity, above all of the past of our Western world; secondly, this interest in history is manifested in contemporary Western philosophy, in the tendency to define man as above all a historical being conditioned, and in the end created, by History. What is called historicism, *Historismus*, *storicismo*, as well as Marxism and certain

existentialist schools—these are philosophies which, in one sense
or another, ascribe fundamental importance to history and to the
historic moment. To some of these philosophies we shall have to
return when we come to examine the meaning of anxiety in
Indian metaphysics. For the moment, we will confine ourselves
to the first aspect of this interest in History; that is, the passion of
the modern world for historiography.

This is a fairly recent passion; it dates from the second half of
the last century. It is true that, from the time of Herodotus, the
Greco-Latin world knew and cultivated the writing of history:
but this was not history as it has come to be written since the
nineteenth century, the aim of which is to know and describe, as
accurately as possible, all that has come to pass in the course of
time. Herodotus, like Livy, like Orosius and even the historians
of the Renaissance, wrote history in order to preserve examples
and models and pass them on for our imitation. But for a century
past history has been no longer the source of exemplary models;
it has become a scientific passion for exhaustive knowledge of all
the adventures of mankind, an endeavour to reconstitute the
entire past of the species and make us conscious of it. Now, this is
an interest we find nowhere else. Practically all the non-European
cultures are without historic consciousness, and even if they have
a traditional historiography—as in the case of China, or the
countries under the Islamic culture—its function is always to
provide exemplary models.

Let us now look at this passion for history from a standpoint
outside our own cultural perspective. In many religions, and even
in the folk-lore of European peoples, we have found a belief that,
at the moment of death, man remembers all his past life down to
the minutest details, and that he cannot die before having remembered and re-lived the whole of his personal history. Upon the
screen of memory, the dying man once more reviews his past.
Considered from this point of view, the passion for historiography
in modern culture would be a sign portending his imminent
death. Our Western civilisation, before it foundered, would be
for the last time remembering all its past, from protohistory until
the total wars. The historiographical consciousness of Europe—

which some have regarded as its highest title to lasting fame—
would in fact be the supreme moment which precedes and
announces death.

This is no more than a preliminary exercise in our comparative
research, and we have chosen it just because it exhibits at once the
risks attendant upon such an approach and how profitable it may
be. It is, indeed, somewhat significant that judged from a wholly
external point of view—that of funerary rituals and folk-lore—
this modern passion for historiography reveals to us an archaic
symbolism of Death; for, as it has often been said, the anxiety
of modern man is obscurely linked to the awareness of his
historicity, and this, in its turn, discloses the anxiety of confronting Death and Non-being.

It is true that in us, modern Europeans, the passion for historiography arouses no presentiments of disaster: nevertheless, seen in
a religious perspective, it signifies the proximity of Death. And
depth-psychology has taught us to ascribe more importance to the
active presence of a symbol than to the conscious experience
which manipulates and evaluates it. In the present case this is
easily understood, for this popularity of historiography is only
one, and that the most obvious aspect of the discovery of History.
The other, the more profound aspect, is that of the historicity of
every human existence and, therefore, directly implies the
anguish of facing Death.

It is in trying to estimate this anguish in the face of Death—
that is, in trying to place it and evaluate it in a perspective other
than our own—that the comparative approach begins to be
instructive. Anguish before Nothingness and Death seems to be
a specifically modern phenomenon. In all the other, non-European
cultures, that is, in the other religions, Death is never felt as an
absolute end or as Nothingness: it is regarded rather as a rite of
passage to another mode of being; and for that reason always
referred to in relation to the symbolisms and rituals of initiation,
re-birth or resurrection. This is not to say that the non-European
does not know the experience of anguish before Death; the
emotion is experienced, of course, but not as something absurd or
futile; on the contrary, it is accorded the highest value, as an

experience indispensable to the attainment of a new level of being. Death is the Great Initiation. But in the modern world Death is emptied of its religious meaning; that is why it is assimilated to Nothingness; and before Nothingness modern man is paralysed.

Let us note, in a brief parenthesis, that when we speak of "modern man", his crises and anxieties, we are thinking primarily of one who has no faith, who is no longer in any living attachment to Judæo-Christianity. To a believer, the problem of Death presents itself in other terms: for him, too, Death is a rite of passage. But a great part of the modern world has lost faith, and for this mass of mankind anxiety in the face of Death presents itself as anguish before Nothingness. It is only that part of the modern world to which we are referring, whose experience we are trying to understand and interpret by situating it within another cultural horizon.

The anxiety of the modern man would seem, then, to be aroused and to feed upon the discovery of Nothingness. What would a non-European say of this metaphysical situation? Let us place ourselves, first of all, in the spiritual position of archaic man, the man who has been called (though wrongly) the "primitive". He too knows the anguish of Death; it is related to his fundamental experience, the decisive experience which made him what he is: mature, conscious and responsible man; which has enabled him to pass beyond infancy and detach himself from his mother and from his infantile complexes. The anguish of Death lived by the primitive is the anguish of initiation.[1] And if we could translate the anguish of the modern man into the experience and symbolic language of the primitive, he would say something like this: This is the great initiatory trial; it is the entry into the labyrinth, or into the bush haunted by the demons and the souls of the ancestors, the jungle that corresponds to Hell, to the other world: it is the great fear that paralyses the neophyte at initiation, when he is swallowed by the monster and finds himself in the darkness of its belly, when he feels himself being torn to pieces and digested, in order to be re-born a new man. One remembers

[1]See above, pp. 198ff.

all the terrible ordeals that constitute the initiation of the young
people of archaic societies, trials that are essential to all initiation,
and such as survived even in some of the Greco-Oriental mysteries.
We know that the boys, and often the girls, leave their houses
and live for a time—sometimes for several years—in the bush;
that is, in the other world, to complete their initiation. Initiation
includes tortures and trials culminating in a ritual symbolising
death and resurrection. This last ritual is the most terrible of all,
for the boy is supposed to be swallowed up by a monster, or be
buried alive, or lost in the bush, which means in Hell. It is in
terms of this order that a primitive would estimate our anguish,
but enlarged to the collective scale; the modern world is in the
situation of a man swallowed by a monster, struggling in the
darkness of its belly; or of one lost in the wilderness, or wandering
in a labyrinth which itself is a symbol of the Infernal—and so he is
in anguish, thinks he is already dead or upon the point of dying,
and can see no way out except into darkness, Death or Nothingness.

And yet, in the eyes of the primitive, this terrible experience
is indispensable to the birth of a new man. No initiation is possible
without the ritual of an agony, a death and a resurrection.
Judged in the perspective of the primitive religions, the anguish of
the modern world is the sign of an imminent death, but of a
death that is necessary and redemptive, for it will be followed by
a resurrection and the possibility of attaining a new mode of
being, that of maturity and responsibility.

Here again, then, we find the symbolism of Death just as we
found it when, looking at ourselves from a different point of
view, we were interpreting the passion for historiography in
terms of popular mythologies. But neither among the primitives
nor in the more highly evolved of the non-European civilisations,
do we find the idea of Nothingness interchangeable with the idea
of Death. As we were saying just now, among Christians and in
the non-Christian religions Death is not homologised with the
idea of Nothing. Death is, of course, an end—but an end immediately followed by a new beginning. One dies to one mode of
being in order to be able to attain to another. Death constitutes

an abrupt change of ontological level, and at the same time a rite of passage, just as birth does, or initiation.

It is also interesting to see how Nothingness has been evaluated in the religions and metaphysics of India, since the problem of Being and Non-being is justly regarded as a speciality of Indian thought. For Indian thinking, our world, as well as our vital and psychic experience, is regarded as the more or less direct product of the cosmic illusion, of Mâyâ. Without going into detail, let us recall that the "veil of Mâyâ" is an image-formula expressing the ontological unreality both of the world and of all human experience; we emphasise *ontological*, for neither the world nor human experience participates in absolute Being. The physical world and our human experience also are constituted by the universal becoming, by the temporal: they are therefore illusory, created and destroyed as they are by Time. But this does not mean that they have no existence or are creations of my imagination. The world is not a mirage nor an illusion, in the immediate sense of the words: the physical world and my vital and psychic experience exist, but they exist only in Time, which for Indian thinking means that they will not exist tomorrow or a hundred million years hence. Consequently, judged by the scale of absolute Being, the world and every experience dependent upon temporality are illusory. It is in this sense that Mâyâ represents, in Indian thought, a special kind of experience of Nothingness, of Non-being.

Let us now try to decipher the anxiety of the modern world, using Indian philosophy as the key. An Indian philosopher would say that historicism and existentialism introduce Europe to the dialectic of Mâyâ. His reasoning would be very much like this: European thinking has just discovered that man is ineluctably conditioned, not only by his physiology and his heredity, but also by History and above all his personal history. This it is that keeps man for ever in a predicament: he is participating all the time in History, he is a fundamentally historical being. And, the Indian philosopher would add: this "predicament" we have known for a very long time; it is the illusory existence in Mâyâ. And we call it illusory precisely because it is conditioned by Time, by History. Furthermore, it is for this reason that India has never allowed philosophic importance to History. India is preoccupied with Being; and History, created by becoming, is just one of the forms of Non-being. But this does not mean that Indian thought has neglected the analysis of historicity: her metaphysics and spiritual techniques have long since included a highly refined analysis of that which, in Western philosophy, is now called "being in the world" or "being in a situation": Yoga, Buddhism and Vedânta have all demonstrated the relativity, and therefore the non-reality of every "situation", of all "conditions". Many centuries before Heidegger, Indian thought had identified, in temporality, the "fated" dimension of all existence; just as it had foreseen, before Marx or Freud, the multiple conditioning of all human experience and of every judgment about the world. When the Indian philosophies affirmed that man is "in bondage" to illusion, they meant to say that every existence necessarily constitutes itself as a rupture, a break-away from the Absolute. When the yogi or the Buddhist said that everything was suffering, that all is transitory (*sarvam dukham, sarvam anityam*), the meaning was that of *Sein und Zeit*, namely, that the temporality of all human existence necessarily engenders anxiety and pain.

In other words, the discovery of historicity, as the specific mode of being of man in the world, corresponds to what the Indians have long called our situation in Mâyâ. And the Indian philosopher would say that European thought has understood the precariousness and the paradoxical condition of the man who becomes aware of his temporality: his anguish follows from his tragic discovery that man is a being destined to death, issuing from Nothingness and on his way to Nothingness.

Yet the Indian philosopher would still be perplexed at the consequences that certain modern philosophers draw from this discovery. For, after having understood the dialectic of Mâyâ, the Indian tries to deliver himself from its illusions, whilst these Europeans seem to be content with the discovery, and to put up with a nihilistic and pessimistic vision of the world. It is not for us here to discuss the why and wherefore of this tendency in European thought; we are only trying to submit it to the judgment of the Indian philosopher. Now, for an Indian, there is no sense in the discovery of the cosmic illusion if it is not followed by the quest of the absolute Being: the notion of Mâyâ is meaningless without the notion of Brahman. In Occidental language, we might say that there is no point in becoming aware that one is conditioned unless one turns towards the unconditioned and seeks deliverance. Mâyâ is a cosmic play and, after all, illusory, but when one has understood it to be so, when one has torn away the veil of Mâyâ, one finds oneself before the absolute Being, before ultimate reality. The anguish is aroused by our becoming aware of our precarious condition and our fundamental unreality, but such awareness is not an end in itself; it only helps us to discover the delusion of our existence in the world. And just at that point there comes a second awakening of consciousness: one finds that the Great Illusion, Mâyâ, was founded upon our ignorance, that is, upon our false and absurd self-identification with the cosmic becoming and with historicity. In reality, explains the Indian philosopher, our true Self—our *âtman*, our *purusha*—has nothing to do with the multiple situations of our history. The Self participates in Being; the *âtman* is identical with Brahman. To an Indian, our anguish is readily understandable: we are in anguish because we have just found out what we are—not mortal, in the abstract sense of the syllogism, but dying, in the act of dying, of being inescapably devoured by Time. The Indian can well understand our fear and anxiety at what amounts to the discovery of our own death. But what is the death in question? he asks. It is the death of our non-Self, of our illusory individuality; namely, of our own Mâyâ, not of the Being in whom we participate—our *âtman*, which is immortal just because it is not conditioned and is not temporal. The Indian, then, would agree with us inasmuch as he admits that anguish in face of the Nothingness of our existence is homologous with the anguish of facing Death—but, he would immediately add, this Death that fills you with such anxiety is only the death of your illusions and your ignorance: it will be followed by a rebirth, by the realisation of your real identity, your true mode of being: that of unconditioned and free being. In a word, he would say, it is the consciousness of your own historicity that makes you anxious, and no wonder: for one has to die to History before one can discover and live true Being. One can easily guess what a European historical and existentialist philosopher might reply to such an interpretation of this anxiety. You ask me, he would say, to "die to History"; but man is not, and he *cannot be* anything else but History, for his very essence is temporality. You are asking me, then, to give up my authentic existence and to take refuge in an abstraction, in pure Being, in the *âtman*: I am to sacrifice my dignity as a creator of History in order to live an a-historic, inauthentic existence, empty of all human content. Well, I prefer to put up with my anxiety: at least, it cannot deprive me of a certain heroic grandeur, that of becoming conscious of, and accepting, the human condition.

It is no part of my purpose to discuss these European philosophical positions: we ought, however, to point out one misunderstanding which distorts the Western picture of India and of Indian spirituality. It is not at all the case that the discovery of the cosmic illusion and the metaphysical quest of Being express themselves, in India, by a total devaluation of Life or belief in a universal vacuity. We are now beginning to realise that, perhaps more than any other civilisation, that of India loves and reverences Life, and enjoys it at every level. For Mâyâ is not an absurd and gratuitous cosmic illusion, it knows nothing of the absurdity that certain European philosophers ascribe to human existence as they conceive it, issuing out of Nothingness and proceeding to Nothingness. For Indian thought Mâyâ is a divine creation, a cosmic *play*, of which the end and aim is human experience, as well as deliverance from that experience. It follows that to become conscious of the cosmic illusion does not mean, in India, the discovery that all is Nothingness, but simply that no experience in the world or of History has any ontological validity and, therefore, that our human condition ought not to be regarded as an end in itself. But when he has come to consciousness of this, the Hindu does not withdraw from the world: if he did, India would long ago have disappeared from History, for the conception of Mâyâ is accepted by the great majority of Indians. To become aware of the dialectic of Mâyâ does not necessarily lead to asceticism and the abandonment of all social and historical existence. This state of consciousness generally finds expression in quite another attitude; the attitude revealed by Krishna to Arjuna in the *Bhagavad Gîtâ:* namely, that of remaining in the world and participating in History, but taking good care not to attribute to History any absolute value. Rather than an invitation to renounce History, what is revealed to us in the *Bhagavad Gîtâ* is a warning against the *idolatry* of History. All Indian thought is insistent upon this very point, that the state of ignorance and illusion is not that of *living* in History, but of *believing in* its ontological reality. As we have said already, although the world is illusory—because it is in a state of continual becoming—it is none the less a divine creation. The world, indeed, is sacred; but, paradoxically, one cannot see the sacredness of the world until one discovers that it is a divine *play*. The ignorance, and hence the anxiety and the suffering, are perpetuated by the absurd belief that this perishable and illusory world represents the ultimate reality. We find a similar dialectic with regard to Time.[1] According to the *Maitri-Upanishad*, Brahman, the absolute Being, manifests himself under two opposite aspects at the same time: Time and Eternity. Ignorance consists in seeing no more than his negative aspect—his temporality. The "wrong action" as the Hindus call it, is not that of living in Time, but of believing that nothing exists outside Time. One is devoured by Time, by History, not because one lives in them, but because one thinks them *real* and, in consequence, one forgets or undervalues eternity.

But we must not pursue these observations; our purpose in making them was not to discuss Indian metaphysics, nor to contrast it with European philosophy, but only to see what an Indian might have to say about our contemporary society. Now, it is significant that, whether we look at it from the standpoint of the archaic cultures or that of Indian spirituality, anxiety appears under the symbolism of Death. This means that, seen and evaluated by the *others*, by the non-Europeans, our anxiety reveals the same signification as we Europeans had already found in it: the imminence of Death. But agreement between our own view of it and that of the *others* goes no further. For, to the non-

[1] *Cf. Images et Symboles*, Gallimard, 1952, pp. 73ff.

Europeans, Death is neither definitive nor absurd; on the contrary, the anxiety aroused by the imminence of death is already a promise of resurrection, reveals the presentiment of re-birth into another mode of being, and this is a mode which transcends Death. Viewed again in the perspective of the primitive societies, the anxiety of the modern world can be homologised with the anguish of death in initiation; seen in the Indian perspective it is homologous with the dialectical moment of the discovery of Mâyâ. But, as we were saying just now, in archaic and "primitive" culture, as well as in India, *this anxiety is not a state in which one can remain*; its indispensability is that of an initiatory experience, of a rite of passage. In no culture other than ours could one stop in the middle of this rite of passage and settle down in a situation apparently without issue. For the issue consists precisely in completing this rite of passage and resolving the crisis by coming out of it at a higher level, awakening to consciousness of a higher mode of being. It is inconceivable, for example, that one could interrupt an initiatory rite of passage: in that case the boy would no longer be a child, as he was before beginning his initiation, but neither would he be the adult that he ought to be at the end of his ordeals.

We must also mention another source of the modern anxiety, our obscure presentiment of the end of the world, or more exactly of the end of *our* world, our *own* civilisation. We will not consider how well-founded this fear may be: enough to recall that it is far from being a modern discovery. The myth of the end of the world is of universal occurrence; it is already to be found among primitive peoples still at a paleolithic stage of culture, such as the Australians, and it recurs in the great historic civilisations, Babylonian, Indian, Mexican and Greco-Latin. This is the myth of the periodic destruction and re-creation of worlds, the cosmological formula of the myth of the eternal return. One must immediately add, however, that the terror of the end of the world has never, in any non-European culture, succeeded in paralysing either Life or Culture. The expectation of the cosmic catastrophe is indeed agonising, but the anxiety is religiously and culturally integrated. The end of the world is never absolute; it is always followed by the creation of a new, *regenerated* world. For, to non-

Europeans, Life and the Spirit are unique in this, that they can never definitively disappear.

We must now suspend comparison with the non-European religions and civilisations. We will not draw any conclusions, for the dialogue has hardly begun: it has to be continued and developed. However, this change of perspective has already been reassuring: we had only to place ourselves on a level with the archaic and oriental cultures to rediscover the initiatory meanings and the spiritual values of anxiety, meanings and values well known to certain European mystical and metaphysical traditions. But this is as much as to say that a dialogue with the *true* Asiatic, African or Oceanian world helps us to rediscover spiritual positions that one is justified in regarding as universally valid. These are no longer provincial formulæ, creations merely of this or that fragment of History but—one may dare to say—oecumenical positions.

But, one may ask oneself, if this dialogue with non-European spiritual traditions simply leads us to rediscover certain neglected sources of our own spiritual heritage, what is the point of going so far afield and interrogating Indians, Africans and Oceanians? As we were saying, our own historic moment obliges us to understand the non-European cultures and to engage in conversation with their authentic representatives. But there is something more: there is this strange and reassuring fact that the change of spiritual perspective takes effect as a profound regeneration of our intimate being. We propose to conclude this chapter with a Jewish story which admirably illustrates this mystery of the encounter. It is a story of the Rabbi Eisik of Cracow, which the Orientalist Heinrich Zimmer unearthed from the *Khassidischen Bücher* of Martin Buber. This pious rabbi, Eisik of Cracow, had a dream which told him to travel to Prague; there, under the great bridge leading to the royal castle, he was to find a hidden treasure. The dream was repeated three times, and the rabbi decided to go. Upon arrival at Prague he found the bridge; but, as it was guarded day and night by sentinels, Eisik dared not dig. But as he continued to loiter in the vicinity he attracted the attention of the captain of the guard, who asked him, kindly, if he had lost something. The rabbi then innocently narrated his dream; and the officer burst into laughter. "Really, poor man," he said, "have you worn out your shoes coming all this way simply because of a dream?" This officer, too, had heard a voice in a dream: "It spoke to me about Cracow, ordered me to go over there and look for a great treasure in the house of a rabbi whose name was Eisik, Eisik son of Jekel. The treasure was to be found in a dusty old corner where it had been buried behind the stove." But the officer put no trust whatever in voices heard in dreams; the officer was a reasonable person. The rabbi, with a deep bow, thanked him and made haste to return to Cracow; there, he dug in the neglected corner of his house and discovered the treasure; which put an end to his poverty.

" Thus," comments Heinrich Zimmer, "the real treasure, that which can put an end to our poverty and all our trials, is never very far; there is no need to seek it in a distant country. It lies buried in the most intimate parts of our own house; that is, of our own being. It is behind the stove, the centre of the life and warmth that rule our existence, the heart of our heart, if only we knew how to unearth it. And yet—there is this strange and persistent fact, that it is only after a pious journey in a distant region, in a new land, that the meaning of that inner voice guiding us on our search can make itself understood by us. And to this strange and persistent fact is added another: that he who reveals to us the meaning of our mysterious inward pilgrimage must himself be a stranger, of another belief and another race."

And this is the profound meaning of any genuine encounter; it might well constitute the point of departure for a new humanism, upon a world scale.

ACKNOWLEDGMENTS

The foregoing essays appeared originally between 1948 and 1955 in the following Continental reviews and symposia:

Chapters I and II of the present work, "The Myths of the Modern World" and "The Myth of the Noble Savage", first appeared in *La Nouvelle Revue Française* in September 1953 and August 1955 respectively.

"Nostalgia for Paradise in the Primitive Traditions" was published in *Diogène*, No. 3, July 1953.

"Sense-Experience and Mystical Experience" was published in the symposium *Nos Sens et Dieu* (Etudes Carmélitaines, 1954).

"Symbolisms of Ascension" and "Waking Dreams" combine three articles which appeared respectively in *Numen*, January 1956, *l'Hommage Van der Leeuw*, (Nijkerk, 1950) and *Homage to Ananda K. Coomaraswamy* (*Art and Thought*, London, 1948).

The previous versions of the present chapters VI, VII and VIII were published in the *Eranos-Jahrbücher*, Vols. XXI, XXII and XXIII, Zürich, 1953, 1954 and 1955.

Chapter IX, "Religious Symbolism and Modern Man's Anxiety" reproduces the text of a lecture given under the auspices of the "Rencontres Internationales de Genève" in September 1953, and published in the symposium entitled *L'Angoisse du temps présent et les devoirs de l'esprit* (Editions de la Bacconière, Neufchâtel, 1954).

I have here tried, as far as possible, to eliminate repetitions and to simplify the references.

As before, it was my good and devoted friend Dr. Jean Gouillard who undertook to read and correct the manuscript of the French edition of this work, and I hereby assure him of my very sincere thanks. Once again I avow my wholehearted gratitude to my friends Olga Froebe-Kapteyn, Dr. René Laforgue and Délia Laforgue, Dr. Roger Godel and Alice Godel: their gentle and affectionate hospitality at Paris and at the Val d'Or has aided me immeasurably in carrying on my work since 1950.

INDEX

247

harper ⚡ torchbooks

† The New American Nation Series, edited by Henry Steele Commager and Richard B. Morris.

‡ American Perspectives series, edited by Bernard Wishy and William E. Leuchtenburg.

* The Rise of Modern Europe series, edited by William L. Langer.

** History of Europe series, edited by J. H. Plumb.

¶ Researches in the Social, Cultural, and Behavioral Sciences, edited by Benjamin Nelson.

§ The Library of Religion and Culture, edited by Benjamin Nelson.

Σ Harper Modern Science Series, edited by James R. Newman.

° Not for sale in Canada.

△ Not for sale in the U. K.

History: Ancient

A. ANDREWES: The Greek Tyrants △   TB/1103
ADOLF ERMAN, Ed.: The Ancient Egyptians   TB/1233
MICHAEL GRANT: Ancient History ° △   TB/1190
SAMUEL NOAH KRAMER: Sumerian Mythology   TB/1055
NAPHTALI LEWIS & MEYER REINHOLD, Eds.: Roman Civilization.   Vol. I TB/1231; Vol. II TB/1232

History: Medieval

P. BOISSONNADE: Life and Work in Medieval Europe △   TB/1141
HELEN CAM: England Before Elizabeth △   TB/1026
NORMAN COHN: The Pursuit of the Millennium △   TB/1037
GALBERT OF BRUGES: The Murder of Charles the Good. Trans. with Intro. by James Bruce Ross   TB/1311
DENO GEANAKOPLOS: Byzantine East and Latin West △   TB/1265
DENYS HAY: Europe: The Emergence of an Idea   TB/1275
DENYS HAY: The Medieval Centuries ° △   TB/1192
J. M. HUSSEY: The Byzantine World △   TB/1057
FERDINAND LOT: The End of the Ancient World   TB/1044
MARSILIUS OF PADUA: The Defender of the Peace. Trans. with Intro. by Alan Gewirth   TB/1310
CHARLES PETIT-DUTAILLIS: The Feudal Monarchy in France and England ° △   TB/1165
HENRI PIRENNE: Early Democracies in the Low Countries   TB/1110
STEVEN RUNCIMAN: A History of the Crusades. △ Vol. I Illus. TB/1143; Vol. II Illus. TB/1243; Vol. III Illus.   TB/1208
FERDINAND SCHEVILL: Siena   TB/1164
SULPICIUS SEVERUS et al.: The Western Fathers △   TB/309
HENRY OSBORN TAYLOR: The Classical Heritage of the Middle Ages   TB/1117
J. M. WALLACE-HADRILL: The Barbarian West   TB/1061

History: Renaissance & Reformation

JACOB BURCKHARDT: The Civilization of the Renaissance in Italy. △ Illus.   Vol. I TB/40; Vol. II TB/41
JOHN CALVIN & JACOPO SADOLETO: A Reformation Debate. △ Edited by John C. Olin   TB/1239
FEDERICO CHABOD: Machiavelli and the Renaissance △   TB/1193
G. CONSTANT: The Reformation in England △   TB/314
G. R. ELTON: Reformation Europe, 1517-1559 ** ° △   TB/1270
JOHN NEVILLE FIGGIS: The Divine Right of Kings. Introduction by G. R. Elton   TB/1191
FRANCESCO GUICCIARDINI: Maxims and Reflections of a Renaissance Statesman (Ricordi)   TB/1160
J. H. HEXTER: More's Utopia   TB/1195
HAJO HOLBORN: Ulrich von Hutten and the German Reformation   TB/1238
JOHAN HUIZINGA: Erasmus and the Age of Reformation. △ Illus.   TB/19
JOEL HURSTFIELD, Ed.: The Reformation Crisis △   TB/1267
ULRICH VON HUTTEN et al.: On the Eve of the Reformation: "Letters of Obscure Men"   TB/1124
PAUL O. KRISTELLER: Renaissance Thought △   TB/1048
NICCOLÒ MACHIAVELLI: History of Florence and of the Affairs of Italy   TB/1027
J. E. NEALE: The Age of Catherine de Medici ° △   TB/1085
ERWIN PANOFSKY: Studies in Iconology △   TB/1077
J. H. PARRY: The Establishment of the European Hegemony: 1415-1715 △   TB/1045
J. H. PLUMB: The Italian Renaissance △   TB/1161
A. F. POLLARD: Henry VIII ° △   TB/1249
A. F. POLLARD: Wolsey ° △   TB/1248
A. L. ROWSE: The Expansion of Elizabethan England. ° △ Illus.   TB/1220
GORDON RUPP: Luther's Progress to the Diet of Worms ° △   TB/120
FERDINAND SCHEVILL: The Medici. Illus.   TB/1010

FERDINAND SCHEVILL: Medieval and Renaissance Florence. Illus.   Vol. I TB/1090; Vol. II TB/1091
G. M. TREVELYAN: England in the Age of Wycliffe, 1368-1520 ° △   TB/1112
VESPASIANO: Renaissance Princes, Popes, and Prelates: The Vespasiano Memoirs   TB/1111

History: Modern European

MAX BELOFF: The Age of Absolutism, 1660-1815 △   TB/1062
ROBERT C. BINKLEY: Realism and Nationalism, 1852-1871. * Illus.   TB/3038
ASA BRIGGS: The Making of Modern England, 1784-1867: The Age of Improvement ° △   TB/1203
CRANE BRINTON: A Decade of Revolution, 1789-1799. * Illus.   TB/3018
D. W. BROGAN: The Development of Modern France. ° △   Vol. I TB/1184; Vol. II TB/1185
J. BRONOWSKI & BRUCE MAZLISH: The Western Intellectual Tradition: From Leonardo to Hegel △   TB/3001
ALAN BULLOCK: Hitler, A Study in Tyranny ° △   TB/1123
E. H. CARR: The Twenty Years' Crisis, 1919-1939 ° △   TB/1122
GORDON A. CRAIG: From Bismarck to Adenauer   TB/1171
DENIS DIDEROT: The Encyclopedia: Selections. Ed. and trans. by Stephen Gendzier   TB/1299
FRANKLIN L. FORD: Robe and Sword   TB/1217
RENÉ FUELOEP-MILLER: The Mind and Face of Bolshevism   TB/1188
M. DOROTHY GEORGE: London Life in the Eighteenth Century △   TB/1182
LEO GERSHOY: From Despotism to Revolution, 1763-1789. * Illus.   TB/3017
C. C. GILLISPIE: Genesis and Geology: The Decades before Darwin §   TB/51
ALBERT GOODWIN: The French Revolution △   TB/1064
ALBERT GUÉRARD: France in the Classical Age △   TB/1183
J. H. HEXTER: Reappraisals in History △   TB/1100
STANLEY HOFFMANN et al.: In Search of France   TB/1219
DAN N. JACOBS, Ed.: The New Communist Manifesto & Related Documents. Third edition, revised   TB/1078
LIONEL KOCHAN: The Struggle for Germany: 1914-45   TB/1304
HANS KOHN: The Mind of Germany △   TB/1204
WALTER LAQUEUR & GEORGE L. MOSSE, Eds.: International Fascism: 1920-1945 ° △   TB/1276
WALTER LAQUEUR & GEORGE L. MOSSE, Eds.: The Left-Wing Intellectuals between the Wars, 1919-1939 ° △   TB/1286
WALTER LAQUEUR & GEORGE L. MOSSE, Eds.: 1914: The Coming of the First World War ° △   TB/1306
FRANK E. MANUEL: The Prophets of Paris: Turgot, Condorcet, Saint-Simon, Fourier, and Comte   TB/1218
L. B. NAMIER: Facing East △   TB/1280
L. B. NAMIER: Personalities and Powers △   TB/1186
DAVID OGG: Europe of the Ancien Régime, 1715-1783 ** ° △   TB/1271
JOHN PLAMENATZ: German Marxism and Russian Communism. ° △   TB/1189
RAYMOND W. POSTGATE, Ed.: Revolution from 1789 to 1906: Selected Documents   TB/1063
PENFIELD ROBERTS: The Quest for Security, 1715-1740. * Illus.   TB/3016
GEORGE RUDÉ: Revolutionary Europe, 1783-1815 ° △   TB/1272
LOUIS, DUC DE SAINT-SIMON: Versailles, The Court, and Louis XIV △   TB/1250
A. J. P. TAYLOR: From Napoleon to Lenin ° △   TB/1268
A. J. P. TAYLOR: Habsburg Monarchy, 1809-1918 ° △   TB/1187
G. M. TREVELYAN: British History in the Nineteenth Century and After: 1782-1919 ° △   TB/1251
H. R. TREVOR-ROPER: Historical Essays ° △   TB/1269
ELIZABETH WISKEMANN: Europe of the Dictators, 1919-1945 ** ° △   TB/1273

2